Henryk Jurkowski's seminal 1988 text, *Aspects of Puppet Theatre*, was ground-breaking in its analysis of puppetry as an important performing art. Focusing on the cultural and social functions of puppetry, Jurkowski traced the role of puppetry in cultural life, from its ritualistic roots to its influence on modernist art and presence in contemporary theatre. This new edition of a classic brings the original text back to life, including four additional essays and a new introduction, edited and translated by leading puppetry scholar Penny Francis.

Henryk Jurkowski is a former Professor at the Krakow and Warsaw Superior schools of Theatre. He is Expert Editor of the *World Encyclopaedia of Contemporary Theatre* and author of *History of the European Puppet Theatre*, volumes 1 and 2. Throughout his distinguished career he has collected a number of awards, including the Polonia Restituta, one of Poland's highest Orders for services to culture.

Penny Francis is Honorary Fellow of the Central School of Speech and Drama, London, UK, where she is Lecturer in Puppetry. She co-founded the Puppet Centre Trust in 1974 and was awarded an MBE for services to puppetry in 1988. She is author of *Puppetry: A Reader in Theatre Practice*, and has written numerous articles for international conferences and journals.

*To my Friends
the Puppeteers*

Aspects of Puppet Theatre

Second Edition

Henryk Jurkowski

Edited by Penny Francis

First edition published 1988 by
PUPPET CENTRE TRUST
Second edition published 2013 by
PALGRAVE MACMILLAN

Palgrave Macmillan in the UK is an imprint of Macmillan Publishers
Limited, registered in England, company number 785998, of Houndmills,
Basingstoke, Hampshire RG21 6XS.

Palgrave Macmillan in the US is a division of St Martin's Press LLC,
175 Fifth Avenue, New York, NY 10010.

Palgrave Macmillan is the global academic imprint of the above companies
and has companies and representatives throughout the world.

Palgrave® and Macmillan® are registered trademarks in the United States,
the United Kingdom, Europe and other countries

ISBN 978-1-137-33843-3   ISBN 978-1-137-33845-7 (eBook)
DOI 10.1007/978-1-137-33845-7

A catalogue record for this book is available from the British Library.

A catalog record for this book is available from the Library of Congress.

Typeset by Cambrian Typesetters, Camberley, Surrey

Contents

About the author and editor

Author
Professor Henryk Zdzislaw Jurkowski

Professor Jurkowski, historian, writer, teacher, essayist. He taught the theory and history of puppetry in the Higher Theatre Schools of Krakow and Warsaw, and as visiting lecturer and speaker in institutions all over the world, including Charleville-Mézières, London, Seville, Chicago, Tokyo, Barcelona, Prague and Sofia.

He is the author of hundreds of essays published in many international journals, and of books in Polish, translated widely. In English his best-known works are *A History of European Puppetry* (1996 and 1998) in two volumes and the first edition of *Aspects of Puppet Theatre* (1988) which has become required reading in the increasing numbers of educational establishments where puppetry is taught.

Henryk Jurkowski is Honorary President of UNIMA (Union Internationale de la Marionnette). His decorations include the Chevalier dans l'ordre des Arts et des Lettres (1994) and Polonia Restituta (2007).

Editor

Penny Francis is a co-founder of the Puppet Centre Trust established in 1974 in Battersea Arts Centre to promote and develop the arts of puppetry in contemporary theatre. She is an editor, critic and until recently lecturer at the Royal Central School of Speech and Drama of which she is an Honorary Fellow. Her book *Puppetry. A Reader in Theatre Practice* was published in 2012. She was awarded the MBE for services to puppetry in 1998.

List of Illustrations

Acknowledgements

This volume follows the previous edition of *Aspects of Puppet Theatre* published by the Puppet Centre Trust (London 1988) thanks to the initiative of Penny Francis.

I owe her thanks also for her editing of my English – not quite adequate for the enterprise – and for her help in making known my writings and thoughts on puppetry in the English-speaking hemisphere. *Aspects* was recognized as an important work, and I have had the pleasure of being quoted by many western writers and academics in discussions on the formal and aesthetic aspects of puppetry.

This edition is supplemented by four new essays, most of them edited by Dr. Mischa Twitchin, to whom I also address warm thanks.

I acknowledge the generous assistance of Olenka Darkowska-Nidzgorski and John M. Blundall in giving permission for the use of photographs from their collections.

Finally, I feel obliged to express thanks to all my puppeteer friends whose creative work and talents were the springboard for my deliberations.

Thank you my friends.

Henryk Jurkowski
Warsaw 2013

Editor's Foreword to the Second Edition

About 25 years have passed since the first edition of *Aspects of Puppet Theatre* was published by the Puppet Centre (1988), with private sponsorship. It became a standard text for educational institutions and individual practitioners, and has been out of print for many years.

It is a matter of pride that these essays are still sought after by the growing numbers of students and puppeteers wishing to investigate the phenomenon of the animated object in its theatrical context, and that a respected publishing house is enthusiastic about producing a second edition. Other books of analysis and theory have been published in the interim, of course, but it is fair to say that the essays of Professor Jurkowski of Warsaw are as valuable as ever they were, and that as an academic specialist in puppetry his influence on the development of the art form has been, and still is, unique.

The present volume brings together only a small part of Jurkowski's *oeuvre*, much of it articles and essays published separately in books and journals all over the world, in Polish and several other languages. Four of these are here added to the collection in the first edition: *The Human among Objects*, *Craig and Puppets*, *The Acting Puppet as Figure of Speech* and *Among Deities, Priests and Shamans*. Mischa Twitchin has been the principal linguistic editor of the last three, and he has the sincere thanks and appreciation of the author and myself.

The need for theoretical analyses of puppetry continues to grow in answer to the steady growth, in global terms, of the numbers of theatre schools which include puppetry in their studies. Similarly, professional and amateur practitioners of most performance disciplines now using animated characters in their work will welcome a basis of theory, as all dynamic practice does. Jurkowski's contribution is a central pillar of the art form.

Penny Francis
London, 2013

1
Literary Views on Puppet Theatre

Performances with puppets are attended mostly by children, a tradition that was established – albeit unconsciously – in the eighteenth and nineteenth centuries, and in even earlier times when French and Italian showmen presented their shows in the palace and gardens of St Germain-en-Laye, to entertain the young Dauphin through many months of the year.

This is not to say that the puppet theatre of the past was only for children; on the contrary, it was a theatre for all ages, enjoyed by all. Children attended performances meant for adults, because in those days the idea of art especially for children was unknown. They were taken, indiscriminately, to see everything.

Some might say that adults enjoyed puppet theatre in the past because of the naivety of the public of those times, but this is not quite true. The main categories of theatre in those days were court theatre and popular theatre, and puppets played the same repertoire for the same classes of audience. Their theatre developed in tandem with actors' theatre, and was accepted in the same way.

In the world beyond Europe puppets have been recognized as a part of theatre for centuries. In the Japan of the seventeenth century it was held in higher esteem than any other form of theatre, and in Indonesia it was almost the only available form, leaving little room for others to develop.

On researching European theatre, the presence of the puppet player is to be found at every stage. Indeed, for many theatre companies, actors and puppets were for a long time simple alternatives.

The classical mimes, Greek, Roman and Byzantine, the members of the Craft Guilds, the priests who organized the Mystery Plays, *commedia dell'arte* players, the English Comedians touring the Continent in the seventeenth century – all these recognized the puppet as an attractive means of theatrical expression. The public was fascinated by the Mystery Play whether performed by puppet or actor; it awaited with equal impatience the transformation of the flesh-and-blood Harlequin or the wooden version manipulated by a complicated system of strings. The plays of Shakespeare and Marlowe were performed in Europe by touring English companies in both a human and a puppet version, and there is no doubt that the success of Marlowe's *The Tragical History of Doctor Faustus* initiated the very important tradition of Faust on the puppet stage. In Italy, opera with humans was no more popular than opera with puppets, with figures immortalized in the sketches of Bernini and Acciaioli, libretti written by Martelli and Metastasio, and music composed by masters of the calibre of Scarlatti.

In general, puppet companies were organized like actors' companies, with their own auditorium, a stage with suitable machinery, and drummers and clowns to advertise the shows. Experienced manipulators were employed and good writers commissioned, of which the list is long: Le Sage and Fuselier, Sheridan and Foote, Mahlmann, Maeterlinck and Schnitzler, and many writers of our own time, such as García Lorca and Michel de Ghelderode.

Nowadays the puppet theatre revival continues to prove the importance of puppetry as a necessary branch of theatre with its own following, its own style, its own aesthetic. For this reason the puppet theatre, rich as it is in ideas and values that are important for any theory of theatre, should be considered in any discussion of the aesthetic problems of theatre art in general.

Since the most ancient times, puppet theatre has been an illuminating source of metaphors, some of which illustrate the relationship between the Creator and his creation. The Creator used often to be presented as an unknown and powerful being, sometimes without a name, omnipresent, pulling the strings of human actions. The metaphor referred both to the relationship between God and man and, equally, to the links between man and man. Horace wrote in his 'Satires':

> ... what am I to you?
> Look how you who lord it over me
> Bow and scrape for others like a puppet on a string![1]

The notion of God as manipulator was actually introduced by the Arabs, whose poets and philosophers expressed Arab determinism. Birri, an Anatolian poet of the thirteenth century, wrote in his *ghazal*:

Wise man seeking for Truth
Look up at the tent of the sky
Where the Great Showman of the world
Has long ago set up his Shadow Theatre.
Behind his screen he is giving a show
Played by the shadows of men and women of his creation.[2]

One could quote hundreds of examples of the use and development of this metaphor. Notice how today it contains new meanings. Vladimir Sokolov, a twentieth-century dancer and puppeteer, expressed it thus:

Striving to reach artistic freedom for his creative will, man invented the puppet theatre. Through its discovery he freed himself from the threat of destiny, creating for himself a world of his own and – through the characters which owe him total dependence – he strengthens his will, his logic, and his aesthetic. In short, he becomes a little god in his own world.[3]

So we see that through the centuries the relationship between the creator and the created, so well illustrated by the mechanism of the puppet theatre, has not changed very much. The only significant change is one of function: the 'Demonstrator of the World' has been replaced by the 'little god'; the 'created' has in a sense taken the function of 'creator' and has grasped his independence. This is evidenced in all forms of contemporary art. The metaphorical use of the structure of the puppet theatre would not be so important if it were not for the fact that it expresses so well the psychological attraction of creative puppetry: the complete, the 'divine' liberty of self-expression, to be found by an artist only in puppet theatre. This question of freedom – autonomy – is valued by many artists other than puppeteers, and particularly by writers and directors of the 'live' theatre.

Lemercier de Neuville, famous satirist and puppet player, wrote about his own experience: 'being unable to find competent actors, the author, wishing to see his plays performed, was obliged to cut his company out of paper!'[4]

Eleanora Duse's opinion of puppets was similar: she wrote to the Italian puppet master, Vittorio Podrecca, 'I envy you. I should have been a director of puppet theatre myself. Your actors do not speak and are perfectly obedient: mine can speak and are not obedient at all.'[5]

These quotations are amusing, but they contain a deeper meaning: they highlight the unique characteristic of the puppet, that it has only one identity whereas the actor has many. The puppet has no private life, living only on stage: to the reformers of theatre at the beginning of the twentieth century this was its special value. They were striving towards a harmonious reality in theatre, one in which there was no contradiction between the artificiality of the scenography and the reality of the actor.

In any theory of puppet theatre, the most important factor is the relationship between puppeteer and puppet. This relationship has changed down the centuries. Very often the puppet players themselves have not been conscious of the change, especially the folk puppeteers of past times who invariably performed spontaneously. They inherited and passed on their professional experience and their repertory from generation to generation, not caring whether they left any recorded evidence of their artistry or of the content of their shows. The first records we have (not counting the written records of the satirical attacks made by fairground 'Polichinelles' on the monopoly of the 'official' theatre in Paris) date only from the second half of the eighteenth century. The author of this evidence was Samuel Foote, actor and playwright, whose company played in London from 1758 to 1773. Before the first performance of *The Primitive Puppet Show* on 15 January 1773 at his theatre in the Haymarket, Foote gave a long talk whose subject was the 'glory of the primitive puppet show'. He insisted that this form of art had bloomed in Ancient Rome and had unfortunately disappeared together with Rome. Foote wished to revive it, and described how actors,

> every part of them, in order to make their figures conspicuous to a numerous audience, were stuffed and raised beyond their natural proportion, their heads covered with masques, and the mouths of those masques lined with brass, in order to convey the voice to the remotest part of their immense theatres; nothing human was visible, the whole appearance was but a puppet; and whether the voice proceeded from within or from behind the figure, the difference could not be very essential.[6]

Foote's interpretation of the theatre of antiquity is very personal, not to say idiosyncratic, but it makes us notice that he was in favour of a theatre of convention, which disguises real life and which, most importantly, even disguises humans. He expressed his interest in *theatricality* thus:

This, gentlemen, was the first state of the stage in Italy: but in the five hundred and fifteenth year from the foundation of Rome this art, by an accident, was brought nearer the puppet perfection. Livius Andronicus, who like your present servant was both author and actor, upon delivering a popular sentiment in one of his pieces, was so often encored that, quite exhausted, he declared himself incapable of a further repetition, unless one of his scholars was permitted to mount the stage, and suffered to declaim the passage, which he would attempt to gesticulate; to this the public assented; and from that period the practice was established of one actor giving the gesture, whilst another delivered the words. This fact will not admit of a doubt, as we receive it from the best authority, that of Livy the historian. Here, gentlemen, by separation of the personage, you have the puppet complete.[7]

Foote's conception of puppet theatre derived from his views on live theatre. In *Tragedy à la Mode* he used flat figures and only one actor who spoke all the roles. In *The Primitive Puppet Show* he applied the principle of the play within a play. When the puppets had finished performing, a second part was played by actors, during which a 'Constable' entered and arrested Foote and his puppets 'under the Vagrancy Act'. The next scene took place in the courtroom where the Constable was found to have no case because, as ever, the puppets brought with them their normal illusoriness. They were not real, therefore they could not be judged – you cannot pass judgment on an object. What was more, Foote himself was equally invulnerable, because, having an artificial leg, he was 'one quarter puppet'! In modern terms, he was a practitioner of 'mixed-media' theatre, mixing humans with puppets on stage, and thus underlining the alienation of the stage character from its surroundings.

However, Foote's ideas on theatricality and his sense of humour were too advanced for the public of the time, which preferred another kind of puppet show, that of 'Punch' and his wife 'Joan'.

With the Romantic Movement in Germany came a new appreciation of the puppet theatre. Lothar Buschmeyer, a twentieth-century writer, said:

The revival of puppetry today would have been impossible without Goethe and the Romantics, because it was they who won for the puppet theatre the interest of the educated classes and of the artists so necessary for its renaissance.[8]

In Germany especially, the help of the Romantics was very necessary as it was here in the previous period that the Rationalists, for example Gottsched, expressed a desire 'to liquidate this tasteless genre'. Romantic writers and their precursors, however, were enthusiastic about anything to do with folk art.

It is interesting to note that, as in older times, the Romantic writers considered the puppet theatre as a source of metaphor. First it served as a satirical analogy of mankind's small-mindedness, so much accentuated during the so-called 'Sturm und Drang' period. The best example of this is in the words of Goethe's Young Werther, expressing his feelings about the unreality of the world:

> I stand as before a peepshow, a magic box. I see small people and little horses passing in front of me and often ask myself if it is not an optical illusion. I play with them, or rather they play with me, like a marionette: now and then I take a neighbour by his wooden hand and recoil in horror.[9]

In Goethe's early plays similar comparisons appear. In *Jahrmarktfest von Plundersweilen* (*Fairground of Plundersweilen*), he presents an image of the fairground of life, or 'the little theatre of the world', meaning the puppet theatre. The same idea was revived in *Hanswursts Hochzeit* (*Hanswurst's Wedding*), published posthumously.

The Polish Romantics exploited the puppet theatre as a source of metaphor to express their opinions on the rules of life. For Adam Mickiewicz, as for Goethe, the puppet theatre was a good analogy for the pettiness of mankind and the world. He wrote:

> It is easy to recognise a talented man from his accomplishments, his arguments, his work. But how deeply hidden are his true character and his soul! These artificial marionettes we call people may embrace us in friendship, smile at us, cry sometimes, but underneath you find egoism, greed and pride manipulating their strings, dominating these figures.[10]

Słowacki, in his drama *Kordian*, mentioned the English 'Punch' to illustrate the machinations of political activity, while Zygmunt Krasiński similarly called politicians 'Polichinelles manipulated by hidden powers'.[11]

Having been used as a symbol of the world to the satirical observer, the puppet theatre then took on a new role, exemplified by Schiller in his concept of *Spiel des Lebens* (the game of life). In the period of early Romanticism it preserved its symbolic function in the so-called *Schicksaltragödie* (the tragedy of fate). Ludwig Tieck, in his novel *Gelehrte Gesellschaft* (*Learned Society*), inserts a story of a puppet performance on this same theme: the hero Hanswurst is a marionette, a symbol of humanity. He is bound – although he does not know it – to another character, undefined, unnamed, disguised. Whenever Hanswurst wishes to take action, for example to meet friends or to give help to another, this other 'formless figure' pulls him back. Hanswurst is at a loss to understand what is wrong.

A little later the marionette acquired an aesthetic importance, also illustrated in the works of Tieck. The negative aspects of the marionette (*Leblosigkeit*, lifelessness) he treated as something of value, since it made the puppet a dependant of the writer's imagination. He also drew attention to the inappropriateness of puppets in the roles they usually portrayed: the lifeless puppet pretending to be a live actor playing 'Faust' or 'Genoveva' seemed to Tieck to be not only grotesque, but ironic. He decided that the writer or the puppet player should exploit this inherent limitation of the puppet for the sake of 'romantic irony', as he did in his own play *Prince Zerbino*. The puppet player should have more importance than the puppet itself; the player should direct its application and use.

Although the Romantics did not write treatises on the aesthetics of puppet theatre, their ideas were expressed within their works, very often works for the stage. Some were specifically written for puppets, and were performed by professional, often folk, puppeteers. When they spoke of the aesthetic value of the puppet, the Romantics clearly thought of it as a virtual actor: one could go so far as to say that they had their own theory of the über-marionette. They were not always satisfied with 'live' actors, whom they frequently found motivated by personal ambition, unfaithful to the author's intentions and over-influenced by traditional, outmoded methods of staging:

> but the marionette, an excellent mechanical creature, overcomes all biological and individual human limitations and appears before us as a first class performer, especially in burlesque and comedy.[12]

These words of Eleonora Rapp echo Tieck and also Jean Paul. August Mahlmann, in the introduction to his *Marionettentheater* (1806), was similarly convinced: 'puppets hewn from wood would present my plays better and more truthfully than the living wooden figures in our

Haupt- and Staatstheaters'.[13] Justinius Kerner also thought along the same lines:

> It may be strange, but for me the marionettes are more free, more natural than live actors. They give me a stronger sense of illusion ... Marionettes have no life backstage: one cannot listen to them nor make acquaintance with them except in the roles they play.[14]

The writer who expressed most precisely the Romantic understanding of the puppet as actor was Heinrich von Kleist in his essay 'On the Marionette Theatre'.[15] In the convention of the time he wrote in the form of a dialogue, beginning:

> Whilst I was spending the winter of 1801 in M–, I met Mr. C. in a park one evening. He had recently become principal dancer at the Opera in the town, and was enjoying an extraordinary success with the public.[16]

This Mr. C. appeared to be a great lover of the puppet theatre, and the author ascribes to him arguments to convince the reader as well as himself, the partner in the dialogue, that the puppet has a real and important value which can creatively influence the live theatre, particularly the ballet:

> He assured me that the pantomimes of these puppets gave him much pleasure and stated emphatically that any dancer who wished to improve his art could learn a great deal from them.[17]

Two arguments support his thesis: one, the roles of the mechanics of dance; and two, the lack of self-consciousness in the puppet as opposed to the overweening self-consciousness of the dancer. Mr. C. seems to be a connoisseur of the mechanics of the puppet:

> Each movement, he said, had a centre of gravity; it sufficed to control the centre of the figure. The limbs, which were no more than pendulums, followed mechanically of their own accord without any prompting.[18]

Naturally, the artist and his talents were not thereby diminished:

> The line which the centre of gravity must describe was very simple and, as he believed, in most cases straight. In cases where it was

curved, the curve seemed to be of the first, or at the most, of the second order. Even in this case it was just an ellipse, a form which was the natural movement of the human body (owing to its joints): it did not therefore demand any great skill from the puppeteer.

On the other hand, this line was something very mysterious, for it was no less than the path of the dancer's soul, and he doubted that it could be found except by the puppeteer transposing himself into the centre of gravity of the marionettes: in other words, by dancing.[19]

With the marionette, the artistry of the performance is not jeopardised by any temptation of the performer to 'charm'. Mr. C. further explains the puppet's advantage over the human:

> The advantage? Firstly a negative one, my good friend: that a puppet does not give itself airs and graces. Affectation appears, as you know, when one's soul (vis motrix or moving energy) is elsewhere than at the centre of gravity of a movement. Since the puppeteer has only that single point under his control, through the string, all the other limbs are as they should be: dead, mere pendulums which simply obey the law of gravity, an excellent characteristic which one seeks in vain in most of our dancers.[20]

Affectation or the desire to charm is much connected with the selfishness of the actor/dancer who places his own soul before the public eye instead of hiding it in the invisible 'point of gravity'. Trying to charm actually results in a lack of charm in the stage character, according to Kleist, who cites many examples to prove his thesis. His conclusion is considerably to the disadvantage of the live performer:

> so grace returns after understanding has passed through infinity. It thus appears in those human forms which either have no consciousness at all or have an infinite one: in the marionette and in the god.[21]

However, Kleist's theory in all its simplicity had no practical influence, inspiring neither the artists of the live theatre nor the puppeteers to transform their fairground booths into an artistic theatre. It was necessary to wait almost a hundred years to see the ideas of the Romantics bear fruit, and for Kleist's theory to evoke the interest of other artists and authors. We cannot be certain of Kleist's influence on Edward Gordon Craig with his own famous theory of the über-marionette –

perhaps Craig did not even read Kleist – but the similarity of the two approaches is obvious.

Little happened to enrich puppetry in the second half of the nineteenth century in ideas or theories, although it was practised by such famous writers as George Sand and her son Maurice, and the group of painters from the Chat Noir cabaret in Paris. The 1852 publication of the *Histoire des Marionnettes en Europe* by Charles Magnin was very important for the dissemination of knowledge of puppet theatre and for its appreciation as a theatre art. . Although several works on the history of puppets have been published since then,[22] for example by Philippe Leibrecht,[23] George Speaight,[24] Paul McPharlin,[25] and John Varey,[26] Magnin's work remains an inspiration to historians and theoreticians of puppetry. Magnin collected much of his evidence searching through various documents, dictionaries, almanacs and diaries. His comments were subtle and his methods surprisingly modern, since he presented the theatre activities of past puppeteers against a broad background of contemporary religious and cultural practice.

Through his work Magnin legitimized the puppet theatre as a separate branch of theatre. He was the first to treat it as a creative art, worthy of scholarly research. He collected an immense quantity of historical evidence, adding a special explanation for his interest in the subject:

> If someone insisted that I give him a reason for my choice of such an unusual subject, and I felt naturally bound to answer, I would have no difficulty in giving him examples of many profound and acknowledged thinkers who were not afraid to compromise their reputation as scholars, poets, even theologians and philosophers, by their close association with these nice, seductive wonders. How many piquant essays, scientific lectures, wise thoughts, caprices or poems could I cite from the work of the greatest writers of all countries and of all times who were inspired by the marionette. I may surprise some of my readers with no more than an introductory list of such excellent patrons: Plato, Aristotle, Horace, Marcus Aurelius, Petronius, Galen, Apuleius, Tertulian; among modern writers: Shakespeare, Cervantes, Ben Jonson, Moliere, Hamilton, Pope, Swift, Fielding, Voltaire, Goethe, Byron.[27]

Magnin was trying to convince his readers that puppets were part of the art of theatre and were thus subjects worthy of research. He wrote:

> A surprising thing! We shall find in the history of these wooden actors the identical stages of development (hieratic, aristocratic and

popular) which we have already noted and which have served us as useful measures in our researches into the grand, real drama. In fact the humble domain of the puppet is like a sort of theatrical microcosm, in which the entire history of theatre is concentrated and reflected, and in which the critic's eye can, with perfect clarity, discern the whole set of laws which regulate the advance of the universal dramatic genius.[28]

Magnin's book determined the views of researchers for many years. In addition, his furnishing of proof of so many famous writers' and philosophers' interest became excellent advocacy for the puppet theatre's re-consideration and re-evaluation.

George Sand and her son Maurice were among the first of his contemporaries to be influenced by Magnin. Maurice Sand made his mark on theatre history as the author of a book on the *commedia dell'arte*, as the author of plays for puppets, as well as a puppet player in his own theatre, in both Nohant and Passy. His work on the *commedia* contains many pages of reference to the puppet theatre. All the information on Polichinelle and Punch, however, he obtained from Magnin's book.[29]

Much more interesting are his mother's views. She took Magnin's theories on the importance of the art a stage further, giving them coherence. Her formulae were probably born in Nohant during the long winter evenings dedicated to theatrical exercises involving live performers as well as puppets. Their parallels of expression as applied in her Nohant theatre strongly influenced her views on puppet theatre.

George Sand considered the history of puppets to be a part of theatre history in general with a common source, their development conditioned by the same factors. They were, she wrote, a common genre in that they were a response to the same human need to enter a world of fiction. The puppet theatre, she concluded, is ruled by the same principles of evolution as the actors' theatre:

> There are not two dramatic arts, there is only one. The introduction of puppets onto a stage is an art that demands as much work and knowledge as the introduction of real actors ... The long history of puppets provides many proofs that they are capable of presenting any subject: these fictive beings are brought to life by man's will so that they move and speak and to some extent become human, inspired with life for good or ill, to move or entertain us.[30]

Most important for her was the creative act achieved by the manipulator of the puppet. Consequently, she declared her doubts about mechanical puppets. They are, she said, 'capable only of astonishing, never of moving their audience'. George Sand's position differed from that of the German Romantics. She did not place puppets in opposition to live actors, but stressed their common factors, showing her deep understanding of the theatrical function of the puppet, conscious of the evolutionary analogy between live and puppet theatre. Here we have two extremes of approach to the relationship between human and puppet drama, both of which were fruitful in their creative and aesthetic conclusion. However, they could not both be applied at once, being mutually exclusive. In one period researchers were striving to find the common features of both genres, and in others they wished to demonstrate their differences. Their positions depended very much on the contemporary situation of drama in general.

At the end of the nineteenth century and beginning of the twentieth, a new consideration of the actor *vis-à-vis* the puppet emerged. The majority of new writers and directors thought theatre to be in a poor way, dominated by the egotistical actor. They called for a new type of performer who could faithfully interpret the ideas contained in the modern, symbolic drama. One of the calls came from Maurice Maeterlinck, who confessed in *Menus Propos* (1890):

> It is possible that we have to remove the living being from the stage. I do not deny that in this way we would return to the art of ancient times, in which the masks of the Greek tragic writers were the last remains. Perhaps someday a sculpture will be used in this respect, for people begin to ask some strange questions about sculpture. Or perhaps the human being will be replaced by a shadow, a reflection thrown on the screen, by symbolic forms or by some being that has the appearance of life but which is lifeless. I do not know: but the absence of the human seems to me essential. When a man enters into a poem, the great poem of his presence dims everything around. A man can speak in his own name only; he has no right to speak in the name of the whole world of the dead.[31]

The tendency was best expressed by Edward Gordon Craig in his theory of the über-marionette,[32] which has provoked a long history of discussion and has given rise to much misunderstanding. Craig was also unhappy with contemporary actors, stating that they were not creative artists. He wanted them replaced by a breed which he chose to call 'über-marionettes' (super-puppets). In his essay 'The Actor and the Über-marionette' he wrote:

> The actor must go and in his place come the inanimate figure – we may call him the über-marionette, until he has won for himself a better name. Much has been written about the puppet, or marionette. There are some excellent volumes upon him, and he has also inspired several works of art. Today in his least happy period many people have come to regard him as rather a superior doll – and to think he has developed from the doll. This is incorrect. He is a descendant of the stone images of the old temples – he is today a rather degenerate form of a god.[33]

As we see, Craig was not choosing a puppet for his model of the future actor: he was thinking of a de-personalized figure. However, 'Puppet' was for him a symbol of creation, so his theory is in support of the dignity of the puppet. At the end of the same essay he wrote:

> Do you see then what has made me love and learn to value that which today we call the 'puppet' and to detest that which we call 'life' in art? I pray earnestly for the return of the image – the Über-marionette – to the Theatre; and when he comes again and is but seen, he will be loved so well that once more it will be possible for the people to return to their ancient joy in ceremonies – once more will Creation be celebrated – homage rendered to existence – and divine and happy intercession made to Death.[34]

It is not surprising, then, that some people understood this to mean that Craig wished the live actor to be driven away from the stage altogether. This was not the case: he wanted only to transform actors into beings properly sensitive to the ideas of the play, meaning that they should serve not their egotism but their art. The old ideas of Kleist were being revived in a new form.

Craig was indeed interested in the puppet, but it would be wrong to judge his views on puppetry only from his essay 'The Actor and the Über-Marionette'. We can find out much more from his periodicals *The Mask* and *The Marionette*, and from his short essay 'Puppets and Poets'.[35]

Like Kleist's Mr. C., Craig believed that 'the puppet is the actor's primer'.[36] The puppet is able to help the actor overcome the 'realistic cliché' and find the way to a new form of gesture and expression. He recognized, however, that the puppet was also itself, with its own expressive capabilities. The puppet theatre owes Craig much, as he gave it new directions. He advised that it should rid itself of the old practice of the imitation of actors' theatre, saying that 'everything is Creation as in Poetry'.[37] Like Kleist, he recognized the puppet's intrinsic value, found only if its own mechanical features are respected. Referring to puppet manipulation he stated: 'You don't move it, you let it move: that's the art.'[38]

The renaissance of puppetry today is owed to a large extent to Gordon Craig. His ideas were developed by other writers and in the practice of puppeteers of the twentieth century. All reveal the importance of the puppet theatre as an artistic genre, corresponding entirely to the evolution of live theatre and many of its artists. Starting with Jarry and Maeterlinck, via Piscator, the Bauhaus and Gaston Baty to Dario Fo and Peter Brook, these and many others have been successors to Gordon Craig through their interest in the use of puppets. We have to take seriously the judgement of so many major artists.

Craig's deliberations were based on his admiration of folk puppetry as it existed in the nineteenth century. He did not, however, examine its nature. Analysis of its features was left to another author, the Bohemian scholar Otakar Zich, one of the Prague Circle, who published a study entitled *Drobné uměni – wytwarne snahy* (Small art – great artefacts) in 1923.[39]

Zich treated the folk puppet theatre as an imitation of the live theatre of the time, and was convinced by his research that the public regarded it in the same way. In his opinion the folk public did not see any difference between the human and the puppet theatre. It regarded the puppet as an actor and judged the one from experiences gathered from the other. It might thus be assumed that in those days the puppet theatre did not possess its own system of signs, but used the same as that of live theatre. However, Zich knew that in puppet theatre there exists an important aesthetic opposition or contradiction between the lifeless figure, a kind of sculpture, and its live voice offstage.

In order to resolve the contradiction, Zich suggested that the puppet be treated either as a live actor or as a lifeless doll. It is important to note that he saw no other solution, no middle way. To regard a puppet as a doll, said Zich, we have to stress its lifelessness. It appears comic or grotesque simply because of its uncanny imitation of human movement:

> it is not primitive but refined amusement that these little figures induce in us as they pretend to look and move like real people. We

regard them as puppets when they wish to be regarded as people, and that amuses us.[40]

It has already been stated that the Romantics were intrigued by the grotesque aspect of the puppet. They recognized its irony of expression, inherent in the opposition between its role as a human being and its limitations as a puppet. On the other hand, said Zich, regarding the puppet as a live thing, imbued with movement and speech, the audience forgets what it is made of and sees it metamorphosed into a magical, mystical creature, beyond rational understanding. The magical aspects of puppetry have their origin in the Middle Ages and were preserved in folk puppet theatre.

However, to categorize the puppet as either 'grotesque' or 'magical' is not enough if we are to define its artistic value. This was a weakness of Zich's theorizing, and one that has provoked much discussion. Erich Kolar pointed out that even in the old Czech puppet theatre the researcher was offered more than two aesthetic categories, as the repertory was rich, including a number of aesthetic values.[41]

Zich was the first scholar to discuss the puppet theatre from a semiotic point of view; even so, he did not believe that the public recognized in it a distinct system of signs. Another scientist of the Prague Circle, a Russian, Petr Bogatyrev, opposed Zich's theories and believed that every genre of theatre has its own distinct system of signs, which the spectators need to learn and recognize if the performance is to be properly received:

If we want to distinguish the badges of military uniforms, to tell a Captain from a Lieutenant-Colonel, we have to learn the insignia of rank. The same applies to art. In order to understand correctly the signs of impressionist painting, we have to learn them.[42]

It appears that Zich was more realistic than Bogatyrev, who aspired to an ideal situation, hopeful but not factual. Zich analysed the public's understanding of the puppet theatre of his time with a truth that one may also observe in our own day, and was doubtless influenced by his very personal observation of the puppet theatre. Although he indicated two possible avenues of development, he knew that the age of 'theatre magic' was over. He recognized the birth of a new theatre art, so he could not encourage puppeteers to preserve the traditional appearance of their figures. He advised them rather to follow contemporary tendencies in art, essential for him since he believed that the basic element in puppet theatre is its visual one, derived from fine art. Naturally, he admitted that the puppet had to be a dramatic character, thereby limiting the freedom of the designer or sculptor; nevertheless, he thought the puppet had to be stylized:

> It should be the result of an unrealistic concept of its model; thus it should become a true symbol of a human being, a type, not an individual, according with the unreality of stylisation.[43]

Zich belonged to that group of puppeteers wishing to renew the Bohemian puppet theatre through the expressive changes in contemporary art. His perception of puppetry as fine art was typical of his time, and can be confirmed by the interest taken in puppets by great masters of that period: Klee, Léger, Picasso, Miró and many others who actually designed puppets for performance. The significance of these performances lay solely in the artistic importance of the figures.

The fascination with puppetry as fine art was also characteristic of the Polish puppet theatre. The director Janina Kilian Stanisławska confessed:

> I was and am attracted by the sculpture, the ineffable charm of movement, gesture – in fact the superiority of form over action, the domination of what is seen over what is heard in the puppet theatre.[44]

At the beginning of the twentieth century the main interest for researchers into puppet theatre lay in the definition of its essence and in the discovery of themes accessible to it. The majority of studies are superficially written, but some more profound writing on the aesthetic problems of puppetry is to be found in German literature. I have in mind three examples: the studies of Lothar Buschmeyer on the aesthetic characteristics of the puppet; of Holger Sandig on the relative values of plays written for puppets and on the expressive potential of the string puppet; and of Fritz Eichler on the essence of the hand puppet and the string puppet.

Lothar Buschmeyer[45] founded his considerations on Schasler's theory of art, perceiving it as the subjective expression of the spirit. This can be easily discerned through a study of his analyses, elaborated from a psychological base of subjective evidence and biographical information. Through these he arrived at his conclusions on the aesthetic influence of the puppet:

This work of art, the product of a human being, is born through the experience of emotion; it is a product which both embodies this emotion and which can, at the same time, transmit this emotion to others.[46]

Deliberating on the problem of the position of puppet theatre in 'arts systems', Buschmeyer posed the familiar question: 'Are we talking about mobile sculptures or is this in essence Spiel (theatre)?'[47] The second case seemed to him to be 'diminished dramatic art' (*verminderte dramatische Kunst*). In the transition of the puppet from the territory of fine art to that of dramatic art, it changes from object to subject, thanks to its apparent freedom of action. Viewed thus, the puppet may indeed be said to satisfy the requirements of dramatic art.

'Diminishment' (*Verminderung*) and other limitations of the puppet as a vehicle of dramatic expression might even be regarded as evidence of its artistic value. Art is, after all, a transformation of reality, and such a transformation may proceed in one of two directions, either to eliminate or to intensify some elements of reality. Thus one writer at least defended the 'minor' art of the puppet theatre, invoking the theory of the 'small' in art.

According to Buschmeyer, there are two groups of characteristics of puppet theatre: drawbacks and advantages. One of the advantages, generally recognized, is the total identification of the puppet with the character it portrays; for example, the puppet figure of 'Kasperle' presents exclusively the character and dramatic function of 'Kasperle'. (This is a re-statement of the observation of the Romantics.)

However, Buschmeyer thought that this characteristic, based on the unity of the scenographic elements of a performance, was over-estimated by theoreticians from the actors' theatre. In reality, it is the use made of the puppet when it is onstage that determines its value in its setting.

In his analysis of the puppet's expressivity, Buschmeyer revealed himself as a clear opponent of the use of puppets as imitators of real life, and a partisan of 'stylization' and archetypes. He believed that each puppet has its own peculiarity of movement, dictated by its centre of gravity and by the materials of which it is made. Puppets, he declared, frequently transcend the limitations of reality (as imposed on living actors) and this is due to the technical peculiarities of their construction: for example, the technique of the shadow puppet is determined by the fact that it is two-dimensional, and so on.

In the main part of his study Buschmeyer confronts the four so-called classic puppet techniques – glove, string, rod and shadow – with various literary forms, such as the fairy tale and the epic saga, and various aesthetic categories, such as the tragic, the sublime, the comic, the parodic and the humorous – altogether 14 genres and categories. He concludes that the expressive capability of the puppet is advantageous in almost every case, though he believes that the 'sublime' and the 'satiric' are accessible only to the shadow theatre. (This conclusion is surprising if we consider the success of the Polish *Szopka*, which includes a kind of satirical revue of famous personalities, played with rod puppets.) The puppets which Buschmeyer finds the most successful in most aesthetic categories are the string and the rod puppet, with the shadow puppet not far behind. He considers glove puppets the least useful, with only 6 out of the 14 categories accessible to it.

At the end of his book, Buschmeyer changed his approach to his subject, abandoning scholarship for a more partisan stance and becoming a propagandist for puppetry. Puppet theatre, he said, should be developed as a panacea for the advancing dangers of industrialization, an aid to the retention of the old values and relationships of society. He believed puppetry to be a rare branch of art, preserving folk customs and thus fulfilling an important role in the revitalization of spiritual vigour against the domination of materialism. Like many other writers of his time in many other countries, including Poland, he strongly supported folk theatre. He was of course right to do so; nonetheless, his views were somewhat limiting to the future of puppet theatre.

Most of Buschmeyer's study, consisting as it does of the confrontation of puppets and their various techniques with dramatic forms and aesthetic categories, is important as the first of its kind. His views are typical of the perception of the puppet theatre during the first decades of the twentieth century. He virtually analyses the puppet as an actor, concluding that although it is an object, it is in its 'materiality' that its greatest value lies. His theories are still valuable today and may be a basis for further deliberation. The weakness of his work lies in the presentation of conclusions as objective facts, although they are based only on subjective premises. For example, his last experiments, on audience reception of dramatic categories as presented by puppet theatre, prove only his personal experience and the influence of a particular environment, separate from other contemporary examples of theatre practice. His opinions and claims tell us only about his perceptions of the puppet as actor, and have little to do with the more general reality of the puppet theatre of the time. His views seem to be *desiderata*.

Holger Sandig, author of a second study,[48] limits his examination of the subject to the discovery of the expressive potential of one technique

Figure 1.1 From *Der aufhaltsame Auforry des Arturo Ui* by Bertolt Brecht, Czelabinsk Puppet Theatre, Russia, 1982

of puppetry only – that of the string marionette. He discusses the dramaturgy of the puppet theatre and the accessibility of the string puppet to some forms of drama and to some aesthetic categories. He lists the characteristics of string puppets, drawing on other theoretical studies, and is fascinated by the aesthetic consequences of the materiality of the stringed figure, believing it superior to the live actor. He is thus in agreement with Buschmeyer's conclusions, and actually goes even further in his enthusiasm for the expressive possibilities of puppets.

In his consideration of the archetypal nature of all puppets, Sandig distinguishes the string puppet as existing on the borderlines of the 'typical' and the 'individual'. He considers its relationship with surrounding objects and concludes that it is well suited to the theatre of surrealism. Sandig looks for the peculiar style of the string puppet – in its natural estrangement from reality – in the 'alienation effect' (*Verfremdungseffekt*), using the theory and practice of Bertolt Brecht.

Sandig thus arrived at what is undoubtedly the right conclusion, namely that the string puppet's repertory should be drawn from that which best suits its expressive capabilities; the demands of the play must accord with what it can actually do. He was inspired by George Polti's *Les Trente-Six Situations Dramatiques*, devoted to the dramatic works of Carlo Gozzi.[49] Of these 36 situations he maintained that puppet theatre might effectively interpret 12: those marked by clear intention, simplicity, potential stylization and the introduction of symbols, with a structure founded on 'pure' action and expressive gesture. This analysis demonstrates beyond doubt the limits of puppet expression *vis-à-vis* those of the live actor; similarly, Sandig leaves no room for doubt about its repertoire, which should, according to him, differ from that of the actors' theatre. The puppet's links with literature are also limited, which is why Sandig prefers the term 'scenic action' (*scenisches Spiel*), because the characteristics of the marionette lead it to mime-play rather than scripted drama. He argues, against Buschmeyer, that tragedy and sublimity can be successfully applied to the marionette stage. He differs from the other also in not attempting to be a propagandist for puppets: he was not as far removed as Buschmeyer from current theatre practice and practitioners. He provides many actual descriptions of puppet shows, although these were, I fear, especially selected to confirm his own theories and preconceptions. His conclusions might have been different had he analysed more diverse material from a wider geographical area.

The studies of Buschmeyer and Sandig arose out of a kind of vogue for puppet theatre at that period. This renaissance, and the interest shown by other kinds of artists, as well as the continuing theory of the über-marionette, provoked a need to define this surprising phenomenon. Scientific investigators, Buschmeyer and Sandig included, as well as puppeteers themselves, believed that the most important problem was to define the peculiar characteristics of the puppet theatre, and to fix its place firmly in the hierarchy of contemporary art.

The majority of those investigators had much sympathy and respect for puppetry, so perhaps it is necessary to note another writer whose views were decidedly more sceptical, Fritz Eichler. His scepticism was based on an analysis of the characteristics of puppet theatre practice in Germany through direct observation.

Eichler simplified his task by limiting his examination to only two techniques of puppetry, the glove and the string figure, then the most popular in Germany. Nevertheless, his analysis was comprehensive and wide-ranging. He was profoundly convinced that one can discover factors of style and the limits of a genre only while observing the creative process, noting therein the relationship between puppet and animator, and the applied technique of the piece to be performed. This, he said, was the only way to establish the place of the puppet and its links to the notion of 'theatre'.[50]

Today his principles are accepted by many authors, but at the time he was alone in reaching one relatively extreme conclusion: that the glove puppet is not to be considered as a 'pure' puppet, for it is actually the hand of the puppet-player which is its soul. The glove puppet is thus a 'prolongation' of the actor. Contrary to the string puppet, the glove puppet acts directly, spontaneously, which is why it should be considered as an extension of mime theatre. From mime, the glove puppet has inherited archetypal characters, above all the 'folk-fool' of Germany, Kasper. Any puppeteer who would animate Kasper – or Kasperle – has to identify with him to achieve success. Everything depends on the performer, on his invention, on his ability to project his folk characteristics to the full.

Kasper has constantly to improvise, especially when talking directly to the audience. He is a comic in the tradition of burlesque, using robust language rich in proverbs, gibberish, idioms and a primitive playing with words: 'The art of mime defines the limits of the glove puppet theatre ... Glove puppet theatre is not an art of style. It is vulgar, coarse, full of rude, simple vitality – it is folk art.'[51] He is right: there is no need to provide proof of the fact that folk art, however well nurtured, becomes less and less vivid, and slowly enters museums.

The string puppet, however, is different; it is an *objectum*, says Eichler. It is separated from the body of its manipulator and has its own mechanical laws, so strongly stressed by Kleist and Craig. Physical separation causes psychic separation and this, Eichler claims, adversely influences the string puppet and explains its passive nature: 'The marionette theatre is a theatre deprived of life, deprived of mimicry.'[52] The statement forms the basis of his dismissal of the whole style of the theatre of the string marionette.

According to Eichler, the marionette theatre has always been a dependant of the live theatre, although the dependence has manifested itself in different ways over the centuries. It is possible for the marionette to achieve its particular and authentic style, but first it must be emancipated from the 'drama' theatre as well as from the mime theatre as represented by glove puppets. A search must be made for what truly suits the genre – for *puppenhaft*. The marionette's best opportunities lie in the grotesque, in fantasy, in poetics. But this is only a theory: Eichler does not really believe that the aesthetic of the marionette theatre can ever attract a wide public, at least in Germany.

This pessimism about the future of glove puppets and marionettes is based on reasoned analysis, and the scholar is left with a feeling of regret, however partisan he may be for this type of theatre. This regret is shared by many of today's marionettists who suffer from the lack of interest, if not of the public, certainly of theatre critics.

These three German studies – by Buschmeyer, Sandig and Eichler – deal with those features of the puppet theatre which distinguish it from other kinds of theatre. This differentiation is well served by the word *puppenhaft* and its opposite *nichtpuppenhaft*, 'puppetlike' and 'unpuppet-like'. Their use was common to both theoreticians and practitioners from the 1930s to the 1950s. In *puppenhaft* they looked for the essence of the puppet theatre and for its *raison d'être*. Take, for example, the words of the most eminent puppet-player of the first half of the twentieth century, Sergei Obraztsov:

> What is the position of the puppet theatre in the contemporary family of genres of the performing arts, and what are the prospects for its development? Answers to these questions demand proof that puppet theatre is necessary to the public at all. This proof will come only when it has been demonstrated beyond doubt that what may be expressed by a puppet cannot be expressed by a human actor.[53]

Obraztsov continues, proving this importance thus – that puppetry is needed by people because it generalizes life's phenomena in a particularly expressive way:

> If satire and romantic heroism exist, if there was ever a Swift or a Homer, a Rabelais or a Gogol, then there must be a puppet theatre. It is needed as a unique and irreplaceable genre of the performing arts. No actor is able to create the representation of a generalized human being, because he is himself an individual. Only the puppet can do this, because it is not a human being.[54]

Puppenhaft (*kukolnoe* in Russian), says Obraztsov, is the essence of the puppet theatre, proved through comparisons with live theatre; but much more important to him is the way to achieve a 'realistic generalization' through puppets. The same words can be seen to serve different aesthetic concepts; we may remember that the German theorists expressed a subjective philosophy of the art, where Obraztsov aims for objective realism.

In Poland, where little has been written on the theory of puppet theatre, Ignacy Matuszewski responded to the publication of Magnin's great work with a study on *Heroes of the Puppet Stage*.[55] More popular was a book by Jan Sztaudynger, *Marionettes*,[56] through which the author wished to promote the puppet theatre. One chapter of interest is concerned with 'the aesthetic values of marionettes'.

Jan Sztaudynger was in favour of a clear differentiation between puppet and actors' theatre. He was closer to the German theories than to Obraztsov, and was rather attached to the old metaphor which compared the destiny of the marionette in the hands of the puppeteer with the destiny of man in the hands of God. Taking his starting point from this metaphor, Sztaudynger argues with Kleist's theory:

> It seems to me that Kleist was wrong in attributing the charm of the marionette to its complete lack of self-consciousness. Its charm more probably lies simply in the point of contact between matter and spirit, particularly when that matter takes on life, completely and without resistance.[57]

He clearly did not understand Kleist's meaning, although he was fascinated by some aspects of his theorizing. Sztaudynger concluded that the puppet theatre was:

> a theatre which permits us to feel the tragedy of the human through that of the puppet; a theatre which gives us the delightful power of the God-substitute; a theatre which enters into the secrets of the human spirit; a theatre which can be an exquisite example of the radiating force of spirit and the metamorphosis of psychic forces into matter – this is something quite different from the usual theatre. The theatre of live people is a human theatre, but the marionette theatre is fashioned after the divine. The human theatre is for adults. The puppet theatre is for children, for simple people, for people of humble spirit and for artists – for all those who are close to God.[58]

There were not many publications on this subject after the Second World War, although some interest remained in Craig's theory of the über-marionette, especially from the famous Polish director Leon Schiller, a correspondent with Craig over many years and in sympathy with many of his theories.

Schiller (1887–1954) spent his youth in Krakow, and became influenced by the ideas of Polish Modernism, including an interest in the puppet theatre, which resulted in a projected foundation of his own puppet company in Krakow in 1917. Unfortunately this was never accomplished and he became a director of actors' theatre, developing the idea of a 'monumental theatre', one which would present imposing images of humanity's most important ideas and achievements. He returned to thoughts of puppets during the German occupation, when all Polish theatres were closed. After the failure of the Warsaw uprising in 1944, Schiller was interned in the Polish prisoner-of-war camp in Murnau. Here he became interested in the work of the soldiers' puppetry group and offered them some lectures, among them a reflection on 'Live Theatre and the Theatre of Artificial Figures'.[59] He stated that since the time of Craig there had been many changes in theatre; the marionette was no more in any position to replace an actor but, in full harmony with the actor, might serve the same cause:

> There was a period of time when the Übermarionette was an aesthetic problem, an instrument in the hands of the enemies of realism ... Today we are inclined to research its development and to value its importance less from the aesthetic point of view, more from a consideration of historical facts including the social background which has made it grow. In this way deliberation on the Übermarionette has taken on a new meaning. The Übermarionette enters the proscenium of theatrical creativity, taking its place next to the actor, this time not to oppose him but to lead the battle for a common cause.
>
> The cause has been common no matter whether the art of theatre wants to teach or to entertain, whether it made its spectators fly above concrete everyday reality, or plunged them into this reality over their ears.
>
> If Hamlet orders Polonius to respect actors, because they are 'a living and summarized chronicle of time', we should give the same privilege to the Übermarionette. It brings us a story of its immemorial history and, by the way, the history of theatre art in general.[60]

It is clear that the puppet (the über-marionette) was gaining more and more consideration, even if at first this was only among theoreticians and theatre connoisseurs.

After 1945, with the end of the Second World War, puppeteers and critics resumed their deliberations on puppets, and again discussed their specificity. Everybody had something to say, so we have many points of view. The situation in France, where hand (or glove) puppets have always received much appreciation among puppeteers, was interesting due equally to George Sand's enthusiasm for them and to the important role of the hand puppet Guignol in French popular culture. Very influential too was the excellent French theatre director Gaston Baty, who used hand puppets in his scenic experiments. André-Charles Gervais, one of Baty's students, described the directing methods of his master, as well as his total embrace of the glove puppet. In his writings we find a new description of the aesthetic values of this puppet's form. Gervais wrote in 1947:

> From the two big puppet families – 'fantoccini' or marionettes and 'burattini' or hand puppets – we chose the second one for our work, because it possessed most completely all the features characteristic of puppets and because its inability to imitate a live actor leads us onto the field of convention.[61]

Gervais was clearly opposed to Buschmeyer's and Eichler's thesis – which is easy to explain. Buschmeyer and Eichler were men of theory, while Gervais presented the practice and, in particular, the experiments of a great master, Gaston Baty. The two theoreticians spoke about the expressive possibilities of various types of puppet, stating that practitioners had not used them to their full potential. Gervais did not analyse the expressive possibilities of each type of puppet, as described by the theoreticians, but presented the results of a theatrical practice, which in France was in favour of the hand puppet.

Some other writers were fascinated by the puppet, its identity and meaning, and that of the character it represented. Puppeteers tried hard to discover the practical meaning of *puppenhaft* and they, together with a few scholars, thought that the best reason for the existence of the puppet theatre lay solely in the fact of its distinction from other forms of theatre.

Erik Kolar, Czech theoretician and director, decided in 1964 to solve the problem once and for all, by publishing a study called 'Puppetness × 26'. It is impossible to present his deliberation as a whole (it is published in the periodical *Československý loutkář*, or *Czech Puppetry*[62]). I give here only his general thesis, which is based on a book written by the German writer Tankred Dorst. Kolar agreed that there is a specificity to puppet theatre:

> Dorst is right to observe ... that the illusionist stage and the psychological theatre are dying out. A new interest is born in other genres of art, in other forms, more appropriate to our times. We agree with him that puppet theatre is this 'old-new' kind of form. It is important however that it exploits its own territory, its own signs, which,

together with the laws of any theatre art, will determine its autonomy. There is no doubt that its specificity will grow and that the puppet theatre will constantly move away from the actors' theatre.[63]

In his 26 'points', Kolar collected all the characteristics of the puppet, but he did so in an eclectic way, with no selection, and here we find puppet characteristics taken from various different aesthetics. When Kolar says, quoting Bogatyrev, that puppets cannot replace humans as they constitute a sign (symbol) of the human, and more precisely a sign of dramatic character; or when he refers to Obraztsov, presenting the puppet's capabilities not available to the live actor, the puppet player may bring to the audience 'the miracle of a sculpture brought to life'. Kolar quotes his Soviet master:

> The puppet does not need to take off its hat and then put it back on to make an impression on its spectators. When a puppet simply sits down on a chair, crosses its legs and smokes a cigarette – that is, when it executes the simplest acts – this is enough to provoke great applause and a fervent reaction from audiences. Why is this the case? Because each act of the puppet transforms immediately into an image (a picture). Spectators see any drawing and any puppet as an object that is not alive. That is why everybody sees its alive-ness as a sort of miracle.[64]

This is a new version of Otakar Zich's earlier observations, and we might think that the circle of deliberation on the nature of the puppet is already closed; that all its expressive possibilities and functions are already researched and described. But the following period shows that such a judgment would be incorrect. Semioticians had many things to say in this respect, but the semiotic theory of theatre needs special treatment, to which I will return later on. For the moment, to complete earlier phases of research, I would like to point to some anthropological aspects of the puppet's evaluation.

   It is true that puppet theatre up until now had not elicited the interest of anthropologists. However, we can find this kind of deliberation in the anthroposophist activists from the circle of Rudolf Steiner, who used puppets for education and treated them as having an 'aprioristic value'. Elke Blattmann, for instance, placed the puppet in a system of human values, as can be seen when reading her definition of the puppet, as well as her differentiation of two types of puppets: the hand puppet and the marionette:

The marionette depends on its central point, the point of gravity. As in the temple of Apollo, where the central point is the most important, so the marionette circles its own 'omphalos'. Its limbs move with charm and harmony, oriented by this point. It follows that as Apollo belongs to the higher gods, a marionette is manipulated from on high. It depends on a dynamic power located above it in the most profound sense of the word. The utterances of the Delphic Oracle signal this unavoidable dependency. The laws of destiny are fulfilled pitilessly in the face of human opposition, as the myth of Oedipus demonstrates. However, the manipulators of the marionette put their trust in these laws and are subordinate to their power. Apollo's instrument is the lyre: in the same way that he moves the strings externally to give them sound, so the marionette player dominates the strings of his puppet from without.

The case of the hand puppet player, who performs the part of Kasperle, is completely different. He himself fills his puppet. His consciousness is so much oriented to contact with an audience that he loses awareness of his own hand. This is because he lets himself identify with this character which is so full of contradictions, who is only the 'clothing' of his hand, and though without legs yet appears to stand firmly on the ground, which can catch things strongly with its rudimentary hands, speak vividly through solid lips, excite the spectators by its careless, anarchic acts. Besides, Kasperle loves playing with words, transformations, and all kinds of contradictions and paradoxes. Dionysus' instrument is the flute, its interior breath causes its sounds. The puppet player slips into Kasperle and lives in his interior. Dionysus belongs to the powers of the underworld. The hand puppet too comes from the depths; it receives its life from below.[65]

Searching for an explanation of the characteristics of various types of puppet within the mythical order of the world might be very productive, but it is also in some cases dangerous – because it is easy to fall into exaggeration and lose the sense of possible or actual analogies. In any case, it is impressive to find that looking for puppet theatre's specificity could be equal to experiencing the values of the mythical world. Nevertheless, Blattmann's surprising thesis also highlighted how little had been done to enlarge the research methodology, as proved by the lack of serious anthropological and symbolic interpretations of puppet theatre.

At the end of the 1950s a new tendency started to develop within puppetry. I would call this 'centrifugal', because it opposes the puppet's specificity for the sake of enriching its means of expression. The first natural complement of the puppet on the puppet theatre stage was the human being. Humans have performed with puppets for centuries, for instance the musician in the Petrushka play, or as a character and thus the partner of the puppet in a special repertory such as *Gulliver in Lilliput*. Miroslav Česal, from the Prague Academy of Fine Art, has published a study of all the possible reasons for such a partnership.[66]

The presence of actors in a puppet production used to be accepted as natural, as long as they acted in the role of compère or the puppet's companion. Although these actors belonged in the puppet's world, critics and historians of puppet theatre did not allow themselves the thought that any mixture of the 'puppet-like' and the human means of expression could be possible. A representative of this conservative way of thinking is the German theoretician Hans Richard Purschke. In an article from 1953, he rejected the possibility of any cooperation of man and hand puppet in a scenic situation:

> The human who appears in the world of hand puppets immediately destroys its puppet-like illusion. Hand puppets immediately lose their power in convincing and charming their spectators, because they are seen in their true nature as papier-mâché, wood, and cloth. Because of this human appearance the spectator can compare the puppet and the human and sees the imperfection of the hand puppet image and its movements. The world of puppets and the world of humans are separate, they exclude each other. This is self-evident especially in the case of the marionette and in the case of the unreal play of shadows. It would be appropriate to adapt Kipling's words: human is human, and puppet is puppet, and never the twain shall meet.[67]

The German tradition deceived Purschke, just as his research instinct misled him. Very soon he was to learn that a cooperation between puppet and actor is indeed possible. The new aesthetics of the puppet theatre consists in an awareness of the fact that a human surrounded by puppets appears more 'human', and that a puppet among humans appears more 'puppet-like'. Purschke understood his mistake and, seeing the inevitable victory of the new aesthetics, allowed Tankred Dorst, in 1958, to pronounce in his (Purschke's) magazine *Perlicko-Perlacko* that the presence of an actor on the puppet stage means a triumph of the 'alienation effect':

The marionette maintains a distance from the spectator in the same way as the 'thing' which it represents. Its movements are not 'natural'. This is true in moments when it is imitative; it affords distance, because it is not presenting but only 'showing' the stage character's acting. Here is the source of the comical acting of the figure, that imitation of the piano virtuoso. One should understand this as something important for the style of performance. If in the 19th century one tried to animate figures in the most invisible, secret and mysterious manner, so today one accepts the revelation of the human who manipulates the puppet ... And this is not an inconsequential thought, simply replacing the threads applied in the 19th century by visible iron wires to operate the figures. The spectators should be aware that the figures are puppets made for acting, that puppet theatre is performing the parable of our reality – a performance observed by those who participate in it.[68]

Tankred Dorst was reacting to the new practices and to the fact that puppet theatre had started to include new forms of expression, such as masks and live actors, giving rise to a new approach to the über-marionette theory. At the 8th UNIMA Congress in Warsaw, Krystyna Mazur gave a lecture on 'The Romance of the Marionette', offering a nice metaphor for the new relationship of the puppet to the live theatre. Recalling Craig, Leon Schiller and the Bauhaus artists, Mazur declared the puppet theatre to be a 'convention of total theatre', the synthesis of every means of dramatic expression, through puppet, mask and living body.

She also listed all the elements of the puppet to be found in the actors' theatre, stating that the renaissance of the puppet was a result of the same development that had brought about the 'objectivization' of the face of the actor:

The relationship between the actor and the puppet figure has been re-evaluated. Today nobody speaks about their competition. On the one hand there is the development of a drama of ideas, alongside the drama of moral sentiment, which is going in the direction of chamber forms, with only limited spectacle. Since the era of extermination camps and the atomic bomb, the human being has given expression to his tragic monologue on a bare stage. The puppet figure tactfully stays away from such territory for which it is inadequate. But when anti-naturalistic tendencies return from time to time to the stage, the door is open for this figure to enter, but this time with no wish to fight the actor, but rather to cooperate with him. The figure has thus become his perfect companion, to present the grotesque and absurd mechanism of the contemporary world.[69]

Although Mazur acknowledged the separate characteristics of the puppet theatre, she doubted whether laying stress on its separateness would be good for its future:

> Insisting on the independence of the puppet as a theatre genre, trying not to see the links with live theatre, though they certainly exist, seems to be pushing puppetry into an artistic backwater, which will sooner or later cause its artistic decline.[70]

Krystyna Mazur's reasoning was developed by the German artist Harro Siegel, who confirmed the rise of interest in the potential links between puppetry and other kinds of theatre when he wrote:

> As puppeteers, we should look at our artistic genre as at an element of a larger whole. We should not be afraid of some sallies into unexplored territory, nor of new means of expression. Within the boundaries of each particular area of theatre, we should not stress what divides but what unites us, to encourage a mutual approach and to strengthen bonds.[71]

The views of Mazur and Siegel were based on their observation of the realities of theatre in the 1950s. Their conclusions, while sounding rather biased in favour of particular artistic tendencies, were in fact confirmed more and more by the development of contemporary puppet theatre practice.[72]

Since then, many writers have continued to concern themselves with the discovery of the essence of puppet theatre and its constitutive characteristics. Janusz Galewicz, another Pole, undertook an experiment to try to define puppet theatre as an art form. He took as his starting point a definition of live theatre elaborated by Janina Makota[73] using a terminology drawn from the aesthetics of Roman Ingarden. Ingarden's theory was that any work of art is a purely intentional entity. It exists through the support given by its material base, the material being of many different things: objects, humans, sound waves and so on. To put it more simply, we can imagine the creator of a work of art as making an 'impression' on a material base after which it is taken over by the 'receiver' (the spectator, the audience etc.).

The material base of live theatre is living people and their actions within defined surroundings and objects, together with the sounds (words, music etc.), appropriate to these actions.[74] In addition, these living beings have a temporal existence and are involved in a process which is clearly manifested by the time and the development of the dramatic action.

The same may be said of puppet theatre: the only difference lies in the function of the things and the people. Janusz Galewicz wrote:

> As for art presented on the puppet stage, the actor lends his voice (word sounds) and the 'appearance' of movement to the stage char-acter but not the visual appearance, which is provided by the puppet itself. The 'appearances', of movement are on a borderline since these, given by a human being, lead to a sort of catalysis which suggests that what is seen is the puppet's *quasi* life.[75]

An actor in the puppet theatre does not take part in the visual appear-ances, which are left to the puppet. He is responsible for the 'appearance of movement', which he shares with the puppet. The 'word sounds' are exclusively his, to the same extent as in the live theatre. From this one could say that the actor's concessions to the puppet are relatively minor, and therefore the similarity of the two genres is relatively major.

The same problem aroused the curiosity of Erik Kolar, who viewed it from another angle: 'Puppetry – Fine Art or Theatre?' The answer to this question, the title of his essay, was, as we might have anticipated, that puppetry is a genre of theatre for these reasons:

- puppet theatre, like live theatre, is an art form developed within time and space;
- it symbolizes the unfolding of characters and events;
- its 'receivers' are the witnesses of a process of creation;
- it is a constantly renewed interaction between puppeteers and public;
- it is always a collective or group work;
- it is always a synthetic work of art.

The difference between live and puppet theatre lies in the fact that the actor is the essence of the first, and the puppeteer is the essence of the second, with the puppet as his instrument.[76]

Galewicz and Kolar were interested in the puppet theatre for itself, as a separate theatre genre. Although puppeteers were searching for means of expression far beyond their own theatre, Kolar and Galewicz deliberately ignored the fact. They did so to stress the essence of puppet theatre, so one could say that their conclusions had a normative intention: they meant to assist in the preservation of puppet theatre as a genre of its own, with its own specific qualities.

An important work concerned with the aesthetics of puppet theatre in recent years was a study by Roger Daniel Bensky entitled *Recherches sur les structures et la symbolique de la marionnette* (Research on the Structures and Symbolism of the Puppet).[77] He was interested in three aspects: aesthetics, psychology and metaphysics. The importance of the work lies in Bensky's additions to the modern understanding of the puppet theatre. Bensky is a theoretician; he knows his subject more from his reading than from first-hand observation of performance. He finds it easy to deliberate on the nature of the puppet, which he defines as follows:

> The puppet is, in exact terms, a mobile object, un-derived, made for dramatic action, operated either visibly or invisibly by whatever techniques its inventor has chosen. Its use is for theatrical performance.[78]

And what is puppet play?

> As a phenomenon of theatre, puppet play implies a dramatic action, a representation of reality, a playing or stage area and an audience. The puppet is first a form of theatrical expression before it is transformed into an expressive idea.[79]

The puppet is an object. Though it is capable of action onstage, its life is nothing more than a projection of the human imagination. This projection is a characteristic of certain human recreational activities (fantasies) that are not always to do with making theatre:

> And so the object offers itself to the individual as an extension of his being in the surrounding universe, an augmented affirmation of his total existence. The 'I' duplicates itself in order to confirm its being.[80]

According to Bensky, the puppet seems to be a simple means of self-confirmation. He used the word 'object' as an alternative to 'puppet', which is rather confusing. The puppet as 'mobile object' has a theatrical nature and when performing onstage it may actually become the 'subject'. Thus it is different from all other 'objects' which may participate in the process of the 'projection of the human imagination'.

Bensky was troubled that some puppeteers extended the word 'puppet ' to toys, mechanical figures, mannequins and so on, demonstrating a fascination for non-theatrical objects. He saw in this fascination a special danger which leads to a kind of limitation of the human imagination, wherein the puppet might become a 'mirror without a soul'.

Bensky is an opponent of the puppet as imitator of the human, especially the puppet which has pretensions to a kind of independent existence. He prefers the puppet to be essentially theatrical. He perceives it as an 'expressive object' which is the vehicle for subjective human thoughts. It gives humans the opportunity to aspire to a transformed reality, to the world of poetry.

Sharing with Bensky his dislike of human simulacra, I am reminded that the puppet of today has become an 'expressive object' in quite a new way, without any attempt to imitate the human. Applying different means of expression, the puppet theatre of today is more and more concerned with the poetic metaphor of the puppet. The phenomenon is discussed in more detail in my study 'Relations between Masks, Puppets and Humans as a Source of Metaphor', written in 1967.[81]

A second weakness in Bensky's deliberations is the substitution of the dramatic function of the animated puppet by the psychological functions of the animated object. While there is no doubt that the psychological aspect of puppet theatre is important, even essential, considered as part of the anthropological approach to the problem, Bensky ignored the different functions of the puppet in its historical development.

The works of theory discussing ontological and aesthetic principles had no influence on the puppet theatre, which goes its own way according to the fashionable impulses of the time. Thus theatre practices using various figures – actors, masks and objects – on the puppet stage, all in one show, demand a critical evaluation. I tried to respond to this in 1966 in an article entitled 'Perspectives of Puppet Theatre's Development'.[82] Having described the tendency to combine 'live' and 'puppet-like' means of expression, I proposed the name 'third genre' for this new style. I meant by this a middle ground between human dramatic expression and the expressiveness of the material puppet. This was not a discovery, but only a statement of fact. In any case, this statement did not disturb the status of 'classical' puppet theatre.

The 'third genre' consists in the mixing of the means of expression of puppet and actors' theatre. It breaks the conventions or principles of the puppet's 'magic' life, but it is not able to break the convention of the actor's biological life. Thus the destruction of the magic of the puppet is not followed by any similar breakdown in the treatment of the actor, and the third genre does not result in an equivalence of aesthetic form. The mixing of the means of expression favours only the actor. Even so, the coexistence on stage of actor and puppet elements does create the opportunity for a new metaphorical language of theatre.

The arrival of the third genre has not impeded the development of the puppet theatre in its pure form: it will always exist as an attractive alternative to the actors' theatre. There will always be a place for it in the theatre, as there has been until now, both in avant-garde and in so-called traditional performance. Besides, we live at a time when the actor wants to present as much artifice in his work as possible, so there is no reason why the artificial puppets should not represent as much realism as possible.

In considering the characteristics of the third genre, I exposed its limitations when simply and mechanically applying it as a means of expression, without any dramatic reason or regard for its consequences. This is why I took the liberty of posing various questions:

> An interesting problem arose – to what extent might the 'third genre' be an extension of puppet theatre? Might its demystification be equally its extension? Certainly it might be. However, the third genre has a certain defect, which warns us to be cautious in formulating our opinions. Breaking the taboo of the magic life of the puppet, the third genre does not intend to break 'the last taboo' – that of the 'physical corporeality of the live actor'. The third genre acts unilaterally: it follows the attitude of the reformers of dramatic theatre from the beginning of the twentieth century, who deliberated on the use of puppets to oppose the domination of the live actor. However, the third genre did not propose a change of theatre philosophy, but limited itself to an enlargement of the means of expression. Naturally, it has its place among the visual arts, but only as a symbiosis of the two genres, which were not transformed into a new quality (as an autonomous genre).[83]

This view of the third genre was the basis of my defence of the values of the puppet theatre – *sensu stricto*. I treated the third genre as a new phenomenon and, in my own sense of it, the presence of the third genre was not a threat to the existence of puppet theatre, which had always been attractive as an alternative to actors' theatre. So I wrote:

There is a place for the puppet in avant-garde theatre, as has been the case up until now. Besides there are still other territories of theatrical art, addressed to spectators of other, less refined, artistic expectations. The theatre has responded to them for many centuries and puppet theatre has done the same. It will continue its art, surprising its audience by its specificity. Of course, I speak about 'good' puppet theatre. Who knows – it might be a traditional or a classic production. We live in a time when the live actor wants to show in his work as much 'artificiality' as possible; why then could not the artificial puppet produce as much life as possible?[84]

Anxiety because of the apparent destruction of puppetry as a theatre genre was voiced by Leonora Shpet at the Symposium on 'Puppet Theatre Today and Tomorrow' held in Lodz, Poland, in November 1967. She described in detail the process of disintegration of the traditional puppet theatre as the result of too much analysis of its characteristics:

We [the puppeteers] have tried everything and now it seems that there is nothing left to be analyzed and dissected. What more can we do? Let us now start to put together again all these parts, like children with toys they have taken to pieces. Sometimes, however, it feels as though we are putting together parts which are not necessarily the right ones.[85]

Leonora Shpet was not an ideologist of Soviet aesthetics; she was open to artistic novelties. Her conclusion tells us about her irritation towards any experiment that was without dramatic meaning: puppeteers should return to the 'true and typical means of expression' if they wish to start once more to convey important emotions or opinions on the problems of our time.

Nevertheless, it became gradually noticeable that heterogeneity in the means of expression served to evoke a metaphorical theatre language. The visible presence of the puppet manipulator with his puppet recalled the ancient metaphor about the dependence of a human being (here the puppet) on supernatural powers (here the puppet-player). An actor removing a mask during a show may be understood as a metaphorical presentation of the human face in opposition to the dead mask.

In 1923, Petr Bogatyrev published his first study devoted to the stylistic value of the folk puppet theatre. However, he only discussed the rhetorical figures of natural language, such as oxymoron, metaphor, metathesis and so on.[86] He did not foresee that half a century later these figures would serve as structures for visual metaphor or visual synecdoche. For many centuries theatre art has exploited metaphorical images, but only recently have these become a subject of analysis and comment.

The puppeteers – artists such as Yves Joly, Jan Wilkowski and Margareta Niculescu – freely used metaphor,[87] the importance of which was pointed out by Niculescu. At the Congress of UNIMA in Warsaw in June 1962, she delivered a lecture on 'Metaphor as a Means of Expression', presenting several examples of its use in puppet theatre. Obraztsov also thought that the puppet itself is a metaphor, because it is not a human being but his image, his presentation. Many puppeteers and critics followed Obraztsov, believing that any plastic deformation of the human image through the puppet is worthy of being called a metaphor. Naturally, they were right, although they did not pay attention to the fact that the stage puppet is already an exhausted metaphor, a petrified one. Nobody among its spectators perceives it as something new; the puppet as metaphor does not reveal anything. For a long time puppet theatre has been socially obvious.

At the present time, however, due to the new artistic context of the third genre, the puppet has rediscovered its metaphorical energy. At the end of the 1960s it became clear that the third genre stands firmly as a distinct and separate genre of theatre art. I came back to this subject in a lecture in Bochum in 1971, entitled 'Co-operation of People, Puppets and Masks on the Theatrical Stage as a Philosophical Metaphor'. Here, for the first time, I called the third genre a theatre of mixed media (*Theater der Mischformen*, or multimedia theatre). I said this because the puppet now exists in a completely new situation:

> Romanticism discovered in the puppet a material object that has its own formal value. For example, in Kleist's theory the puppet is not a little human, but an object with a centre of gravity and its own expressive ability. Our times have discovered the puppet as an interesting partner of the actor – in a mask or without one. The puppet is no longer an homunculus or an isolated object. It has become an element of theatre art, which cooperates with many other means of expression, and in this role it has achieved a special importance. This happened exclusively in the theatre of mixed media.[88]

The organizers of the international conference 'The Puppet in the Service of Metaphor', during the festival at Bielsko-Biala in May 1972, identified the same issue, as indicated by the title of the conference. The majority of participants talked about double-level metaphor – at the level of the puppet itself (with which I was arguing earlier) and at the level of the production, with the possibility of a dynamic metaphor, originating from the juxtaposition of various elements. Most representative of this view was the lecture of Hungarian critic Ede Tarbay:

> The first and most basic metaphor in puppet theatre appears at the moment when the player takes the puppet in his hand, and it exists as long as the player demonstrates it on stage. At such a moment the animated substance loses its material qualities and transforms into its own negation.
>
> Another metaphor is connected with an object that is presented on stage. In this case, it is important whether we are able to convince a spectator that the given object is alive. It is important whether we are able to transform the wooden ball into a human figure. In this case we can speak of a concrete metaphor. The essence of the metaphorical presentation consists in the spectator's emotional and intellectual reaction to the creative impulses of an artist.
>
> That is why I am not able to accept the multimedia theatre, in which a player is seen next to the puppet, as a metaphorical presentation. In this case, the puppet has lost its metaphorical meaning due to the alienation effect. Also, the artist ignores the theatrical competence of the spectator, trying to explain to him the principle of metaphor.[89]

Tarbay's submission in 1972 proves that some puppeteers and critics opposed the idea of multimedia theatre. They protested especially against 'demystified' theatre, which also transformed it into a self-referential art. It did not present a story, as with classical theatre, but showed the process of creation, hidden until then behind a screen. That the protesters were not right, however, is suggested by the cultural theorist Jurij Lotman:

> The puppet theatre uncovers theatricality within the art of theatre. When theatre art reaches the highest level of naturalism it has to recall to itself as well as to its spectators the need to think about its specificity. Thus the folk art of puppet theatre becomes one of the models for the live actors. By contrast, in periods when the theatre

strives to conquer its conventionalism – seeing in it its capital sin – puppet theatre is pushed off to the peripheries of art and aesthetics.

The art of the second half of the twentieth century intends to a certain degree to develop an awareness of its own specificity. The art presents ... the art itself, striving to get the measure of its own limits. For that the art of puppetry became situated at the centre of contemporary artistic problems. The juxtaposition of magic stories (children's and folk worlds) and the images of automatic, inanimate life open huge possibilities for expressing the eternally living problems of contemporary art.[90]

The critics were wrong when faced with the developing tendencies of theatre art. In spite of many traditionalists' reservations, metaphor, born from the visible cooperation of actor and puppet, will be the central subject of research into the language of contemporary puppet theatre.

Deliberation on the means of expression as well as the cultural function of puppetry was complemented by the psychoanalytic interpretations of the puppet offered by Annie Gilles, a French psychologist.[91] She was a diligent observer of the festival's shows in Charleville-Mézières, where she gathered rich comparative material. Applying structural and psychological methods, she proposed some general theses, although her conclusions might come as a surprise to those who have not followed psychoanalytic methods of explaining the secrets of artistic creativity.

We have to note that psychoanalysis has the merit of many important impulses in researching literature and art, but at the same time it has provoked much resistance due to its one-sidedness. Arnold Hauser has expressed this reservation well. He wrote in 1958:

Research into the work of art considered as a medium for the transmission of sexual symbolism was from the very beginning a beloved branch of psychoanalytic inquiry. It was a charming activity, which might be accomplished more or less mechanically and which allows one, apparently, to formulate an unlimited number of brave hypotheses with surprising results.

However, as time passed, the effect of surprise disappeared, diminished, and at the end everybody was accustomed to (and even bored by) the statement that each material object might be a symbol for the genitals, that almost all human relations might be linked with the Oedipus complex, that art is full of maternal images, and that epic and tragic heroes have no other fear than that of being castrated.[92]

Puppeteers can hardly speak about being bored, because until now psychoanalytic critics have not dealt with the puppet (except for some occasional remarks and references). We should be grateful to Gilles for filling this gap, although her thesis represents a one-sided view of the world, as already mentioned.

We will not be surprised, then, by her first conclusion, when she declares that all the puppet shows that she saw and analysed originated either from the fear of castration, or the Oedipus complex, or some narcissistic deviations. Taking the opinions of Jan Kott and René Sieffert as starting points, she tries to convince us that the two famous plays by the 'Japanese Shakespeare', Chikamatsu Monzaemon – *The Banished Priest* and *The Double Suicide in Sonezaki* – express the threat of castration by political power on the one hand and familial power on the other. The same motif exists in Marivaux's play (produced by the Compagnie Dominique Houdart) in which Harlequin opposes the wooing of an elderly fairy. In this, he is defending himself from maternal, incestuous, castrating love.

There is no reason to argue with applying such methods of analysis. However, we must note that all the literary examples given by the author suggest that the fear of castration is a characteristic of all characters from the puppet repertory, as well as characters from the majority of literary works, as was suggested already in the quote from Hauser.

Another of Gilles's conclusions refers to the relationship between puppet player and puppet, which very often – according to her view – has a narcissistic character, or which is the expression of a complex concerning the 'father figure'. She found a confirmation of this approach in the character of Geppetto, the carpenter who carved the Pinocchio puppet, as well as in many stories that tell about the attachment of puppeteers to the puppets they have made. She ended her deliberations with a question: Is not a puppet a symbolic son, an object and mirror of the puppeteer's libido?

Gilles also spoke about the puppet's ability to manifest the process of projection. Although she did not say anything new in this, it was a starting point for discussing the most important question, which I refer to below.

Unquestionably, the constant – and at the same time unique – element of puppet playing is the coexistence of the puppet and its manipulator. This is a situation of necessary duality both in the speculative sense and on the technical level. There is no need to recall that puppet playing is a distinct form of theatre. However, it is a form in the state of dissociation, and as such it offers numerous examples of expressive possibilities and variations.[93]

In making this remark, Gilles was obliged to confront the puppet theatre with Brecht's theory of alienation. So for her, puppet theatre seemed to be a theatre of paradox, one that proposed the double play of illusion and reality. She is conscious that the parallel is not absolute, so she prefers to say that puppet theatre presents an 'extreme position'.

It is important in the case of child audiences that with the artist's guidance they see the 'objective-ness' of a puppet. In this situation the puppet has the function of the 'transitional object', so important in child psychology, aided by the 'anthropomorphism' of the classical puppet. (Gilles does not agree that the modern use of the name 'puppet' should include any kind of object.) These deliberations led her to a basic thesis, which I now quote at length:

> If we remember that the puppet is a sign of the manipulator's power, that the puppet is an object marked by the libido of the person who manipulates it and also for the person who sees this manipulation, that it knows the state of abandonment and the state of no-life, which is not synonymous with the state of death; that at the end the puppet is a sort of appendix, separate from the manipulator's body, that giving its life reveals the sense of the 'true image of the ego', we would be inclined to think, that the puppet's latent value is that of a substitute phallus. If we agree, following Freud and Lacan, that the phallus is a basic signifier of the unconscious; and if we agree on the phallic meaning of the puppet, we will understand the universal importance of the puppet. We will understand its surprising energy for survival in spite of the competition of cinema, as well as the passions that it evokes: the fundamental signification of puppet theatre is phallic. This latent phallic value does not contradict other values discovered in studying the relations between a child and puppet. These same people may, unconsciously, be sensitive in their childhood first to each other and next to the phallic symbolism of the puppet.[94]

We have to acknowledge that particular and highly differentiated puppet techniques caused many difficulties for being categorized in terms of this analysis. It was easy in the case of the rod puppet, where Gilles addressed the idea of André Tahon's figures, simple rod puppets called *marottes*. In one of his variety shows Tahon showed a striptease by the puppet which ended with the revelation of the protruded stick. The issue is more complicated when we speak about the hand puppet, because this puppet may only start its acting after its penetration. So it is a contradiction of the phallus, and seems to be an equivalent of the feminine sex. Gilles found a solution here in separating the study of children's and adults' reception. For children, the hand puppet remains a phallic symbol. Only adults, who know the hand puppet's construction, understand it in an ambivalent way. Marionettes (string puppets) express the complex of the father figure or paternal ideal. Their phallic function is confirmed by their complete dependence on the demiurgic power of the manipulator.

I doubt whether this kind of interpretation of the puppet's symbolism is to be fully accepted. There is a large group of puppets that are operated with penetration – besides hand puppets, the Japanese puppets *ningyo joruri* and the Court puppets of Thailand – and we should not forget the feminine characteristics of puppets. Noting the duality of these attributes (the coexistence of feminine and masculine elements), we should consider the possibility of accepting the puppet's androgyny. On the other hand, we should analyse the coexistence of phallic symbolism, belonging to the human unconscious, and the distinct and consciously marked sexuality of puppets in some ritualistic examples from 'primitive' cultures.

Gilles is immune to such thinking. She thinks that, independently of puppet technique and puppet morphology, puppet means phallus and the puppet show is its exhibition. In this perspective, an act of manipulation is a substitute act of masturbation, and when we see a puppet's manipulator we have something to do with the masturbation being exhibited. Our culture rejects public masturbation as something pathological and illegal; however, the scenic play transforms it into its sublimated image, so that it becomes acceptable in the case of ludic or aesthetic presentation. Gilles refers to works of such psychologists as Melanie Klein and Jos Van Ussel, and states, following their opinions, that the puppet player excites the spectators less through his stories, and the indecency of action and language, as through his lack of respect for authority and, even more, through the latent eroticism of his playing. This is the basis of her definition of the puppet:

> The puppet is a ludic object that allows the reconciliation of the contrary needs of the social and individual orders through liquidation of the feeling of guilt. Again the puppet appears once more as a transitional, or intermediary, object. If ever such an object existed it had to be the puppet. The name 'object' points to its real nature, but also to its semiological and psychological values. It is an object, which exists as a sign in the ideologically determined system of

images, and which might very easily respond to narcissistic needs in the counterpoint of a fundamental 'signifier' and its latent meaning. The term 'intermediary' points to the objective relation between puppet player and his audience, but also points to the theatrical territory where the transformation and all ludic acts take place.[95]

Scholars as well as artists have applied various methods of thinking and creation, and their works of art or theory influence their recipients in different ways. Annie Gilles's interpretation had a small number of adherents; furthermore, it did not provoke any important continuation of her analysis.

The growth of semiology brought with it the temptation to apply semiotic methods to define the characteristics of the puppet theatre. The theory of theatrical signs seemed to be appropriate for the examination of what has nowadays become a theatre of different means of expression. In a study of my own, I tried to define the territory of possible research. For me it was not a question of 'pure puppet theatre' but the puppet theatre as it actually is. We must face the fact that despite all warnings, contemporary puppet theatre aims to enrich its means of expression, to the detriment of the puppet as 'expressive object'.

Significant inspiration came from the work of Polish semiotician Tadeusz Kowzan, whose observations on puppet theatre confirmed the earlier theses of Foote and Galewicz. Kowzan wrote:

> It is a typically theatrical problem, to understand the relationship between the speaking subject and the physical source of the speech. In spite of normal theatre practice they do not always constitute a unity. What is more, this incompleteness of the character brings with it certain semiological consequences.
>
> In puppet theatre the characters are presented to the view, onstage, while their words issue from the mouths of invisible artists. The movement of each puppet during the dialogue suggests which one is speaking, which gives the reply: a sort of bridge is created between the vocal source and the speaking character.[96]

Watching a puppet show we know immediately the importance of the skilful 'source of motor energy' that is the puppet manipulator. He is not always the 'voice giver': the actor speaking the text as well as the puppet's manipulator might be visible or invisible, a matter of great importance for the content and style of the show.

As a result of this analysis, I came to the surprising conclusion that the puppet is not the most characteristic element of today's perform-ances. Its characteristic features are the changing relationships between its iconic signs of character, its driving power and the source of its vocal expression:

> Puppet theatre is a theatre art: the main feature that differentiates it from live theatre is that the speaking and performing object makes temporal use of physical sources for its vocal and driving powers which are present beyond the object. The relationship between the object (the puppet) and the power sources changes all the time and these variations are of great semiological and aesthetic significance.[97]

This definition is, I think, adequate for the present state of puppet theatre, because regardless of form – be it realistic or highly stylized – puppet theatre avails itself of the changing relations between the means of expression and their sources of power. We should remember that this changeability of the relations between the components of puppet theatre is realized also when choosing some particular technique – string puppet or hand puppet, for example.

The constant oscillation of the relationship between the puppet and the physical sources of its motor and vocal powers has caused a vital change in the understanding of the puppet. Suddenly, the arrangement of correlations between puppet and power is more substantial than the components of this arrangement. The arrangement remains even when its most distinctive feature – the puppet – may have disappeared, to be replaced, for example, by a prop or a crude object.

The semiological analysis of a theatre performance is a complicated task, due to the abundance of signs and their correlations. So what can be said about the analysis of a puppet production where, from its very nature, the signs and their connotations are in constant motion, build-ing every now and again new relations between themselves? Semiological analysis helps us to prove that the puppet theatre belongs to those contemporary artistic manifestations that, due to the abun-dance of their means of expression and their interchangeability, and due also to their rich and fertilizing traditions, exist as universal phenomena.

Thus, from our review of views on puppetry through the centuries we arrive almost at the present. However, this survey is by no means complete and it is not intended to be an inventory of every theory or opinion on the subject, interesting as it might be to undertake such a task. I have preferred to show only the main aesthetic problems evoked by puppetry considered both as a popular and a sophisticated art form. As such, this essay may serve as an invitation to further research.

A special issue of the journal *Semiotica* in 1983 provided an important direction for semiotic research in puppet theatre. The 300-page volume was edited by Frank Proschan of the University of Texas under the title, 'Puppets, Masks, Performing Objects from a Semiotic Perspective'. Here I will focus on puppets.

In his introduction, Proschan prepared a historical review of semiotic studies on puppets up to the present day, rightly giving priority to Zich and Bogatyrev. He also republished one of Bogatyrev's last studies about the links between the similar semiotic systems of puppet and live actor theatres.[98] Then, in a chapter entitled 'Some General Considerations', he inserted three studies that are worth presenting in outline.

The first, a long study by the Czech semiotician Jiří Veltruský (then living in Paris), is entitled 'Puppetry and Acting', and offers detailed analysis of all aspects of scenic acting from the semiotic perspective. The work, in large part, consists in applying semiotic terminology to well-known views and theories about acting, leading to the discovery that semiotic language allows a more thorough investigation of various aspects of theatre practice.

Veltruský sees that the puppeteer's acting differs a great deal from the actor's. An actor's acting engages his or her body and speaking organs. The puppet player, even when hidden, may enter the realm of acting if his whole body is engaged in the puppet's manipulation and if he or she delivers its words. Veltruský wrote:

> The puppeteer's performance is closely related to, and yet different from, acting. In some respects the two coincide but in others they have hardly anything in common. And the area of their overlapping keeps expanding and shrinking from one form of puppetry to another.
>
> The puppeteer's speaking belongs to the realm of acting. In various forms of puppetry, however, this component is separate from the manipulation. Its separateness is sometimes enhanced by the inclusion of other elements of acting – facial play, expressive gestures, etc. – in the performance of the actor who delivers the words. Bunraku is the most outstanding example, but the same procedure is also important in other forms of puppet theater, for instance, in the performance of French classic plays by the Dominique Houdart Company. On the other hand, in certain forms of puppetry there are no

speeches. The puppet ballet flourished in eighteenth-century Italy; the futurist Balli Plastici, a program of five short performances chore-ographed by Gilbert Clavel and Fortunato Depero, were presented at the Teatro dei Piccoli in Rome in 1918; several contemporary puppet companies, including the Salzburg Puppet Theater, perform ballets or mimes; some joruri plays have contained dancing scenes since the late seventeenth century; and more recently pure dance plays, such as the Lion Dance, have been adapted from the Kabuki; and all types of puppet dances with music but without words exist in Africa.[99]

Reading this, it is easy to note that Veltruský was trying to create or at least to grasp a universal theory of acting with puppets. And if this conclusion is true, it is astonishing that he was doing so by way of acting with actors. Puppetry, as much as human theatre, has many vari-ants. The existence of the puppet ballet or puppet opera is hardly surprising given the example of human ballet and opera. Veltruský compared acting with puppets with the different sorts of acting in the art of human theatre, as he chose this as the theme of his study (quite different from Bogatyrev's perspective, for instance).

Striving for universal theories, referring to global artistic phenomena, is characteristic of the American school of research which focuses on intercultural links. Certainly, this opens new perspectives, especially in cultural anthropology, but it also gives rise to a loss of research into specifics. This is Veltruský's error, that in comparing actors' acting with puppeteers' acting he takes examples from every continent: from Bunraku and storytellers (using puppets) to ventriloquists and partici-pants in African rituals. For this reason, only his most general conclu-sions can be accepted without reservation, such as his statement about how the antinomy between acting and performing with puppets varies with different epochs and cultural forms:

> This multifarious nature of acting, and its consequent flexibility, may help to explain the persistence of the antinomy opposing live actors' theatre to puppet theatre. The concrete shape of the antinomy changes from period to period and from culture to culture. The changes are due to the fact that not only do puppeteers adjust to different structures of acting, but, equally, the actors respond to different structures of the puppet show.[100]

This is absolutely right. Our doubts start while reading about the Petrushka show in its traditional form as an argument for fixing the characteristic features of 'acting' with puppets in contemporary theatre:

> All the factors on which the sense of the dramatic character depends in acting also obtain in puppetry. What distinguishes puppetry from acting in this respect is above all the relative weight of these factors. Though the question remains largely unexplored, two moments are likely to be significant. First, the performer's image may be twofold, relating to the puppet on the one hand and to the puppeteer on the other, or even threefold when there is a separate speaker. Second, all the available evidence suggests that in puppetry there is a definite tendency to make the directly represented character prevail and, concomitantly, to fashion all the other images in such a way as to support it and build it up.[101]

If earlier we talked about the dangerous aspects of synchronic analysis (for example, in comparing Bunraku and the *Pupi Siciliani* without any reservations), now we have an opportunity to see the danger of applying uncritically a diachronic analysis. The theatre of popular heroes (such as Petrushka) already belongs to the past and it is doubtful whether its structure and style may serve to interpret today's puppetry.

Veltruský's study has, all the same, the great value of being the first semiotic attempt to analyse the different aspects of acting with puppets. He successfully gathered almost all the uses of puppets in theatrical art and confronted them with theories of acting. Even if we do not agree with parts of his thesis, we cannot deny the value of the vast amount of material that he collected and prepared for further study.

Completing my arguments in relation to Veltruský's research, I will now offer my own study: 'Transcodification of the Sign Systems of Puppetry', published in the same issue of *Semiotica*. My starting point was the thesis that the mere fact of using puppets cannot be a basis for defining its semiotic system. This had its source in my observations about the importance of relations between the puppet, its manipulators and the voice donor (where one existed). These *relations* determine the nature and functioning of the semiotic system and so I claimed that the puppet belongs to many sign systems. I wrote:

> So it seems that the puppet, during its long history in Europe, has belonged to four different sign systems. Since all four systems still exist, it means that the puppet still belongs to them at this moment. I will try to discuss them briefly in four separate sections: (1) The

puppet in the service of neighbouring sign systems, (2) The puppet in the sign system of the live theater, (3) The sign system of the puppet theatre, and (4) The atomization of all elements of the puppet theatre and its semiotic consequences.[102]

By 'neighbouring sign systems' I understood those rituals (including the use of automata) which involve 'magic' puppets, pre-eminently the use of puppets by storytellers to illustrate their words, always very popular in both West and East.

Puppeteers who imitated the live actors' theatre, even in its deformed, popular version, certainly used sign systems borrowed from that theatre. As we might remember, the puppet copies of Parisian live theatre in the nineteenth century were famous throughout France. An awakening consciousness among some puppeteers of the separateness of puppet theatre from human theatre formed the basis for the wish to fix their own system of signs, which meant promoting a separate language.

In the second half of the twentieth century the structure of puppet theatre changed due to many innovations. Puppeteers let their spectators see the mechanisms of the puppet stage, revealing the cooperation between puppet-player, puppets and other animated objects. Thus the images that the puppet theatre presented disintegrated into smaller parts, into theatre atoms, as I wrote. So I called this process the 'atomization of the puppet theatre'. One thing did not change, however, as I emphasized in the conclusion of my study:

> The puppet theater became a theater characterized by the constant pulsation of the means of expression and their relationships.
>
> This last sentence, true of the contemporary puppet theater, should be related as well to the history of puppetry as a whole. The puppet theater throughout its history has been a theater of the constant pulsation of the means of expression and their relationships.[103]

Thomas A. Green and W.J. Pepicello in their turn discussed the 'Semiotic Interrelations in the Puppet Play', meaning the semiotic description and interpretation of the puppet show's structure. They were interested in the process of communication between the theatre and its receiver, and first of all in the way in which the 'message' of the show was composed and which codes were used for its transmission, a transmission which is through two channels: visual and auditory (in theatre art we do not know other channels, although there have been some attempts to use the gustatory or olfactory channels):

> In an attempt to explain the transformation of the message in puppet theater, we shall focus on a number of codes. In the auditory channel we shall discuss the voice as a sign; in the visual channel we shall discuss the kinesics code, the physical appearance of the puppets in performance, scene, and the semiotic nature of interactions between humans and puppets in performance. Specifically, we shall investigate how various of these channels serve to create ambiguity in the puppet performance, while others serve to resolve ambiguity, at the same time intensifying and focusing on selected elements of the resolution.[104]

Green and Pepicello also analysed with great accuracy the choice of codes and the functioning of channels, focusing, however, on the so-called traditional theatre. They developed interesting deliberations on the limits of applying voices in the puppet theatre and on redundancy, which in puppet theatre seems to be inevitable. Redundancy in puppet shows means numerous repetitions of a text, extravagant costumes and exaggerated facial features. Naturally, this observation is not confirmed in contemporary artistic theatre.

The authors deliberated also on the nature of the puppet in its function as a sign. They were willing to place it in each of the sign groups identified by Peirce: icons, indexes and symbols (where icons are based on similarity, indexes are the effects of some cause and symbols are the result of social agreement). In contrast to Obraztsov, Green and Pepicello are convincing when they propose that puppet theatre does not have a metaphorical character but rather a metonymical one, from which they draw the following conclusion:

> Yet if, as we have seen, the puppet figure has strong components of icon and symbol, as well as index, we might well ponder the role of the visible puppeteer, and whether the visible puppeteer bears any relation to the human actors or interlocutor in puppet theater. The first part of our inquiry may be clarified if we consider the devices by which puppet theater functions. We have noted that the codes in puppetry involve distortion and reduction of normal human communicative modes. This distortion and reduction result in contradiction and incongruity when viewed from the perspective of human-oriented drama. While the various reduced systems are in

many respects complementary, the whole that they form is still an attenuated representation of conventional signs, or perhaps a separate, self-contained code defined by transformations of distortion and reduction.

The truncated nature of this representation can be better understood if we relate the indexical aspects of puppetry with which we are dealing to the notion of metonymy mentioned previously. Elam (1980) points out that index is related to metonymy as icon is to metaphor. That is, an icon gives a fairly direct representation of a signatum, whether it would be an image, diagram, or metaphor. An index, however, is an indication of a signatum, one part that stands for a whole, i.e., a metonym of sorts. Indeed, each of the reduced and/or distorted systems of puppetry is metonymic in that it consists of only parts of the human system on which it is modeled. This being the case, we can see puppet theater as a metonym of human theater, which is itself a sign; therefore, puppet theater, and the puppet itself, is a sign of a sign, standing in metonymic relationship to human drama.[105]

Faced with this dictum Bogatyrev would certainly turn in his grave, because during his life he wanted so much for puppet theatre to be recognized as a separate sign system, independent of live theatre. I have less reason to protest. Bearing in mind the exemplary material taken from the folk and popular theatre of the nineteenth century, Green and Pepicello could not reach any other conclusion. Their mistake was in not mentioning that their research into puppet theatre belonged to a particular period.

Besides the general articles, two detailed studies are included in the puppet issue of *Semiotica* that encourage the use of semiotics as a method of research. The first is an investigation by the Italian researcher Antonio Pasqualino, 'Marionettes and Glove Puppets: Two Theatrical Systems of Southern Italy'.

Pasqualino has undertaken a comparison of *Pupi Siciliani* (large rod marionettes) and Neapolitan glove puppets. Although he is conscious of the fact that both theatres differ immensely, heis attracted by the hope of finding common elements – which, in the end, he does.

Pasqualino starts his study by presenting a semiotic description of each of these theatrical genres, looking for its specific elements equally in details of costume, in voice delivery, in the convention of gestures within a schematic action and so on. When he analyses the linguistic code, for example, he is also interested in the voice code, in which he

Figure 1.2   Sicilian Marionette. Photo by Carl Schröder

distinguishes the voice's volume, its tone, its timbre, rhythm and vibration. Also, when he speaks about *Pupi Siciliani* he makes a typology of its characters, separately for the Palermo version and for the Catania one, taking into consideration heraldic emblems, as well as helmets, cuirasses, shields, skirts and feathers.

He also presents a very interesting thesis on the existence of a schema of events, responding to the chivalric story presented by the *Pupi Siciliani*:

> (1) Solemn council; (2) private council; (3) battle; (4) liberation of a prisoner by force; (5) secret conversation heard by eavesdropper or soliloquy overheard by hidden person; (6) surprise of a sleeping personage; (7) receipt of news from an encountered personage; (8) liberation from a spell; (9) evocation of devils who give news and/or receive orders; (10) apparition of angels who bring news and/or orders; (11) glorification and ascent to Heaven of the soul of a dead hero; (12) damnation and descent to Hell of the soul of a traitor; (13) arrival of a personage bringing news; (14) departure or dispatch of a personage to perform a task; (15) dialogue; (16) secret advice; (17) soliloquy.[106]

Pasqualino similarly presents the glove puppets called *guarattelle* in the south of Italy. The hero of the show is Pulcinella, who fights everybody, including Death at the end. Here is Pasqualino's conclusion:

> The opera dei pupi and the guarattelle, we have demonstrated in our analysis, present the following similarities: the frequency and importance of the physical encounter; the fact that this encounter is represented in symmetrical dancing movements with resounding, rhythmic blows; the conclusion of the encounter with the death of one of the contenders; and the identifiability of the glove puppet Pulcinella with the masques of the opera dei pupi: Nofriu, Virticchiu, Peppenninu, and Pulcinella himself.[107]

Although the stories presented by chivalrous *pupi* and dynamic glove puppets are different, their structure, as Pasqualino shows, is similar. They are a product of the same imagination of the same folk culture. *Pupi* present their heroic ambitions in grandiloquent fashion, while the glove puppets offer their comic abilities in a grotesque style.

The study by Joan Gross, 'Creative Use of Language in the Liège Puppet Theatre', has a similar value.[108] She researched popular puppet theatre in Liège, demonstrating its social context and social functions, which manifest themselves in the manner of shaping and using the spoken text. Gross wrote, however, mainly about how the famous puppet player Defour used his voice in the shows, pointing out the changes of tempo, rhythm, tone and intensity, timbre and emotional interpretation. Semiotics in this case appeared to be an exquisite instrument to describe traditional theatre.

In 1984 Beata Pejcz presented a semiotic description of a particular show, without addressing its specifics.[109] Discussing the problems of describing a puppet show, she presented an analysis of a show within the illusionist convention, with the actors hidden behind a screen (*Rymcimci, the Bear* by Jan Wilkowski), as well as an anti-illusionist show with the actors visible – puppet players without a screen (*Winnie the Pooh*, after A.A. Milne). This attempt confirmed the usefulness of semiotic methods of description in both traditional theatre and modern theatre. It did not aspire, however, to offer a general thesis on the nature of this theatre.

Other semiotic studies of puppetry have dealt with such different aspects as the status of the scenic characters[110] and the poetic languages in puppet theatre, discussing its various tropes.[111] We can only guess at how these will be continued.

The first essays discussing the influence of Bertolt Brecht's theories on puppet theatre appeared in the 1980s. Nobody had researched this as a whole, but now and then some aspects were discussed. Chronologically the first was the Soviet historian Natalia Smirnova's statement that the influences of Gordon Craig and Bertolt Brecht were decisive for transformations in puppet theatre. She wrote:

> Puppet theatre has paid close attention to the views of Gordon Craig and Bertolt Brecht. During our century many new companies found inspiration in their views. They produced surprising shows due to their use of new means of expression.[112]

Some pages later we can read further:

> Twentieth century puppet theatre in its most excellent and meaningful achievements represented Gordon Craig's ideas. Considering the professional and aesthetic points of view we may say that the best puppet masters demonstrated the maturity and accuracy of their political positions. The theatre of the twentieth century took a noble place in the progressive fight of humanity for justice and ethical

ideals. It also proved that, entering a new stage of existence, it was able to remain in contact with real life, in its development and the fight for progress.[113]

We can agree neither with Smirnova's political phraseology nor with her idea of seeing Craig and Brecht as reformers with a similar artistic programme. The former was interested in the aesthetics of art theatre, while the latter was interested in its ideology and political functions. The former researched the very nature of theatre art, the latter its social reception. Brecht's concept of epic theatre did not originate from aesthetic premises but from the political attitude of the artist.

There is no need to discuss once again the importance of Craig's ideas in the renewal of the art of puppetry. From my own feeling and knowledge, the influence of Brecht's theory was rather limited. The epic theatre style in its pure form was applied by Jan Wilkowski in 1956, in his show *Guignol in Trouble*, at Warsaw's Lalka theatre. All other applications, even in productions of Brecht's own plays, offered rather its transformation.

Brecht's theatre was popular, but his theory was very little known. The term 'alienation effect' (*Verfremdungseffekt*) was the cause of many misunderstandings. Normally, artists connected it with Brecht's theory, not knowing that it has a wider meaning and that many writers and artists before Brecht used it to mean a break with scenic illusion. The German researcher Joachim Fiebach wrote about it as follows:

> Craig, Tairow and Meyerhold also used the 'alienation effect' understood in a general way. It consists in the opposition of an actor and his role, in the use of mask, in the special stress on gestures, in the use on stage of visual documents, in separating the text from gesture, in quotations, and in direct address to audiences.[114]

I agree with Fiebach that we should apply this term in its wider sense as a break with scenic illusion, since scenic action is no more true than the fiction presented on stage. Such an understanding of *Verfremdung* is different from that of Brecht's theory and practice. Brechtian *Verfremdung* breaks with scenic illusion but does so for social reasons: it proposes a new way of seeing represented events in accordance with the ideological attitude of the artist. This is why I use the term 'alienation effect' in connection with Brechtian theory and in all other cases I refer to a 'break with illusion' or a 'theatricalization of events'.

The precondition of any 'break with illusion' (including the Brechtian *Verfremdungseffekt*) is the pre-existence of illusion. In other words, the break with illusion is not possible if the scenic illusion does not exist in the first place. A theatre that does not practise illusion may be called an anti-illusionist theatre, but it already loses the possibility of exploiting the *Verfremdungseffekt*. The 'alienation effect' needs contrast, the element of opposition. That is why the 'theatre of narration' – which is anti-illusionist, linking narration and diverse images, and is so much beloved by puppet-players – has nothing to do with Brecht's concept, which consists of the interchangeable coexistence of illusion and reality. The possible presence of a *Verfremdungseffekt* in the theatre of puppeteer Peter Waschinsky from East Germany is linked with this meaningful paradox:

> To return to 'Verfremdungseffekt' in the puppet theatre. It is its immanent part and, in principle, it is always present. Puppets are only material. Let us discuss a little Chekhov show ['The Witch' at the Neubrandenburg Puppet Theatre]: the characters are true and realistic. Thus their movements and words should also be very 'natural' in the human sense of the word. But what does this word 'natural' mean in relation to the puppets? It means that they are behaving as inert material; that is, they are completely motionless or they produce as best they can sweeping movements. However, the matter of the puppet acted upon externally imitates human movements and becomes alien to itself. This is exactly the alienation effect. The most naturalistic puppet creates the strongest alienation effect.[115]

Again, here we have to do with an interpretation of the alienation effect, seeing its presence in puppet theatre as a paradox. The phenomenon disturbed many researchers, especially within German cultural circles. Konstanza Kavrakova-Lorenz, a Bulgarian scholar living in Berlin, focused on the specificity of the *Verfremdungseffekt* in puppet play. She wrote:

> There is the basic difference between 'Verfremdung' as a method and technique in actor's theatre, and the constant 'alienation effect' in the puppet play. An actor who plays ignoring 'Verfremdung' is acceptable but the puppet show without the presence of 'Verfremdung' is unthinkable, because it is part of its essence, consisting in the tension of its developing duality.[116]

Here again, we should have some doubts as to whether the use of the term *Verfremdung* is correct in this case: in Brecht's practice it meant the sharp opposition between illusion (actors as characters) and reality (actors as humans). In puppet theatre, the elements of artificiality, counterfeit and reality are juxtaposed, seldom in sharp opposition. The material puppet that moves links elements of reality and illusion. In the course of a performance a slight change in its relations exposes one or the other, reality or illusion. So in puppet theatre we have to do with processes of a pulsation between values and not with processes of opposition.

Bogatyrev was aware of the existence of relationships between these opposite notions. That is why he spoke about the need for controlling aesthetic signs, as those which an artist uses purposely. Considering the intentional playing between fictive and real elements, I have spoken about the same phenomenon, calling it 'opalization':

> When movement fully dominates an object we feel that the character is born and present on stage. When it is the nature of the object that dominates we still see the object. The object is still the object and the character at the same time. Sometimes however this unity splits for a short while, to be regenerated after a moment. This is what I mean by 'opalization'.[117]

Further deliberation on this subject led me to the field of puppet theatre rhetoric, suggesting research on tropes applied in puppetry. Deliberating on both the metonymical and the metaphorical puppet's character as a means of expression, I came to the conclusion that the puppet is a special form of metaphor – an oxymoron:

> Oxymoron is the figure of speech by means of which contradictory terms are combined so as to form an expressive epithet such as 'black sun', 'cruel kindness', and last but not least 'living object': The material puppet combined with the appearance of life, supplied by movement and vocal delivery, is an oxymoron.[118]

The young American researcher Steve Tillis presented his own analysis of this phenomenon, proposing to call it 'double vision':

> What is willful in the live theatre is native to the puppet: a process of representation that is inherently make-believe, and is predicated on a double-vision that acknowledges the 'object' of the puppet as having 'life'.

It would be incorrect to say that all puppetry consciously strives to create double-vision; in fact, such a striving has not been central to the phenomenon of the puppet. As we have seen in Jurkowski's example of the Italian theatre company that alternately performed live and with puppets, double-vision might well have frequently been considered an undesirable side effect. Nonetheless, double-vision is a constant in all puppet performance, whether intentionally or not, and thus provides the basis for a synchronic explanation of the puppet's widespread and enduring appeal, for it creates in every audience the pleasure of a profound and illuminating paradox provoked by an 'object' with 'life'.[119]

I have quoted all these definitions to emphasize that the opposition of reality and fiction in puppet theatre has many aspects. To see them as a simple *Verfremdungseffekt* is a mistaken simplification, which restricts our knowledge of the puppet and its theatre.

I have already mentioned the East German researcher Konstanza Kavrakova-Lorenz. In 1987 she published her paper 'Puppetry as a Synergetic Genre of Art: Examination of Process, Dialectics of Constructing Images, and Presentations in the Creative Process of Communication in Puppetry'. This is a fundamental study dealing with all the principal problems of the creative process in puppet theatre based on theories of communication and semiotics, drawing mainly on Ernst Schumacher's work, 'Theory of the Art of Performing'.[120]

Kavrakova-Lorenz, like most puppeteer-artists from Eastern Europe, considered puppet theatre as an art of theatre; she presented the creative problems of puppet theatre, viewing them against the background of the experience of actors' theatre. She used the general German term *Darsteller*, which has a different meaning to the word 'performer'. In principle, a *Darsteller* may appear in two forms of presentation: he or she may be a *Schauspieler* (actor) or a *Puppenspieler* (puppet player):

Using the notion 'Darsteller' we designate two categories, which reveal its principal basis in the art of acting and the art of playing with puppets. They are manifested by the different use of mimetic material serving the creation of a figure or character, which is the starting point and the end point of the show, according to the medium used.[121]

There is no doubt that Kavrakova-Lorenz considered the puppet-player to be an actor, which corresponds to Polish artistic practice, as proved by the cycle of Jan Wilkowski's works published in the 1980s.[122] Nevertheless, the process of creation of stage characters consists of something more than the mechanical transmission of an actor's feelings. It consists of a cooperation between 'puppet' and 'player':

> Connecting both as one entity, which shows sometimes their differentiated characteristics, is a result of the communication between internal and external processes. Inwardly this connection is accomplished as a contact between subject-puppet player and object-puppet. It serves the existence of the synergetic phenomenon, whose elements interact mutually, alienating its basic characteristic – to be a subject and to be an object – and so they exchange their functions in the show. Outwardly they are oriented for a receptive process, to give a basis to this synergy; that is, to create 'what is essential' in the mind of the spectators.[123]

The term 'synergy' was applied in philosophy, and more precisely speaking in theology. Philipp Melanchthon (1497–1530) introduced it to designate the cooperation of the Holy Spirit and human free will striving for redemption. It seems that puppet theatre cannot escape religious metaphor. It is worth noting, however, that Melanchthon's synergy dealt with two subjects, while in Kavrakova-Lorenz's interpretation it is limited to subject and object. Here we have her explanation of this:

> We understand synergy as the dynamic principle for formation and development of structures, which are achieved in processes of reception, interaction, and activity. Through synergy we will imagine a complex of processes which include existing elements, with such activities as choice, transformation and other changes. These are processes of cooperation and competition. They give life to synergetic images, which means no more than a certain caesura. Inside this caesura, which is a turning point, some structures come into being, that help to strengthen the potential of the cooperating elements. In general, acts of a synergetic character will be experienced (revealed or hidden) and evaluated through the organizing power of the leading element (or group of elements), which gets imposed as the constitutive component. The playing of puppets acts as a synergy of the plastic and representative forms using the tension between the starting elements and their functions. To solve this

contradiction one should strive for an exterior, objective dynamic that will alienate both constitutive elements. Dynamics achieved with the help of movements, gestures, poses, decide on the process of animating things, which demands alienation, the 'objectivization' of performers.[124]

All these complicated (typically German) deliberations find support in the classic concept of subject and object, which in this case cooperate closely: 'The specific approach of subject and object in the performance of a puppet play shows the true aesthetic content of this form of art and its means of expression.'[125] This conclusion is of course correct, although the Americans, sensitive to the crisis of 'the subject' in their philosophy and art, might reject this thesis as contradictory to ideas of 'postmodernism'.[126]

Americans have also taken a clear position in relation to the parallelism of acting in actors' and puppet theatre. Roman Paska's opinion in this respect is significant:

Puppetry or puppet theatre? If puppetry can function as a performing art in various contexts (cinema, drama, cabaret, circus, television, performance art, avant-garde theatre), what exactly is the meaning of the expression 'puppet theatre'?

Puppet theatre in the West has been largely dependent on (and derivative of) the dramatic actors' theatre. But apologists and defenders of the art who hope to legitimize puppetry as theatre by citing its similar nature as a composite theatrical form (using Craig's variation on Wagner's concept of the *Gesamtkunstwerk*), are only asking to board a sinking ship.

If puppetry is an art form in its own right (or at all) according to modernist criteria, it has to manifest qualities that distinguish it from the theatre in general – qualities both inherent and unique that define its essential 'puppetness'. (Even if the puppet itself is only implied or virtual, as in the hand mime or object theatre.)[127]

So, after almost an entire century of research into the specificity of puppets and their performances, it appears that there is always the same need to define the essential features of puppets and puppetry as an artistic genre. Does this mean that the previous considerations have been unsatisfactory? I do not think so. However, they belonged to other times; today we require a new commentary on our art. Moreover, Paska is trying to suggest a definition that extends the notion of the puppet into a theatre of objects.

In the late 1980s, new themes appeared in deliberations on puppet theatre. We have long been told that the puppet is an object manufactured by man for playing in the theatre. The fact that it was a 'theatrical play' distinguished the puppet from other objects also manufactured by man. For a long time one remembered, even subconsciously, the old aesthetic concepts which situated the puppet in a series of theatrical subjects – imagined, but subjects nonetheless. Recently, however, one more often forgets about the 'subjectivity of puppets', highlighting rather its 'objectivity'.

This trend is associated with the rapid development of so-called object theatre (although this relates not to puppets but utilitarian things). Increasingly, the real subject, which is the human in this theatre, takes a central, and clearly demonstrated, place. Previously the subject was a human subordinated to a puppet; the human served the puppet. After a long period of transition, where the relationship between puppet and human underwent continual change, the human being decided finally to reveal the truth about the hierarchy and dependencies in puppet theatre. The human is the deity, the true creator of the theatre. The ancient metaphor renewed its life. The human artist gained true freedom, both in the choice of theme (formerly dictated by the specificity of his puppets) and the means of expression (formerly dictated by the puppet's technique). This freedom has become so far advanced that in the choice of means of expression the artists can dispense with the dolls. They can replace them with props, objects, even with themselves and their body parts.

It would seem that in this way the borders of puppet theatre were ruptured. Meanwhile, it appeared that a new generation of artists wanted to preserve the notion of puppets, puppetry and puppet theatre. In this regard, the statement by Roman Paska (already referred to) was significant: while remaining on the side of puppetry, he expands the concept of the puppet. He divides puppeteers into two groups: 'illusionists' and 'primitives':

> Primitivism differs from illusionism in consciously directing audience focus back and forth between the outward sign and the inner process of simulation. And the primitive puppet is flagrantly exhibitionist in exposing its own emptiness as a vehicle for expression in performance.
>
> In effect, puppet primitives let the puppet 'die' … and, discarding the pretense of realism, take it for the inanimate object (dead thing) that it is. The dead thing can only be reborn as a puppet from one

moment of performance to the next. While illusionists hope to produce an unbroken series of such moments so that the puppet seems always alive, primitives aim for a series in which the illusion of being is consciously fragmented by the intrusion of awareness into the structural mechanics of animation, the real nature of the objects employed, and the real time of theatrical activity.

In the pure puppet performance, focus oscillates between the real time and nature of the puppet as an object, and the illusory time and nature of the puppet as a character sign. The puppet seems to come alive without pretending to be alive, with an effect closer to magic than technology.[128]

In sum, this division provides a clear characterization of the opposing trends in contemporary puppet theatre, but primarily gives a description of the intentions of the 'primitives'. In another part of his article, Paska stresses the importance of how the actor (performer, puppeteer) acts, as this changes the meaning of the term 'puppet':

Like a fish out of water, the puppet out of performance is a dead thing, as potential signifier only. As demonstrated most recently by the theatre of objects, the signifying properties of the puppet as a passive formal object or sculpture are 'ultimately unnecessary to the object's kinetic signifying activity as a puppet actor' in a performance context. The puppetness of an object is determined by use, not latency, and is a renewable, not a permanent quality.[129]

Taking this position, Paska could view the theatre of objects as identical to puppet theatre: 'In the theatre of objects, puppetness is only ever a concept or possibility. (But the object is a virtual puppet before it is anything else, which is why the theatre of objects is still puppet theatre.)'[130]

Here we meet with a fairly widespread view that everything, every object that serves the artist in making a stage character exist, is a puppet; that a puppet is a thing in *statu nascendi*. It becomes a puppet in the process of animation, as is allegedly confirmed in the theatre of objects.[131] This issue requires detailed examination. Indeed, we are entering into language that is not only the property of the puppeteers' milieu, but can serve in communication to groups of many millions of people.

According to tradition, puppets are divided into various basic types, such as the hand puppet, marionette, rod puppets, clavier puppet and others. At this level there are no difficulties. No one tells the umbrella that it is a rod puppet or marionette, but there are many who consider that the umbrella is a kind of doll, because it can function like a puppet.

The object's features can offer a starting point for clarifying the matter. A puppet (stick puppet, marionette, hand puppet) is an object made for theatrical use. This cannot be said of the umbrella or the brush, even when it is present as a stage character in the theatre of objects, because they were made for another purpose: to protect against rain, or to sweep the floor. Each type of puppet incorporates a programme of theatrical action (visually expressive, technical and method of manipulation). Each object contains certain utility properties, enabling it to perform its functions. The puppet is ready to go onstage. The object must renounce its utility functions before it takes its role as a stage character, when it has to assume a new function.

The puppet corresponds iconically to its depicted role; the object (except in rare moments of impersonation) contrasts with the iconicity of the role. Puppets can create an illusion of stage character that the object will never attain; the object will always be recognizable as an object, which in a certain type of theatre is somehow automatically a great advantage. That is not to say that the figurative puppet is more perfect, only that it is different. Of course, you can forget about the linguistic tradition, you can forget about the functional differences between puppets and objects, you can focus on the process of creating an oscillating effect ad hoc, as Roman Paska wanted to do. In this way we will preserve the ancient notion of 'puppet', giving it a very wide meaning. But is it not more appropriate to call new things by new names?

To be fair to the puppeteers' milieu, it must be said that in the last 20 years several attempts to introduce a new terminology have been undertaken. Thus there is the 'theatre of animation', the 'object theatre', the 'other theatre'; but the greatest success, because it is well accepted in Italy and Germany, has been with the term 'theatre of figures' (*teatro di figura*, *Figurentheater*). In 1990, puppeteer and teacher Werner Knoedgen published the book *Das Unmögliche Theater. Zur Phaenomenologie des Figurentheaters* (The Impossible Theatre. Towards a Phenomenology of a Theatre of Figures[132]). He attempted to define the place of puppet theatre among its related genres, and above all to determine the characteristics of modern derivative forms of this theatre as a 'theatre of figures'. Here is an example of what is, and what is not, the theatre of figures:

'Theatre of figures' – what does this term mean? Is it a conceptual re-evaluation of folk art, thought to refer to a toy? Or is it just a 'better' word for 'playing puppets', to cover up the old inferiority complex? Or by means of a 'theatre of figures' do we designate a newly created 'discipline', of material and object animation, mixing different kinds of shapes and techniques? Does this mean that one can open forms of dissemination of play, in which animators are visible alongside the theatrical figures?

Indeed, some changes have taken place and the new forms of artistic expression are symptomatic. There is a new awareness that is expressed in terminology, as the previously dominant term 'puppet play' was replaced by 'theatre of figures'. In Germany, 'theatre of figures' as a notion has existed for two hundred years but only now does it begin to be used as the name of a theatrical genre.[133]

The 'theatre of figures' also characterizes the 'theatre of material' (*Materialstheater*), which has different variations. The first of these is a theatre based on unformed material (receiving its shape during the show), and this is proper to the 'theatre of material'. Its second characteristic is a theatre which uses material that is already shaped, to which belongs the theatre of objects, mask theatre, puppet theatre, mixed media theatre and theatre using only parts of the human body, such as a theatre of human hands. The task of the player (that is, the *Darsteller*) in the theatre of figures is the creation of a role. Knoedgen consistently avoids the term 'stage character', using instead the formal term 'role'. In any case, in the theatre of figures the creation of the role differs from the tasks of the actor in drama theatre:

> Due to the suggestion of life in things devoid of life, due to the presentation of the active by use of the passive, the actor of the figure theatre differs from the dramatic actor. He transfers his role into the material object, and thus takes a distance from this role; even if he could abandon himself, he knows that that object-role cannot replace him. He is the only present subject: the object-role remains the means of expression, the ordinary instrument of its production.[134]

It might be assumed that this analysis is of value for all variants of material theatre, were it not that the separation of the object (material) and subject (the acting actor) is not as simple as Knoedgen presents it. It is often the case that subject and object are involved in a joint presence within the role; that is, they cannot be clearly separated (for example,

in cases where the material supports the equivalent of an actor's role
with the help of facial expressions of the actor's own face).

Knoedgen analyses many different aspects of working with materials, shaped or still virginal. It is interesting that, while he constructs
an autonomic playing theory in 'his' material theatre, we can redis-
cover phenomena from earlier deliberations on puppetry.
'Opalisation' of the puppet, and 'double vision' in the puppet theatre,
he calls the 'duality of theatre' (*Doppelung des Theaters*), which means
the same as the constant playing between fictive and real elements. It
is true that in the material theatre there is no place for an actor's identification with the role, as is familiar in drama theatre. The image
presented in material theatre is broken, split into two components,
which leads Knoedgen to suggest a centripetal tendency in the following synthesis:

> Due to the fact that the images in the figure theatre are split, each
> scenic subject may freely choose the form of appearance, inside a role
> or outside the role. However, the fact that the picture is 'inconsistent'
> – and this is a fantastic freedom – is perceptible as both functional
> and at the same time auctorial, meaning that this theatre allows spec-
> tators, through its feedback loop, to participate in an incredible act
> of creation: human action solidifies into matter, matter starts to act.
> Objects become actors. Playing their roles, subject and object enter
> into the highest, dialectical synthesis of a united presentation.[135]

The flavour of Knoedgen's book lies in its details, which there is no
room to discuss here. It is one of those rare books that attempt to
describe in a new way, and with a new language, the state of contemporary theatre, as it emerged from the earlier forms of puppetry.
Knoedgen's struggle with the wealth of artistic phenomena renders its
descriptions more complicated than these quotations might make them
appear.

Actually, all these reflections on the puppet and its theatre have
resulted from its current state, which is extremely diverse and distinguished by the richness of its forms. There is nothing surprising in the
fact that in the twentieth century, especially its second half, a number
of commentaries on puppet theatre were published, even though only
a few of them refer to its theory and aesthetics. In this review, although
I could not cover all the work worthy of interest, I have attempted to
describe the fundamental issues that have moved and provoked reflection in theoreticians and in the puppeteers themselves.

First published as Z djiejów poglądów na teatr lalek (Literary views on puppet theatre), *Pamiętnik Teatralny* (Memories of theatre), Warsaw 1968, 1: 3–52. Translated and edited by Penny Francis and Mischa Twitchin 2013.

Notes

1   Horace, *The Satires* Book II, Satire 7.
2   Aslan O., *L'Art du Théâtre*, Paris 1963, 133.
3   Sokolov V., *Gedanken zu meiner Theater musikalischer Dynamik* (Thoughts on the musical dynamics of my theatre): *Das Puppentheater* vol. 1, Leipzig 1923, 33–8.
4   Lemercier de Neuville L. *Nouveau Théâtre de Pupazzi*, Paris 1882, vii.
5   Boehm M. von *Dolls and Puppets*, Boston 1956, 395.
6   Foote S. 'Piety in pattens', *Biografia Dramatika or Companion to the Playhouse. III*, London 1812, 150.
7   Ibid.
8   Buschmeyer L., *Die Kunst des Puppenspiels* (The art of puppet play), Erfurt 1931, 2.
9   Goethe J.W., *The Sorrows of Young Werther*, trans. David Campbell, London 1999.
10 Mickiewicz A., *Dzieła* (Works) vol. V., Warsaw 1948, 26.
11 Krasiński Z. *Listy Zygmunta Krasińskiego do Augusta Cieszkowskiego* (Letters of Zygmunt Krasiński to August Cieszkowski) vol. I, Krakow/Warsaw 1912, 212.
12 Rapp, E. *Die Marionette in romantischen Weltgefühl*, Bochum 1964, 70.
13 Ibid., 71–2.
14 Ibid.
15 Kleist H. von 'On the marionette theatre', *Animations*, 1983, 6(6): 3–4.
16 Ibid.
17 Ibid.
18 Ibid.
19 Ibid.
20 Ibid.
21 Ibid.
22 Since the first edition of 'Aspects' appeared, a two-volume treatise on *A History of European Puppetry* by Henryk Jurkowski (1996 and 1998) has been published by the Edwin Mellen Press, New York and Wales.
23 Leibrecht P., *Zeugnisse und Nachweise zur Geschichte des Puppenspiels in Deutschland*, Borna/Leipzig 1919.
24 Speaight G., *The History of the English Puppet Theatre*, London 1955.
25 McPharlin P., *The Puppet Theatre in America*, New York 1949.
26 Varey J.E., *Historia de los Titeres en España*, Madrid 1957.
27 Magnin C., *Histoire des Marionnettes en Europe*, Paris 1852, 1–2.

28   Ibid., 9
29   Sand M., *Masques et Bouffons*, vol. I, Paris 1860, 141.
30   Sand G., *Dernières Pages*, Paris 1877, 128.
31   Maeterlinck M., 'Menus propos', *La Jeune Belgique*, 9: 1890.
32   Craig E.G., 'The actor and the über-Marionette', *The Mask* vols. I–II, Florence 1908.
33   Craig E.G., *On the Art of the Theatre*, London 1911, 81.
34   Ibid., 94.
35   Craig E.G., 'Puppets and poets', *The Chapbook*, February 1921, 20.
36   Ibid., 13.
37   Ibid., 4.
38   Ibid., 18.
39   Zich O., *Drobné uměni – wytwarne snahy* (Small art – great artefacts), Prague 1923.
40   Ibid.
41   Kolar E., 'Ke korenum Česke loutkarske estetiky' (The roots of the aesthetic of Czech puppetry), *Divadlo*, 1964, 68.
42   Bogatyrev P., *Lidové divadlo ceské a slovacké* (Czech and Slovak Folk Theatre), Prague 1940, 124.
43   After Kolar, op. cit., 71.
44   Kilian-Stanisławska J., 'Po piętnastu latach o teatrze lalek' (Puppet theatre fifteen years later), *Państwowy Teatr Laleka*, 1944–55, 13.
45   Buschmeyer L., *Die Kunst des Puppenspiels*, Erfurt 1931.
46   Ibid. 55.
47   Ibid. 169.
48   Sandig H., *Die Ausdruckmöglichkeiten der Marionette und ihre dramaturgischen Konsequenzen* (The expressive potential of the puppet theatre and its dramaturgical consequences), Munich 1958.
49   Polti G., *Les 36 Situations Dramatiques*, Paris 1895.
50   Eichler F. *Das Wesen des Handpuppen und Marionettenspiels*, Emsdetten 1937.
51   Ibid. 22.
52   Ibid. 26.
53   Obraztsov S.V., 'Znaczenie teatru lalek i jego miejsce wśród innych rodzajów sztuki teatralnej' (The importance and place of the puppet theatre among the other theatre arts), *Teatr Lalek*, 1958, 6: 12.
54   Ibid.
55   Matuszewski J., 'Bohaterowie Jasełek. O stałych typach teatru ludowego w Europie' (Heroes of the puppet stage: on the perennial characters of European folk theatre), *Swoi i obcy*, 1903, 362–403.
56   Sztaudynger J., *Marionetki*, Lvov and Warsaw, 1938.
57   Ibid. 133–4.
58   Ibid.
59   Sztaudynger J., Jurkowski H., Ryl H., *Od szopki do teatru lalek* (From szopka to puppet theatre), Lódż, 1961.

60   Schiller Leon, 1887–1967 (ed. M. Waszkiel), *Teatr Lalek*, 1987, 1–2: 2.
61   Ibid. 34.
62   Kolar E. '26 x loutkovost' (26 times puppetness), *Ceskoslovensky Loutkař*, 1964, 8–9: 196.
63   Ibid., 197.
64   Ibid.
65   Blattman E., 'Märchenspiel mit Handpuppen?' *Puppen- und Figurenspiel*. Arbeitsheft 2. Herausgegeben von der Dektion für Redende und Musizierende Kunstler/Abtg. Puppenspiel, Goethenaum-Dornach, 1991, 33.
66   Česal M., *Živy herec na loutkovym divadle* (Live actor in the puppet theatre), Prague 1983.
67   Purschke H.R., 'Puppe und Mensch', *Perlicko-Perlacko* 1958, 2: 134–5.
68   Dorst T., 'Das Marionettentheater der Gegenwart' (The contemporary puppet theatre), *Perlicko-Perlacko* 1958, 2: 134–5.
69   Mazur K., 'Romanse marionety czyli o powiązaniach teatru lalek z teatrem dramatycznym – i nie tylko ...' (Romance of the marionette or the links between puppet theatre and actor theatre – and more ...), *Teatr lalek i jego związki z innymi dziedzinami sztuki*, Warsaw 1962, 22.
70   Ibid.
71   Ibid. 29.
72   Siegel H., 'Schauspieler und Puppenspieler' (Actor and puppet player), *Puppentheater der Welt*, Berlin 1965, 24.
73   Makota J., *O klasyfikacji sztuk pięknych* (On the classification of the Arts), Krakow 1964, 183.
74   Ibid.
75   Galewicz J., *Próba określenia widowiska lalkowego jako jednej ze sztuk pieknych* (An attempt to define puppet performance as an art form), *Teatr Lalek* 1965, 33: 5.
76   Kolar E., 'Lalkarstwo – sztuka plastyczna czy teatralna?' (Puppetry – fine art or theatre), *Współczesny teatr lalek w słowie i obrazie* (Contemporary puppet theatre in word and image), Warsaw 1963, 31.
77   Bensky R.D., *Recherches sur les structures et la symbolique de la marionnette*, Paris 1971, 22.
78   Ibid.
79   Ibid. 23.
80   Ibid. 114.
81   Jurkowski H., 'De Relatie tussen Mens, Pop en Masker het Toneel ais menselijke Metafoor' (Relationships between men, puppets and masks as a source of metaphor), Instytut voor Kunstanbachten, Mechelen 1973.
82   Jurkowski H., 'Perspektywy rozwoju teatru lalek' (Perspectives on the development of the puppet theatre), *Teatr Lalek*, 1966, 37–8: 3.
83   Ibid.
84   Ibid.

85 Shpet L.G., Speech at symposium 'Teatr lalek dziś i jutro' (Puppet theatre today and tomorrow), *Teatr Lalek* 1967, 41–2: 58.

86 Bogatyrev P., 'Czeskij kukolnyj I ruskij narodnyj teatr' (The Czech and Russian folk puppet theatre), *Sborniki po teorii poeticheskogo języka*, vol. VI, Berlin and St Petersburg 1923.

87 Niculescu M., 'Metafora jako środek wyrazu lalki' (Metaphor as a means of expression in the puppet theatre), *Teatr lalek i jego związki z innymi dziedzinami sztuki* (Puppetry and its relationship to other arts), Warsaw 1962, 35.

88 Jurkowski H., 'Die Verbindung von Menschen, Puppen and Masken auf die Bühne als philosophische Metamer', UNIMA Almanach no. 2 *L'Art de la marionnette à notre temps* (The art of puppetry in our time), Warsaw 1972, 23.

89 Torbay E., 'Teatr lalkowy i metafora' (Puppet theatre and metaphor), *Lalka w służbie metafory* (Puppet in the service of metaphor), V Festiwal Teatrów Lalek w Bielsku – Białej, 15–20 May 1972, 54.

90 Lotman J., 'Lalki w systemie kultury (Puppets in cultural systems), *Teksty* 1978, 6: 51–2.

91 Gilles A., *Le jeu de la marionnette. L'objet intermediaire et son metathéâtre* (Puppet play. The intermediary object and its metaphor), Publications-Université Nancy II, 1981.

92 Hauser A., *Filozofia historii sztuki* (Philosophy of history of art), Warsaw 1970, 59–60.

93 Gilles, op. cit., 126.

94 Ibid. 128.

95 Ibid. 133.

96 Kowzan T., 'Znak w teatrze' (Sign in the theatre), *Wprowadzenie do nauki o teatrze* (Introduction to theatre science) (ed. Janusz Degler), Wrocław 1976, 307.

97 Jurkowski, H., *Język współczesnego teatre lalek* (The language of the contemporary puppet theatre), Teksty 1978, nr. 6, 61.

98 Bogatyrev P., *Semiotyka kultury ludowej* (Semiotics of folk culture), Warsaw 1975.

99 Veltruský J., Puppetry and acting, *Semiotica*, 1983, 14: 73–4.

100 Ibid. 77.

101 Ibid. 105.

102 Jurkowski H., 'Transcodification of the sign systems of puppetry', *Semiotica*, 1983, 14: 131.

103 Ibid. 144.

104 Green T.A., Pepicello W.J., Semiotic interrelationships in the puppet play, *Semiotica*, 1983, 14: 147.

105 Ibid. 158.

106 Pasqualino A., 'Marionettes and glove puppets in southern Italy', *Semiotica*, 1983, 14: 256.

107 Ibid. 276.

108 Gross J., 'Creative use of language in a Liège puppet theatre', *Semiotica*, 1983, 14: 281.

109   Pejcz B., 'Problemy semiotycznego opisu przedstawienia w teatrze lalek' (Problems of semiotic description of the puppet performance), *Studia o sztuce dla dziecka* (Studies on art for children), 1987, 1: 59–65.

110   Jurkowski H., 'The mode of existence of characters of the puppet stage', in L. Kominz, M. Levenson (eds.) *The Language of the Puppet*, Vancouver 1990, 21–36.

111   Jurkowski H., 'The acting puppet as a figure of speech', in M. Waszkiel (ed.) *Present Trends in Research of World Puppetry*, Warsaw 1992, 92–104.

112   Smirnova N., 'Iskusstvo igrajushchikh kukol' (The art of the performing puppet), Moscow 1983, 106.

113   Ibid. 109.

114   Fiebach J., *Von Craig bis Brecht. Studien zu Künstlehrtheorien in der ersted Hälfte des 20. Jahrhunderts* (From Craig to Brecht. Studies in art theories in the first half of the twentieth century), Berlin 1975, 299.

115   Waschinsky P., *Théâtre des marionnettes entre illusionisme et distanciation*, Gennevilliers 1980, 57.

116   Kavrakova-Lorenz K., 'Das Puppenspiel als synergetische Kunstform' (Puppet play as synergetic artform), In M. Wegner (ed.), *Die Spiele der Puppe*, Köln 1989, 235.

117   Jurkowski H., *Aspects of Puppet Theatre*, London 1988, 41.

118   Jurkowski, 'The acting puppet as a figure of speech', op. cit., 100.

119   Tillis S., *Towards an Aesthetics of the Puppet. Puppetry as Theatrical Art.* New York 1992, 65.

120   Kavrakova-Lorenz, op. cit. 230–41.

121   Ibid. 232.

122   Wilkowski J., 'Zrywam pieczęć omerty' (I reveal the secret), *Teatr Lalek* 1986, 2–3.

123   Kavrakova-Lorenz, K., op. cit. 234.

124   Ibid. 235.

125   Ibid. 241.

126   Baran B., *Postmodernizm*, Krakow 1992, 188.

127   Paska R., 'Notes on puppet primitives and the future of an illusion', in Kominz and Levenson, op. cit., 37–8.

128   Ibid. 41.

129   Ibid. 39.

130   Ibid. 41.

131   Jurkowski, H. 'The theatre of objects', in *The Theatrical Inanimate. A Conference of Changing Perceptions.* New York, 1992, September 11–12.

132   Knoedgen W. *Das Unmögliche Theater. Zur Phänomenologie des Figurentheaters* (The impossible theatre. Towards a phenomenology of puppet theatre), Stuttgart 1990.

133   Ibid. 1.

134   Ibid. 19.

135   Ibid. 109.

2

Towards a Theatre of Objects

Theatre is transformation. It is a vision created by an artist, transforming himself or a puppet or even an object into an imagined character. This is a well-known fact which I recall in order to discuss the situation of the contemporary puppet theatre and particularly that of the puppet itself. I need a widely accepted truth as a point of departure for my arguments and conclusions.

While we are involved in theatre activity, we hardly notice the new impulses as they come and bring their changes. However, when it occurs to us to look from a distance, we can see all the new tendencies which have appeared in our own time, giving new colouring to the face of the art.

Some years ago I presented a sort of judgement on the development of European puppetry, at a conference in Moscow. Then I stated, giving as my example the production of the DRAK theatre *Final Appearance – Circus Unikum*, that we had just come to the end of a cycle in the history of puppet theatre. This cycle, started centuries ago by ritual puppetry, included different periods of theatre development and had now come full circle in today's ritual manner of the puppets' handling. It was precisely there, in *Circus Unikum*, that we saw that the play's most important character, Nadezhda, had no movement. She was inanimate – or almost. In spite of that she was 'alive' because all the other characters, played by live actors, treated her as a live person.

This is the ritual way of making a figure live, which can be referred to as the 'animization' of the figure.

During the last year I have had other opportunities to see productions of this kind, with variations, and for this reason I invite you to share my thoughts. Let us go back to the beginning, since the contemporary situation must derive from the past. Although this is not the place to recount the whole history of puppet theatre, I would like to recall the various functions which puppets have had, to give you an idea of their variety.

In the beginning there was animism. People believed that stones, trees, clouds, animals were invested with some spiritual force – anima. In the same way their ceremonial figures, as they became participants in their rituals, were also believed to be imbued with life. In this way these figures became idols.

The next stage was the animation (manipulation) of the idols, which resulted in their transformation into puppets. Then the puppets were given functions, which fall into two groups:

- Ritual and magic, still fulfilled among many African and indigenous American tribes (Europeans are rarely accepted at such ceremonies).
- Theatrical functions which have changed from century to century, depending on cultural and social life, and that of the theatre.

At first the puppet was considered as an object of curiosity, then as something more spectacular than theatrical. Only by degrees did it attain its place as a theatre performer.

I will not discuss here the ritual and magic functions. It is undoubtedly a fascinating subject, but is far beyond our present concern, which is about the puppets' theatrical functions. These may be classified thus:

- The puppet as android. It was seen as an artificial human which amazed its audiences by its resemblance to the real thing. The apparently lifeless figure becoming filled with life was the first stage of the theatrical transformation of the puppet.
- The puppet as a substitute for the actor. The puppet came on to the miniature stage just as an actor did, since when the puppet has represented its own life as well as the life of the character, claiming to be a little homunculus. This kind of puppet never admitted that it was a puppet, striving to prove its equality to the human actor. This was the second stage of its theatrical transformation.
- The puppet as an artificial actor. Samuel Foote and later the German Romantics wanted to present the puppet as an artificial performer. For them it was a puppet and nothing more than a puppet, not to be considered as a live actor. The confrontation of the dead, wooden figure with the real live actor became a main principle of the productions of their time.
- The puppet as a 'transforming' figure, especially as seen in the 'metamorphosis' or 'trick' puppets which were well known to British puppeteers.
- The puppet as a 'puppet-like' thing. This tautology means 'the

puppet which presents its own special characteristics'. This notion was born as an opposition to the puppet which was 'human-like' and designed to imitate man. The idea of the puppet-like puppet resulted from the revival of the Romantic approach to puppetry at the beginning of the twentieth century, seen clearly in the theatre of Paul Brann and Ivo Puhonny, and in some productions of Sergei Obraztsov.

- The puppet as an artificial actor of definite origin. It emerges from the puppeteer's basket, it descends out of the frame of the folk picture, it comes to life under the influence of music and so on. To make it quite clear we should say that often this puppet is an actor of a play within a play; for example the actor of the puppet show within the living actors' play, as in the majority of the productions of Jan Wilkowski, such as *Guignol in Trouble* and *Zwyrtala the Musician*.

- The puppet as anything that is material and impersonal and may serve as a stage character. This function of the puppet was a real revolution started by Yves Joly and Sergei Obraztsov. The puppets which up to this century had been solid figures made for a long performing life were replaced, in Obraztsov's case, by bare hands and plastic balls, and that of Yves Joly by paper figures and ephemeral objects. The work of the sculptors and manufacturers was replaced by the work of the imagination of the artist, the kind of imagination which suggested the use of an umbrella, perhaps, instead of a carved figure.

- The puppet as a puppet character in the hands of its creator and companion. The revolution mentioned above did not destroy it, although it influenced it a great deal. In the case of this function attendance and assistance are given to the puppet character by the puppet player who is seen on stage.

- The puppet as a puppet character in the hand of its creator and/or companion, which becomes a magical creature in revolt against its master, like the 'Pierrot' of Philippe Genty and the 'Pulcinella' of Henk Boerwinkel. Here magic appears to rescue the puppet, proving that although puppets are pure artefacts, something more may be found within them.

- The puppet as partner of the actor, who is visibly manipulating the figure onstage. The puppet and actor cooperate to create a theatre character. The puppet is the mobile picture of this character, the actor giving to it his voice, feelings and even his facial expression. Many such productions can be seen in European puppet festivals. In this case the actor has replaced the puppet player, quite a new situation.

- The puppet as a sort of prop or accessory for the actor. Here the function of the puppet is degenerating. Again, the actor creates the character, using the puppet as an iconic sign, but paying no attention to it as a true acting subject.
- The puppet as an idol, like Nadezhda in *Cirkus Unikum*, already mentioned.
- The puppet as an object as such, deprived of theatrical life, even of the attendant belief in it of actors or public. When the actors as well as the public no longer believe in the life of the puppet, the wonder of the transformation into a live character does not occur. Though the puppet is an object manufactured especially for theatrical use, in this ease it is completely dead. This lack of belief results in the degeneration of the puppet and onstage it seems to be useless. That is why the puppet when treated as an object is today often replaced by actual objects taken from everyday life.

All these examples of the modus vivendi of the puppets are present in the puppetry of today. Though some originated far back in its long history, they exist still and give a sense of richness to the art. We still meet puppets used simply as replacements for actors, though more often we see them as the actor's partner. Sometimes the puppet is there in the function of the 'idol'. More and more often puppets are being used as objects per se or replaced by real objects.

The characteristics and qualities of different kinds of puppet provoke me to think that we are not at present within one cycle of the puppet's history but in two. They touch and even penetrate each other. The first is the cycle which deals with magic, rites, religious and similar sorts of puppets, all based on animism and the supernatural. Because of the ritual uses of the figures in some modern productions, puppetry comes back to its starting point. The second cycle is the one which deals with profane and secular puppets, wherein all interest lies in the process of creation. Of course it is the actor who appears onstage who is the 'creator'. The puppet is at most a participant of the actor's work.

This process of creation on the stage has become more important than the puppet by itself. That is why there are nowadays so many strange items in the theatre that are very often dubbed 'puppets'. Not so long ago the puppet was a manufactured figure made to be moved and animated in a theatre context. Now, according to modern practice, anything may be called a puppet, because 'being a puppet' means for many people 'being transformed'.

So puppets are any items which can be transformed into characters – even the human body (if treated like a puppet) or some part of it (the hands for example), and all sorts of objects as well as different kinds of materials adapted during the process of invention into stage characters. All of these are no more than objects, the majority of them taken from everyday life. They have nothing to do with the sacred or magic, as puppets once had. On the contrary, they have much to do with our profane civilization. In spite of this they are today produced onstage with much more enthusiasm than the puppets.

The reason for this is not hard to discover. We have lain aside magic. Besides, the constant presence of the actor on the puppet stage encourages directors to hand him not only puppets but props and objects for him to try to bring alive.

Out of this one discovers a special characteristic of the phenomenon we call 'transformation'. The puppet, which is only a pictorial representation of the character, passes through one stage of transformation only. It was dead and now it comes to life, but it remains the same thing. The puppet remains the puppet and nothing more.

On the other hand, the object passes through two stages of transformation. First it has to take on life, and second it must become a character, or vice versa. This is a double transformation – and still there is something more. The manufactured object is an iconic sign of a character; the puppeteer adds movements and words which tell the public that the object is a living, scenic character. Though it may be considered an iconic sign, it nevertheless belongs to a class of objects in everyday use and has nothing to do with the theatre. Introduced onstage, it becomes a character by means of movement and sometimes words, but it lacks the iconic resemblance to a true character. In contemporary theatre this is considered an advantage, since the transformation has to be more sophisticated and more intense.

And there is still something more – the effect of what I choose to call 'opalization'. When movement fully dominates an object, we feel that the character is born and present on the stage. When it is the nature of the object which dominates, we still see the object. The object is still the object and the character at the same time. Sometimes, however, this unity splits for a short while, to be regenerated after a moment. This is what I mean by opalization.

This constant exchange of the functions of components is characteristic of the contemporary puppet theatre as well as the theatre in general. It is not new to the puppet, which has been producing the opalization effect since the eighteenth century. The puppet was then considered a puppet and a live character at the same time; sometimes it was even conscious of its own puppet-like existence. This happens today too when we see the opalization of magic and reality. The opalization of the object, on the contrary, is quite another thing: it is the opalization both of the effect and of reality.

Opalization is only a possibility for the puppet in performance, while it is a fixed prerequisite of any play with objects. The puppet exists in many different ways, as was shown in the first part of this essay. However, the object has only one way forward and this is through opalization.

The opalization effect of the puppet depends on the story presented to the audience; when playing with objects the effect seems quite natural, existing per se, independent of the production. This is attractive and modern; but those are not the only reasons for which some puppeteers have abandoned puppets in favour of objects. The reason for that is more philosophical.

Each puppet embodies a programme of its acting self. It is its plastic expression, its technique of animation and its tradition of movement that give the impulse to the puppet-player. If the player wants to realize this programme, he has to submit to the puppet. And this is the model of the relationship between the 'magic' puppet and its puppeteer. The puppeteer serves the puppet; that is, he serves its magic.

The object holds no programme of acting: the performer must invent one from his own imagination. So he does not serve the object; it is the object which serves the imagination of the performer. That is why some contemporary puppeteers want to change their puppets into objects, depriving them of the remains of their ancient magic power and submitting them to the actor so that he may be the sole creator on the puppet stage.

The creator and his creation as such thus become much more important than the puppet alone, as we have noted already. But it must be said that this is not an exclusive characteristic of the puppet theatre: the same situation can be found in the actors' theatre of the avant-garde. The most important element is the creative process, dominating all other elements of theatre.

Edward Gordon Craig many years ago wanted to liberate the theatre from the domination of literature. He also wanted to liberate it from the egoism of actors to make possible creation in the theatre. It was Bertolt Brecht who liberated the theatre from illusionism. He allowed the actor to stop inhabiting a character in favour of speaking to the audience as himself. This was the famous alienation or distancing effect. In his turn, Antonin Artaud wanted to enrich theatrical expressiveness. He imagined a total theatre in which actors would cooperate with masks, mannekins, moving pictures and props, with the intention of attacking the spectators' sensibility in a 'total' way.

Craig gave a sceptre to the theatre artist; Artaud transmitted it to the actor, who was meant to be the theatre's driving force. The stage became the space for the actor's activities. Today, when an actor enters onstage he first plays the role of an actor who, if needed, is able to create some stage characters with the use of every possible means of expression. Contemporary avant-garde theatre closely approaches the experience of contemporary puppet theatre. They express the same idea: theatre is a creation, and creation is *statu nascendi*. This means that the development from the first impulse to the final effect is executed by its creator – the actor or puppet-player.

This is a phenomenon of our time. It seems that we are arriving at the point of being able to talk about a unity of approach for puppets' and actors' theatre. However, does this unity in fact exist? No, it does not! For some transcendent reason the puppet theatre still has a separate existence. Is this because its response to human psychology is unique, not to be found in any other branch of theatre? To answer the question it is necessary to observe the puppet theatre over the coming years. Today there are no answers – there are only questions.

First published in *Animations*, 1984, 7(3); revised 1988.

3
Between Literature and Plastic Art

Theatre, being a synthetic and diverse art, contains a plastic element, in which fine art plays its part. The identification of a sub-genre called 'plastic theatre' or 'visual theatre' testifies to the emancipation of the plastic element which for many reasons has here become dominant. The domination of any single dramatic element usually acts to the detriment of the others. Literary, discursive theatre limits stage action; mime excludes literature. The opera does not eliminate the text but makes it almost unintelligible, and so on. A theatre in which the visual element is dominant subordinates both the text and the acting.

It would seem that the matter presents itself quite differently in the puppet theatre, where the puppet, a stage character, is a work of plastic creation. Thus one would expect its natural language to be the language of fine art. However, this is so only in the sphere of theory. In practice, the issue is and has always been much more complicated.

In the first period of the history of puppets in theatre, they were received not so much as an object of art as an artificial substitute for a human being. Because of this puppeteers were often accused of magic-making, and the creators of mediaeval and Renaissance androids were persecuted by the Church for violating God's rights. For a while the puppet onstage remained mute; then it started to speak, but in a distorted voice. Its audiences grew, mainly attracted by the semblance of life that it held.

As late as the eighteenth century the prince Hieronim Radziwill praised puppets for their 'lifelike-ness', not for their beauty. Even in the nineteenth century the imitation of the human within a variety of circus performances was the factor which defined the status of the puppet.

Of course, the puppet has always remained in the sphere of plastic art, and has been present in all variants of the performing arts including actors' theatre (which during some phases of its development used man-sized puppets). It was present too at the birth of modern 'visual

76

theatre', whose roots lie in many ancient court and church ceremonies which can be viewed as the foundation of visual theatre. Good examples are the religious festivals of fifteenth-century Spain, in which special performances featuring groups of figures – often mobile – were organized. The same can be said of triumphal entries by monarchs of the sixteenth and seventeenth centuries, the age of the Renaissance and Baroque, which included caravans of vehicles carrying allegorical tableaux, a specific propaganda programme. They were not so much theatrical performances as a free spectacle offered by the ruler to his subjects, with no immediate contact between artist and public.

Other origins of plastic theatre can be found in performances given by travelling players, starting in the Middle Ages: minstrels, storytellers, *Moritatensingers, cantatores dei storie*, many of whom carried paintings or boxes containing sets of figures in separate compartments, as in a portable Gothic altar or *retablo*. Each set of paintings or figures constituted a complete story, like the modern strip cartoon but without the words. Here the words were provided by the storyteller, who drew his listeners and viewers into the events contained in the pictures. Thus it was a demonstration of independent plastic art with the storyteller as commentator. This tradition is still continued in Sicily.

Italian sculptors and architects of the seventeenth century, like Bernini or Acciaioli, built complete puppet theatres for the home, with machinery, puppets and décor. Each was an independent work of art and during a performance each became a synthesis of almost every artistic medium, most often used for the staging of Italian opera.

The first truly visual theatre, as opposed to actors' theatre, was born as a result of secession. After an argument with Garrick's successor, Drury Lane's famous designer Philip de Loutherbourg walked out of the royal theatre and founded another London theatre of his own called the Eidophusikon. This was indeed a plastic theatre, although in those days such places were called 'optical' theatres. There Loutherbourg gave demonstrations of pictures of cities, sunrises and sunsets, sea storms and so on, using spectacular décor, mobile figures and lighting effects. It was not entirely a new idea, but the execution was of a supreme excellence. Previously, in Spain, a mechanical puppet theatre had developed called Mundinuevo; a similar one grew up in Central Europe and was known as Theatrum Mundi. In Poland this kind of show was popularized by the painter Antoni Wolski and the Romanian Jordaki Kuparenko. Despite the carefully elaborated show and visual effects, the last mentioned functioned as a curiosity, like the later *fotoplasticon* (magic lantern show), and disappeared almost completely with the development of cinema. In some places within Poland, it remained in the form of crèches or *szopkas* with moving figures, like the one in Karmelitow Church in Miodowa Street in Warsaw or at the Jesuit Church in Wambierzyce.

From the seventeenth century puppeteers made great efforts to simulate the actors' theatre as much as possible, soon achieving their goal in the performance of dramas, comedies and operas which were its loyal copy and substitute. In this way a 'synthetic' puppet theatre was created, or in other words a theatre which was a synthesis of the arts, using design, words, music and characters, just like the actors' theatre. It is in this direction that the Polish puppet theatre has been and is developing.

In a puppet theatre which is a synthesis of the arts, the artist creates an iconic expression of the stage characters – although this does not change the character of the genre. Behind the puppet stands the puppet actor, who completes the full picture of the stage character with movement and speech.

Similarly, the live actor also contributes to the iconic expression of the character, except that he gives it as his natural self. It is thus possible to say that the actor is a natural stage sign while the puppet is an artificial one. This fact does not affect the plastic or the non-plastic character of the performance. If the harmony of all the theatrical components is preserved, we remain within the sphere of a theatre which is a synthesis of the arts.

Like the 'dramatic' theatre, a synthetic puppet theatre can also fall victim to an erosion of the genre if one component starts to dominate. It is for this reason that we sometimes speak of literary, actors' or 'plastic' puppet performance – and this last term is no tautology.

In puppet stage practice, especially in Poland, the multi-component synthetic theatre is dominant. At the time of writing, it is possible to say that Polish puppet theatre has abandoned the world of plastic art, so much its essence in past centuries, and has adopted the means of expression of the actors' theatre, often defined by literature. To return to the lost paradise, it must pass through the door that remains open to all creators of modern visual theatre in its strictest sense.

To tell the truth, the puppet has participated only theoretically in the creation of this kind of theatre. The development of the modern theatre in Poland was initiated on the one hand by Stanisław Wyspiański and on the other by the author of the theory of the über-marionette, Edward Gordon Craig.

Wyspiański expounded the concept of theatre as a synthesis of the arts. He not only demonstrated how diverse elements can cooperate with each other, but also how they can merge. Wyspiański was able to inject the element of the plastic into the literary framework of his dramas, such as *Acropolis* or *Wyzwolenie* (Liberation). Productions by Kantor or the late Jan Dorman originated from Wyspiański's conception. Their manner of expression realizes the principle of the inter-penetration of elements, experienced for example in the musical structure of their work, in the ebb and flow of selected visual motifs, in the total domination of what is seen over the words. It is difficult to say whether Wyspiański would recognize these two men as his heirs, as in the last analysis his art was dominated by the word, which determined the meaning of the performance.

Edward Gordon Craig contributed to the development of plastic theatre as the author of the super-puppet theory and the creator of the category of 'theatre artist'. In the first case he attacked the place of the actor in the theatre, and in the second, the domination of literature.

Craig was not the first to use the puppet (or über-marionette) to stab the actor in the back. A century before, Heinrich von Kleist and (even earlier) Samuel Foote (in his *Tragedy a la Mode*, 1769) did the same. Third time lucky, they say, but Craig's attack on the actor was not successful either, and he met with strong resistance from supporters of the actors' theatre. Nevertheless, the über-marionette entered theatre through the back door.

In attacking the actor in the interests of art, Craig created a new tyrant – the modern theatre director. He intended to oppose the actor's egoism, but only replaced it with another kind. The 'artist of the theatre', at first called the producer, demanded the right of his own subjective interpretation of dramatic works. Gradually increasing his demands, he took over even the rights of the author, hoping that gradually his *raison d'être* might fall into oblivion: literature as the vehicle for dramatic art was replaced by the producer's concepts, either through adaptation or by 'writing on the stage', as it is sometimes called today. This new situation was accompanied by changes in dramatic literature. A disintegration of dramatic structures occurred: linear stage action was replaced by sets of scenic images connected by common themes to be combined into one message.

The artist 'writing on the stage' did not have to be a playwright; it was enough to compose pictures. And from here it takes only one short step to make the pictures dominate the theatre performance. The 'super-puppet' gave way to Galatea.

Similar processes occurred within the European puppet theatre. The disintegration of classical dramatic structure accelerated the puppet

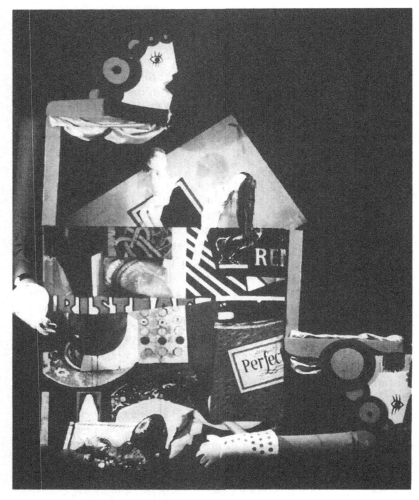

Figure 3.1   From the Hungarian State Puppet Theatre production of *Motel* by Van Itallie, Designed by Ivan Koos, 1972

theatre's withdrawal from the position of substitute for the actors' theatre and encouraged a return to its natural function as a vehicle of visual art. This process went hand in hand with an expansion of its means of expression. Alongside the puppet appeared masked players, props, artefacts and actors. The cooperation of all these was used for the communication of visual metaphors. As if from a different starting point, puppet theatre now became true visual theatre in its strictest sense – a theatre which, as we already know, is one with a variety of means of expression.

I have myself raised objections to the term 'plastic theatre', but I wish to preserve it in order to see, within the same phenomenon, trends of diverse genealogy. The first and best example of the puppet theatre's plastic character was a performance by Die Klappe from Göttingen in the early 1960s. Through the seemingly poor plastic medium of pieces of rag on string, it was possible to represent the fanaticism of a mob subjected to political tyranny. Later, the outstanding Swiss puppet-maker Fred Schneckenburger created surrealist figures and presented them in absurd sketches. The trend towards a plastic theatre was even visible in solo and cabaret programmes. Albrecht Roser of Germany showed each of his marionettes not as a live character, but as a character formed by a specific material. He played with materials – thus with plastic form. Today, new masters of this convention are appearing. Eric Bass from the United States in his performance *Sand* plays out a psychological analysis of his protagonists by means of plastic images, including the pouring of real sand. The startling popularity of the shadow theatre in France and Italy is also a sign of the domination of the visual: there are some excellent companies, among them Gioco Vita, Jean-Pierre Lescot and Amoros et Augustin.

And what of the development of 'object theatre'? Herein lies another proof of the inclination of Western puppeteers towards plastic art. In Poland there has in fact been no such inclination. During the 40 years of its postwar existence there have been superb artists and outstanding performances, but we have not had a true plastic puppet theatre. Even if Janina Kilian Stanisławska and, following her, Adam Kilian stood for the importance of the visual element in puppet theatre, they did it in the name of increasing participation in puppet performances, but neither was in revolt against the domination of the text. Today the Polish puppet theatre, although using a heavily illustrative visual style, is increasingly inclined towards literature. It seems that this is as much the outcome of its passivity as of conscious choice.

There are some exceptions to this: Jan Dorman, as we said, directed a theatre of plastic and literary collage; even more emphatically, Zygmunt Smandzik wrote and directed *Ptak* (Bird), in which he gave a picture of man's existential situation, using simple puppets on sticks. There is also Grzegorz Kwieciński's Theatre of Fire and Paper, in which plastic forms are animated by the power of fire.

This is not much, but it would be surprising if things were any different. The puppet theatre in Poland is formulated as a replica of actors' theatre and until it liberates itself from this pattern, it will not be liberated from the domination of literature. Of course, I am not an opponent of literary theatre and I can appreciate its quality if it is well done. However, I think that the presence of plastic theatre as an alternative is very desirable, if only for the sake of the puppet theatre's creativity and psychological well-being.

First published as 'Teatr lalek – między literatura i plastyką' (Puppet theatre – between literature and fine art), *Teatr Lalek*, 1986, 2: 7–10.

4
The Language of the Contemporary Puppet Theatre

The originator of the discipline of semiotics, Ferdinand de Saussure, understood it as an exceptionally broad one intended to include in its research every kind of sign used by man. Nonetheless, the main choice for modern semiological research resides in linguistics, and it is this which is the point of reference for all its other areas of research. It is surely for the same reason that we use the term 'language of theatre', and we may thus devote this work to 'the language of the contemporary puppet theatre'. It is generally agreed that this phrase has a metaphorical sense, denoting the various means of expression used in theatre. To employ the word 'language' instead of the phrase 'means of expression' is to put the emphasis on the theatre's function as a vehicle of communication. Theatre communicates with its audiences through its language, its particular means of expression, so there is nothing surprising in the fact that not only theoreticians but also practitioners of theatre make use of semiological terminology when they use the terms 'language', 'sign' or 'theatre code'. The basis of the semiological approach to art lies in the principle that any work of art is a 'sign'.

In the case of actors' theatre, which we will call the 'drama theatre', such signs are the spoken word, intonation, facial and bodily expression, gesture, the actor's use of stage space, make-up, coiffure, costumes and properties, the set, the lighting and the music, as listed by Tadeusz Kowzan. This classification is the generally accepted one, but using others the list can be lengthened or shortened. We may equally well apply it to the puppet theatre, provided that we complete it with some missing elements, essential to the sign system of this kind of theatre. In place of 'facial expression' and 'make-up' we must introduce 'plastic expression' and 'the crafting of the puppet'. In place of the stage gesture and movement appropriate to the actor, the gesture and movement of the puppet. However, this exercise will only serve to enumerate the puppet's signs and not its mode of existence, which is more important and which needs to be separately examined.[1]

The first and – up to now – only semiologist to have taken an interest in the puppet theatre as a system of signs is Petr Bogatyrev. He was moved to make his first pronouncement on the subject by a study written by Otakar Zich on the public's reception of puppet theatre and Zich's own conclusions on theatre practice.

Zich noted that puppet theatre contained two ways of involving its audience. The first is by accentuating the material (crafted) nature of the puppet, thus compromising its ambition to imitate the human. In this way the puppet becomes a caricature, a grotesque figure. The second is by accentuating the life-like properties of the puppet, thus underlining its magical origins. In this way the puppet evokes wonder and mystery.[2]

Bogatyrev criticized Zich's approach, saying that it presupposed the drama theatre as the point of reference for puppet theatre. He therefore proposed that the latter be considered as an entirely separate genre of art, that is to say one with its own system of signs. In this way the puppet would become an independent performer, with its own particular properties. Bogatyrev declared:

> If we wish to distinguish military rank, the Captain from the Lieutenant-Colonel, we need to learn how to distinguish the badges of rank on military uniforms. The same applies to different areas of art. To be receptive to the signs of impressionist painting, we need to learn what those signs are.[3]

Of course Bogatyrev was right, but the fact remains that many people do not know how to distinguish military rank and are not in the least ashamed of it. Worse, many do not understand impressionist painting and are equally unconcerned. The puppet theatre's sign system has its own place in the general system of signs of the theatre arts. Kowzan ranks puppetry alongside drama, ballet, mime and opera. However, this is not correct. Puppet theatre is actually in opposition to the theatre of live performers – actors, singers, dancers and so on. The puppet opposes the human. But let us for a moment stick to the common view, that puppet theatre is one of the genres of theatre art. Following this, another opinion has been generally accepted, that puppetry is the genre of theatre that most closely resembles the drama theatre. In spite of all his foregoing arguments, Bogatyrev himself ended with this conviction, writing:

I agree with Kolar when he states that puppet theatre is a theatre art where the first and basic feature differentiating it from any other lies in the replacement of the actor by the puppeteer indissolubly linked to the puppet.[4]

On this basis, Bogatyrev affirmed that drama theatre and puppet theatre represented two separate but neighbouring semiotic systems of theatre art. Puppet theatre and drama theatre are indeed two separate semiotic systems, but they are no more 'neighbouring' than, for example, the theatre of opera is to the theatre of mime. Using the present state of puppetry as a starting point, we can demonstrate that the differences between the sign system of drama and puppet theatre are actually enormous. Above all, we do not know what Bogatyrev meant by 'puppeteer'. We may assume that he had in mind a manipulator and speaker of the text in one person. If so, the puppeteer – in spite of Bogatyrev's conclusions – is not indissolubly linked to the puppet; quite the contrary. What has occurred is a complete rupture of these 'indissoluble links', if indeed they ever existed. It would appear that as an entire genre puppet theatre denies any such natural links – and many hundreds of years of its history confirm this.

These links, these relationships, are what ought to interest us most when we study the sign systems of this branch of theatre. Theatrical signs cooperate to complete, reinforce and define themselves and each other. Their cooperation or, alternatively, their alienation has certain semiological consequences. Kowzan said: 'Here is a typically theatrical problem, to understand the relationship between the subject speaking and the physical source of the speech.'[5] In spite of normal theatre practice, they do not always constitute a unity. What is more, this incompleteness of the character brings with it other semiological consequences. Kowzan again:

> In the puppet theatre the characters are presented to the view, onstage, while their words issue from the mouths of invisible artists. The movement of each puppet during the dialogue suggests which one is speaking, which gives the reply: a sort of bridge is created between the vocal source and the speaking character. Sometimes actors have been known to employ this puppet convention; but if they do, the semiological role of the procedure is entirely different.[6]

This separation of the speaking subject and the physical source of its voice is only occasionally used in actors' theatre; however, in puppet theatre it is the distinctive feature, manifested through centuries with exceptional force. In the most ancient performances of which we have any knowledge, the puppets were usually dumb. The words were spoken either as a commentary or as indirect speech. In fact, the narrator stood in front of the stage and told the story illustrated by the puppet play.

Next came a period in which the puppeteers attempted to suggest to their audiences that the puppets – the speaking subjects – were able to talk by themselves. To this end, the puppeteers used a small instrument (a swazzle) which distorted the voice. This attempt to eliminate the separation of the puppet from the voice source has definite semiological significance.

These two trends continue, with variations, in today's puppet theatre. Even now, the Japanese Bunraku theatre maintains the distinct separation between the vocal source (the special reader or, more precisely, the *joruri* singer) and the puppet (operated by three visible manipulators). In the Toone theatre of Brussels, a single performer speaks for all the characters. He is seen through a small window in the proscenium, while the puppets are worked, in elaborate settings, according to this traditional and popular style. In most puppet theatres of the Communist-ruled countries, each character has his own animator, who at the same time provides the voice for the puppet. In this case the physical source of the words and the speaking subject (the puppet) constitute a unity, at least territorially.

The same can be said about the separation of the moving subject (puppet) in relation to its source of movement. In the drama theatre, in this respect, there is total unity. The actor accomplished all the demands made on his body through his own power. In the puppet theatre, the puppet depends on a source of motor energy independent of itself (usually human but occasionally mechanical). Remember that the physical source of the words is not necessarily always the same as that of the gesture and movement. One puppeteer can be the manipulator and another the speaker for the same character.

These relationships between the acting subject and its sources of energy have serious semiological implications. Put in another way, the question is whether the performance hides or does not hide the puppet's operator, the method of its operation and the person speaking for it.[7] For centuries, puppeteers looked for ways in which their puppets might be taken for human beings with a life of their own, perhaps even a magic life. So of course they concealed, as the closest professional secret, the manner of their animation. Nowadays it is fashionable to display the operators and the speakers. Often you can see the puppeteer onstage beside his puppet; that is, beside the acting subject. In this way he demonstrates who is the passive object and who the principal of the action.

As a consequence, we must return to the notion of the 'acting subject' as two simultaneous signs: the puppet and the animator. This is particularly necessary when the puppet as much as its operator – each in its own way – aims to play a single character. Further still, one could cite various examples of a single operator playing several characters in one performance, but that would require a whole essay of its own.

The changes in the relationships between the stage subject and the physical source(s) of its speech and motor power form the one factor which distinguishes puppet theatre from all other genres. If the drama theatre calls on similar methods, it does so only very rarely, whereas these methods are natural to puppetry. They arise out of its own poetic, with all the attendant semiological implications.

On this basis we can construct a definition of puppet theatre in keeping with that formulated by Bogatyrev. Puppet theatre is a theatre art distinguished from the theatre of live performers by its most fundamental feature, namely that the speaking, acting subject makes temporal use of vocal and motor sources of power which are outside it, which are not its own attributes. The relationships between the subject and its power sources are constantly changing, and this variation has essential semiological and aesthetic significance.

This definition seems adequate for the present state of puppet theatre. Whatever form it takes, realistic or highly stylized, puppet theatre makes use of the variable relationships between its means of expression and their driving forces. These variations are even demonstrated in the choice of technique – string or glove, say – meaning that tradition still underpins the style of contemporary puppet theatre and that any new relationships between the means of expression and the power sources arise from the characteristics of the whole genre.

The relationship between the puppet and its sources of energy has brought changes in our understanding of the puppet. It has been stated that the system of dependence existing between puppet and power source was more concrete than the component parts themselves. The system itself did not change, only the components were variable. However, the principal element, the puppet itself, has also been undergoing change, and in that lies the proof that the real essence of puppet theatre lies in the relationships between its component parts.

These changes have at last led to the destruction of the 'classical' rules and at the same time have contributed to the diminishing use of puppets as a substitute for humans. In place of the 'classical' puppetry, or rather alongside it, a new theatre rich in sign systems has grown up. On the stage have appeared masks, many new kinds of props and appurtenances, and objects. Puppet theatre has become a heterogeneous art drawing on many different sign systems: the human with the puppet, the masked human, the object alongside or in place of the puppet. Sometimes these combinations are an expression of the truly surrealistic; all are exponents of metaphor. Modern puppet theatre, or at least some forms of it, has become the art of juxtaposing different means of expression (or 'signs'), all able to evoke metaphor and so to complicate still further the language of this form of theatre.

Semiological analysis of any theatre performance is a difficult task, given the multiplicity of signs and their relationships. How, then, can we analyze a puppet theatre production in which, by its nature, signs and meanings are in perpetual motion, building new correlations? The analysis becomes more difficult and more challenging.

These preliminary deliberations serve to demonstrate that puppet theatre can be counted among those contemporary artistic phenomena which, because of the abundance of their expressive means and their potential variations, and because of their rich and fertile traditions, have a universal function. Contemporary puppet theatre is not only at the service of children and of the simple-hearted, but is also conquering and enlarging the frontiers of the artistic avant-garde.

Notes

1   Kowzan T., 'Znak w teatrze' (Sign in theatre). In *Wprowadzenie do nauki o teatrze* (Introduction to the science of theatre). Selected and compiled by J. Degler. University of Wrocław 1976, 299–326.
2   Zich O., *Psychologie loutkovego divadla* (Psychology of puppet theatre). Prague 1923, I: 8–9.
3   Bogatyrev P., *Lidové divadlo ceské a slovenské* (Popular Czech and Slovak puppet theatre), Prague 1940, 130.
4   Bogatyrev P., *Semiotyka kultury ludowej* (Semiotics of popular culture), Warsaw 1975, 136.
5   Kowzan, op. cit., 308.
6   Ibid.

7   Cervantes M. de, *Przemyślny szlachcic Don Kichot z* Manczy (The ingenious gentleman Don Quixote of La Mancha). Trans. A. L. Czerny, I Z. Czerny, Warsaw 1955, II: 200.

First presented at 1978 UNIMA Conference, Budapest.

5

The Sign Systems of Puppetry

When I addressed the problem of the language of contemporary puppet theatre a few years ago,[1] I mentioned Petr Bogatyrev as the first semiotician to consider the puppet theatre as a system of signs. I presented his first such pronouncements, remarks provoked by the 1923 article of Otakar Zich on the audience's reception of puppet productions.

Bogatyrev criticized Zich's approach of taking the live theatre as a point of reference for the puppet theatre. Bogatyrev argued that the puppet theatre should be looked upon as any other art form; that is, as a system of signs. Only then could the puppet become an independent actor and reveal its own unique features.[2]

I agreed then with Bogatyrev and his declaration in favour of the puppet theatre as an independent sign system. Today, however, it seems to me that, intrigued by Bogatyrev's opinion, I under-estimated the importance and scientific consequences of Zich's article, just as Bogatyrev did. Let us come back to this article. Zich wrote:

> In fact, it is an argument about two forms of perception: the puppets may be perceived either as living people or as lifeless dolls. Since we can perceive them only one way at a time, we are faced with two possibilities:
>
> (a) We perceive the puppets as dolls, that is, we stress their inanimate character. It is the material they are made of that strikes us as something that we are really perceiving. In that case, however, we cannot take seriously their speech or their movements, in short, any manifestations of their life; hence, we find them comical and grotesque. The fact that the puppets are small and, at least in part (especially in face and body), frozen, and their movements consequently awkward and 'wooden', helps create a comic effect. The result is not, of course, crude comedy but subtle humour which these small figures produce by appearing to act like real people. We perceive them as figurines, but they demand that we take them as

people; and this invariably amuses us. Everyone knows that puppets really make such an impression.

(b) But there is another possibility; we may conceive of the puppets as living beings by emphasizing their lifelike expressions, their movements and speech, and taking them as real. Our awareness that the puppets are not alive recedes, and we get the feeling of something inexplicable, enigmatic and astounding. In this case, the puppets seem to act mysteriously.[3]

Zich's purpose was to provide suggestions to theatre practitioners. He was aware that the theatre he knew and talked about was the folk theatre, with all of its values and limitations. He noticed that folk puppet theatre was stylized and he took this as being characteristic of puppet theatre in general. So he suggested that puppet practitioners develop two kinds of stylization: the plastic-art one (with caricatured puppets) and the symbolic one (with symbolic puppets), according to two kinds of perception. In this way, he wanted to influence puppet theatre to develop its own characteristics.

Zich was aware, then, that puppet theatre is quite different from live theatre. If he talked of puppetry having the live theatre as a background, it was to show distinctly the *differentia specifica* of puppet theatre.

Zich's article also deserves to be appreciated because its analysis is very concrete. He did not write about puppetry in general, but about the puppetry of his time, the theatre he saw and knew. And, equally important, he wrote about the perception of the public he knew. Even if Zich did not mention it directly, we recognize in his descriptions the perceptions of two kinds of public: the folk audience (puppets are mysterious) and the erudite audience (puppets are puppets).

Criticizing Zich's approach, Bogatyrev demanded that the public (both folk and erudite, we assume) learn the signs of puppet theatre. Learning the signs is a general requisite for the proper understanding of all messages. He wrote:

> If we want to distinguish the badges of military uniforms, if we want to tell a Captain from a Lieutenant-Colonel, we must learn the insignia of rank. The same applies to art. In order to understand correctly the signs of Impressionist painting we have to know them.[4]

Of course he is right. The fact is, however, that many people do not know the insignia of rank and they are nonetheless untroubled. What is more, some people do not appreciate impressionist painting and they do not worry about that either. Bogatyrev did not pay attention to such obvious facts, so he did not consider them as arguments. His efforts were to identify the principal faults of Zich's discussion. He wrote:

> Whenever we perceive artistic signs in comparison with a real thing, that is, proceeding from a real thing and not from the sign system that constitutes the work of art, we have the same impression that Zich describes.[5]

Today, considering the advances of semiotics, we can easily argue with Bogatyrev. Bogatyrev contested the perception of artistic signs in constant comparison with real things. Today our attitude is quite the opposite: we realize that we do perceive the theatre by comparing it with reality. Drawing on Peirce's tripartite typology of signs (icon, index and symbol), many scholars have applied the notion of icon in their theatre research.[6] Iconicity becomes the principal characteristic of the theatre, although the examples of iconic signs given by Peirce himself do not include theatrical signs.[7] As Elam remarks:

> The governing principle in iconic signs is similitude; the icon represents its object mainly by similarity, between the sign vehicle and its signified. This is, clearly, a very general law, so that virtually any form of similitude between sign and object suffices, in principle, to establish an iconic relationship.[8]

The contemporary meaning of 'sign' seems to be quite different from that applied by Bogatyrev. He undertook to chart the basic principles of theatrical semiosis and, like almost all of the Prague Circle scholars, he gave primacy to the representing function of the performance elements. He classified them as signs of objects and signs of signs. According to Peirce, the nature of the sign is much more complex, and today it is much more completely known. The sign fulfils its function in being represented or interpreted. It replaces something for someone. Its structure is based on trichotomy. Its typology depends on different functions that are subject to variation as related to its context.[9] The puppets, whether producing a comical or a mysterious impression, continue to be theatre signs no matter which impression is intended.

Another question has to do with the problem of perception. Bogatyrev stated that Zich employed the wrong sign system to decode a puppet presentation. Bogatyrev acted as if he were identifying himself with a puppet-player disappointed that his audience misunderstood his performance because they applied the wrong decoding system. Let us remember that perception is only a part of the greater process of theatrical communication. The understanding of the message depends not only on the public and its ability to understand, but on the artist and his ability to be understood as well.

An artist who wishes to be understood should choose that system of signs that is the best vehicle for the ideas he wants to communicate to the audience. This means that he should know the sign systems existing potentially in the minds of the audience. What is so valuable in Zich's article is his view of the puppet theatre as an active communication; he looked at it through the eyes of putative spectators. In our day there is no doubt that for successful communication, both partners (sender and addressee) should do their best to learn the necessary codes; that is, cultural codes and theatrical and dramatic subcodes.[10] Responsibility for possible misunderstanding of the puppet theatre sign system lies with both partners.

The relationship of live theatre and puppet theatre troubled Bogatyrev throughout his life. In 1973, 50 years after his first publication on the puppet theatre, a posthumous article summed up his thoughts on this subject: 'The interconnection of two similar semiotic systems: the puppet theatre and the theatre of living actors'. At the very beginning he wrote:

> The perception of one semiotic system in comparison to another system is an especially interesting problem. Thus someone familiar with only one language often regards a related language as a distorted version of his own native tongue. There are many examples where a Russian interprets another Slavic language against his own linguistic background defining, for example, Ukrainian as distorted or corrupted Russian.[11]

In spite of his awareness of the similarity of the two systems, he persisted in criticizing Zich's article, repeating the arguments with which we are familiar. However, while forming his definition of puppet theatre, Bogatyrev took the live theatre as a background for it:

> We agree ... that puppetry is a theatrical art. The principal characteristic that differentiates puppet theatre from live theatre is that in puppetry 'the actor is replaced by the puppet operator in inseparable unity with his puppet'.[12]

This definition cannot be satisfactory, for many reasons. Bogatyrev proceeded to analyze contemporary puppets, pointing out stylization and caricature as their characteristics. He showed himself to be much concerned with the problems of the cooperation of two sign systems: live theatre and puppet theatre. He saw this cooperation in the union of human beings and puppets as actors in the same theatrical space, as, for example, happened in the comedy of Petrushka in the nineteenth century. He was preoccupied, too, by the distorted 'puppet voice' of this comedy, the result of employing the instrument called, in English, the swazzle. However, Bogatyrev's presentation of contemporary puppets is not a real analysis of the subject. It is, rather, a sort of register or index of different kinds of puppets and of different relationships between live actors and puppets. Bogatyrev did not intend to produce a detailed analysis like that of Zich. He wanted, instead, to show the profusion of puppet theatre components that warrant semiotic treatment.

Thus Bogatyrev and Zich presented different approaches to puppetry. Bogatyrev, concerned with semiotic problems, discussed puppetry as a totality, looking for materials of semiotic value. Zich, concerned with a concrete theatrical epoch determined by territory and cultural tradition, discussed the puppet theatre of his time, giving a detailed analysis and taking into consideration the perception of this theatre by its audience.

An approach like Bogatyrev's happens to be applied rather often by contemporary scholars who discuss the characteristics of puppet theatre. Puppetry for them seems to be a synchronically unified monolith, although the contemporary puppet theatre is a rich and differentiated totality, taking in cultural elements of different provenance and from different epochs. Contemporary puppetry includes puppet forms ranging from indigenous African ritual puppets, through the puppets of different cultural circles such as Europe and the Far East, to folk puppetry and an unlimited quantity of modern artistic puppetry.

If one takes this entire range of puppet theatre as a field of scientific investigation, a preliminary task is to make a register or index of its various elements, as Bogatyrev did. This register may be of some use as a demonstration of the puppet theatre's means of expression, but I am afraid that it will not tell us much more about puppetry than we know already.

The most interesting subject discussed by Bogatyrev, one that fascinated him throughout his life, was the problem of the relationship between the live actor and the puppet. Some theatres have involved the collaboration of a storyteller, narrator or some other kind of human intermediary. This was the case for the Renaissance theatre described by Cervantes in *Don Quijote* as well as Petrushka's comedy and that of Punch and Judy. Though the intermediary was present in front of the stage, the manipulators of the puppets were hidden in the booth or behind the *retablo* (the puppeteer's stage). However, there exists a theatre with an intermediary in which the puppets' operators are not hidden: the Japanese Bunraku theatre. Increasingly, many European and American theatres introduce the manipulators on the stage alongside the puppets, as though the function of intermediary were almost forgotten. These are the most familiar examples of the coexistence of two sign systems (actors and puppets) in contemporary puppetry.

Listing such intermediaries together implies that all of them belong to the same class of objects. Let us see if this is really true. The Renaissance puppet theatre of Cervantes' Master Pedro is a sort of storytelling performance. A boy stands in front of the *retablo* and points at the puppets while recounting the story of Don Gaiferos and Melisandra. The boy's text is mostly narration, only occasionally including the direct speech of the acting figures. The principal role of this presentation belongs to the boy; he is the main actor. The *retablo* and its puppets are but illustrations. When necessary, the boy responds to remarks made by the audience. He is, then, a real intermediary, but he mediates the reaction of the public towards the text (words) and not towards the puppets.

The comedy of Petrushka was performed in a portable booth, with a (human) musician in front who talked with Petrushka. The musician fulfilled a number of functions. He was, of course, playing on one or other instrument; he was an actor partnering Petrushka (their talks were a sort of frame for the action, which might be described as theatre within theatre); when necessary he acted as a real intermediary, interpreting Petrushka's words since they were distorted by the swazzle. Petrushka, on the other hand, was an acting figure, a speaking one, although his speech was distorted; he was easily recognized as a puppet, both because of the proximity of the musician-intermediary, a real man, and because of his distorted speech.

There is no doubt that in the case of Don Pedro, the *retablo* puppet served the storyteller/musician, while in the case of the Petrushka comedy, it was the actor/musician who served the puppets. In the first case the story is the constitutive element of the presentation; in the second it is the puppet hero. I would dare to say that the puppets entered into two quite different sign systems.

We find a much more complicated situation in Bunraku theatre. On the stage we have puppets, each puppet manipulated by three men who are visible to the public. Sitting on a platform to the side are a *joruri* chanter and a musician playing the *samisen*. The puppets do not speak or chant. It is the *joruri* chanter who speaks and chants for every character. Though he remains sitting, he moves while chanting, expressing all of the feelings and emotions of the characters. His means of expression include both his chant and his facial mimicry. The three manipulators do not speak. Two of them work with hoods hiding their faces. The head operator is the only one who ever appears unhooded. His face frequently expresses the emotions of the character. Though the operators do not speak, they add to the sound sphere of the performance by the drumming of their feet, important for the rhythm of the action.

It would be hard to compare the sign systems of Bunraku with any other system already mentioned here. Even in Japan, experts disagree on what is the constitutive part of Bunraku theatre. Ando wrote: 'Actually one should 'hear', not 'see', Bunraku since the narrator's chant called Gidayu-bushi is the most important part of the performance.[13] Adachi sees, instead, three balanced components that together constitute Bunraku:

> Sometime just before 1600, a notable event occurred to change Japanese cultural development. Puppetry, narrative storytelling, and samisen music were joined to create a new popular dramatic form known today as Bunraku.[14]

The definition given by Adachi is closer to my understanding of Bunraku. The puppets are not simply illustrations to accompany the storytelling, they are visual components of the characters. As such, they enter into cooperation with the voice of the *joruri* chanter, with his emotional mimicry and with the sound of the drumming of the puppeteers' feet. Only in the collaboration of these different elements are the scenic characters of Bunraku created.

In the storyteller system (like Don Pedro's puppet theatre) or in the Petrushka comedy, human beings and puppets are separate units that cooperate to fulfil their dramatic functions. In Bunraku theatre, these units (especially the humans), so that they may serve as scenic characters, are submitted first to the process of atomization, with the atoms obtained used to construct new units that exist only as theatrical beings. This system may be compared with the most advanced artistic puppet theatres of our time in Europe and America. This cross-cultural comparison may raise the problem of the relationships of the different 'atoms' employed to create a scenic character. The historical and cultural backgrounds of the two systems (Japanese and European) are so differentiated that they need further discussion, especially since the Bunraku system was born at the end of the seventeenth century, while similar European trends are two-and-a-half centuries younger.

The Bunraku system has its origin in the rich tradition of Japanese puppetry. Though the puppets often entertained people of different social classes, they were used more frequently in ritual. As we are informed by Ortolani,[15] the *joruri* chanters were monks who, by associating with puppet players, founded Bunraku theatre. Puppets were often presented in the shrines or close to them; even today, in the ceremonial atmosphere of the theatre, the public performance carries the atmosphere of ritual. As explained by Ando:

> Next the narrator picks up the libretto which is on the ornate reading stand in front of him, lifts it above his head with both hands, and bows. This bow has three meanings; it expresses respect for the author of the play, it is a sort of prayer that the narrator 's performance will be worthy of the work, and it expresses gratitude for the presence of the audience and a request that they listen to him.[16]

The Bunraku system is closed, as all classical systems are. To cooperate within this system means to maintain it. If so, one is obliged to accept it and to subordinate oneself to it, otherwise the system will cease to exist. The artists of Bunraku seem to be aware of this, seeing themselves as modest artists in the world. This is the confession of the famous puppeteer Tamao:

> The tayu's narration is essential, of course, but my movements must give his words that other dimension that makes them convincing. The tayu is an artist: he is interpreting, and I can't tell him how to express the feelings I too am trying to convey. The samisen is the third force. Our work is distinct. Usually we complement each other well, but sometimes ... if we're fortunate, we mesh perfectly.[17]

The European system, which I once called 'the third genre'[18] between live theatre and puppet theatre, is obviously an open system. In the course of the 1950s and 1960s, all the elements of puppet theatre were atomized. There exists now an unlimited number of 'atoms' just waiting to be introduced as components in new theatrical 'units'.

Let us look at how this system works in the performances of the well-known Czech director Josef Krofta. In the Poznan Theatre in Poland in 1977), he directed his own script, after Cervantes' *Don Quijote*. Onstage we saw a number of live actors and some puppets. The principal characters (Don Quijote and Sancho Panza) were doubly represented by men and puppets. At one time we saw the characters represented by men, at another time by puppets, and sometimes by both. The scene of Don Quijote's defeat in the inn was performed using different means of expression. One actor with a stick in his hand beat the bench where the Don was supposed to be lying; another actor pretending to be beaten shrieked like a madman; another was damaging the puppet of Don Quijote, while the rest of the actors observed the action, adding various exclamations.

All of this together was to convey Don Quijote's punishment and suffering. This particular combination of 'scenic atoms' will never be repeated in Krofta's work. Looking for originality is the first principle of European art. That is why in each performance of Krofta we may find a new combination of the means of expression and so, to some extent, a new system of signs.

I hope that I have succeeded in proving that the presence of a puppet is not always and inevitably constitutive of one fixed sign system of puppet theatre. In the case of Don Pedro's theatre, the puppetry belonged to the sign system of storytellers' performance. The Petrushka comedy represents, for me, a true system of puppet theatre signs. In Bunraku theatre we see two possible interpretations, since even the Bunraku puppeteers admit that their puppets have a secondary role in the whole performance. For modern European puppetry, I would rather think of quite a new and special sign system, one based on the personal and impersonal elements of theatre. And this is perhaps true because the impersonal elements are introduced so often into the production of live theatre.

The results of my deliberation encourage me to discuss the puppet's long journey through different sign systems, seen in historical perspective. There is no doubt that the puppet theatre as such was preceded by the puppet. Without the prior existence of the puppet, the existence of puppet theatre would be impossible. Thus, the first serious evidence of European puppet theatre begins in the seventeenth century. Before then there were many puppet demonstrations, but they were not theatre, they were *Puppenspiel* ('play with puppets'), as they are called quite correctly by Purschke.[19] Let me explain that for us 'the theatre' will mean actors (human or puppet) who in a special space present imagined characters, according to a given or improvised drama, being seen by a public gathered especially or by chance. Until the seventeenth century, however, the puppet demonstrations always lacked some elements; they did not have dramas, or the puppets were not characters.

Though the puppet in Europe seems to be as ancient as the live actor (maybe even older), it is obvious that the actors' theatre outstripped the puppet theatre. The first 'real' theatre into which puppets entered was the theatre of live actors, and for many centuries the puppet remained the slave of the live theatre's rules. However, some people tried to discover that which was characteristic of puppets – to form their unique style and in consequence, though unconsciously, to form their unique sign system. They succeeded by developing the artistic puppet theatre of the nineteenth and twentieth centuries, which brought new elements to the genre. At first they were looking solely for the puppet theatre's characteristics, which meant that they accepted the puppet-like (*puppenhaft*, *kukolnoe*) elements on stage. Later they started to analyse the puppet theatre's means of expression, finishing with an atomization of the puppet theatre (getting rid of the screen, for example) and giving birth to a new form of theatre whose characters are created of both personal and impersonal elements.

So it seems that the puppet, during its long history in Europe, has belonged to four different sign systems. Since all four systems still exist, it means that the puppet still belongs to them at this moment. I will try to discuss them briefly in four separate sections: (1) the puppet in the service of neighbouring sign systems; (2) the puppet in the sign system of the human theatre; (3) the sign system of the puppet theatre; and (4) the atomization of all elements of the puppet theatre and its semiotic consequences.

The puppet in the service of neighbouring sign systems

The evidence left by the writers of antiquity tells us about the existence of certain kinds of puppets and dolls. However, the information is poor as concerns their shape, construction and use. The most complete descriptions relate to automata, which included little mechanical figures. One of the automata, 'The Apotheosis of Bacchus' by Hero of Alexandria, was a sort of mechanized altar and belonged to sacred art. It tells us a great deal about the possible origin of puppets as such. Another automaton, which performed 'The Tale of Nauplios', was a mechanical theatre presenting the story in five scenes with characters and changeable settings. The story itself belonged to mythology; one would have seen Greek deities on the stage.[20]

The two automata were – as we may guess – miniatures of the cult manifestations practised either in a temple or in a theatre, and, as such, they were expensive products. They surprised the spectators because of the engineering skill of their maker.

There is no doubt that puppets could surprise spectators for other reasons. Although puppets were deities at the moment of their birth, they later gave up their sacred functions for those of entertainment. While they were deities their movement seemed to be quite natural for them: deities are omnipotent. Later, when representing a man and continuing to move, the situation became new and unusual, in fact miraculous. And this surprised the spectators.

Reading the different texts, we do not feel that the antique writers were surprised by puppets – not Plato, Xenophon or Athenaeus. They treated puppets as something routine, which suggests that they were popular at that time. Plato, in his famous metaphor on the perception of reality, tells us about 'the partitions puppet-handlers set in front of the people and over which they show the puppet'.[21] Xenophon suggests that the mime group of Syracuse used puppets in their perform-ances,[22] and Athenaeus tells us about Potheinos' puppets presented in one of the Hellenic theatres.[23] Plato's evidence might well be a sign of the existence of a real puppet theatre, but he conveyed insufficient information for us to be sure. The references of the others also suggest the participation of puppets in the sign systems of mime and live theatre; but here too we do not know enough.

In the Middle Ages, puppets were used by wandering players: *jongleurs*, bards and storytellers. The last certainly used puppets as well as scroll paintings and dolls. They significantly influenced the puppetry of the time. Both bards and storytellers, chanting or telling their stories, used puppets as illustrations. This may be seen in the puppets illustrated in the *Hortus deliciarum* by Herrade of Landsberg.[24] These puppets were very simple and rather poor illustrations of the narration, but in the following centuries, when figurative painting and sculpture were wide-spread in mediaeval churches, new cult objects appeared that could be used by storytellers.

At the beginning they exploited painted or sculpted altars (*reredos, retablos*) as illustrations for their sacred stories. Later they added devices that enabled them to move parts of puppets, whole figures or, finally, a set of them. And so storytelling was changed into a combined demon-stration of narration and puppets. We should not be deceived by the fact that some of the references give primary attention to the puppets rather than to the narration. The narration was already known, but the puppets were the new ingredient that might attract the public.

The majority of the puppets at that time were moving figures included in the sacred tableaux. For this reason, the sets of puppets used by storytellers were called in France *retable*, in Spain *retablo*,[25] in Poland *tabernaculum*,[26] in England motion[27] and in Germany *Himmelreich*.[28] These words derive either from religious implements or from the notion of movement.

This kind of puppetry developed through the centuries. Some of the boards or boxes with sets of puppets changed into the mechanical theatre, others into elaborate theatres with successive scenes to perform real dramas. However, those changes occurred rather late, at the beginning of the seventeenth century.

Although puppets used by storytellers were those most often described, they existed among a large variety of other kinds of puppets. Let us start with those not connected with any specific real or imaginary subject, but with human beings in general. These puppets did not pretend to present a definite character: they were just puppets that tried to be alive like a human. Of course they were not alive, and thus they seemed to be caricatures. And so the puppet-player associated them with monkeys because monkeys were also caricatures of man.[29]

Other puppets claimed to be something more than caricatures. They pretended to be *Kobolds*, then a kind of magic being.[30] Their operators endeavoured to hide the system of manipulation in order to convince the spectators that they were looking at unusual creatures. In both cases, the puppets were not theatre characters; they attempted to be something real, and being real they became an object of spectacular and public interest. They were living artefacts. Their lifelikeness was the goal of the 'artistic' efforts of the puppet players. They were like circus puppets whose only wish is to imitate human circus performers as closely as possible.

However, there is some reason to think that in the Middle Ages a specific puppet stage was already being constructed. Looking at four-teenth-century miniatures by Jehan de Grise, we see a sort of puppet booth in the shape of a castle. Perhaps that is why the French booth is called *castelet*. In this booth we see puppets ready to fight, some of whom are knights. These were possibly an advanced form of puppets designed to illustrate *chansons de geste*. Besides this evidence, there were other indicators of the puppets' disposition to fight. One of them is a German figure, Meister Hamerlein,[31] which probably represented the mediaeval devil in conflict with heaven and human beings. Fighting seems to be rather 'puppet-like' if done by hand puppets.

I hope that it is clear now why I am insisting that puppets have belonged to many different sign systems. Puppetry itself does not constitute a single, monolithic system. Systems are constituted by the relations between puppet and puppeteers or actors, thereby producing different functions of the puppet. This was proved by the use of puppets in antiquity and the Middle Ages: in live theatre, the puppet was a copy of an actor; in jugglers' presentations, a copy of human beings; in the storytellers' system, an illustration; and in the embryonic puppet theatre, a real theatrical puppet.

The puppet in the sign system of the live theatre

In antiquity (the mimes, Potheinos) and in the Middle Ages (liturgical puppets in Whitney), the later managers of live theatre used puppets in their productions. Groups of Italian *commedia dell'arte* players brought puppets to many countries. References in Poland indicate that Italians in 1666 performed one day as comedians and another day as puppeteers.[32] Dutch engravings of the seventeenth century show that they inserted puppets into their live productions.[33] The puppets were either the equivalent of an actor or 'guests' on the stage of live comedians.

The puppets were also 'guests' in the official Italian theatre during the Renaissance. Sebastian Serlio declared that he wanted flat figures on the stage as a complement to live actors:

> While the stage is empty of characters, then the architect should have ready some groupings of little figures, as large as space will allow them to be, and these will be of heavy coloured pasteboard and cut to shape; they should be on a rule of wood crossing the stage between some arches, with grooves in the stage into which the wooden rules will be put, and thus a person behind the arch will make them pass slowly, sometimes to show musicians with instruments and voice, while behind the stage there will be subdued music.[34]

Gradually, puppets became actors in their own theatres, constructed according to established models. These were true miniatures: the puppets were flat figures or marionettes with one wire and four strings, as documented by Domenico Ottonelli.[35] The first puppet theatre opera production was presented in 1668 in Rome, at the palace of Pope

Clement IX who, as Cardinal Giulio Respigliosi, had written the drama *La comica del cielo* (The divine comedienne). This play was performed, with music by Anton Maria Abbatini, in a theatre 'apparatus' prepared by Gian Lorenzo Bernini. It should be noted that the puppet apparatus was made by the same master who constructed theatres and settings for live actors. It was a real Baroque theatre in miniature, with a box stage, curtains, wings, perspective prospect and all the necessary devices.

This kind of theatre was used by famous puppet opera manager La Grille[36] and the English puppet master Martin Powell.[37] Differing from the live theatre, the puppet stage was often furnished with a network of fine wire stretched across the proscenium opening. Domenico Ottonelli was the first to mention its existence[38]; the function of this network was to hide the wire and strings of the puppets, to further the illusion that the puppets were miniature live actors.

In announcements of the time, the puppet theatre managers assured the public that their puppets would act like live actors. Today it is hard to believe that a puppet could imitate an actor so perfectly that it might be treated as his miniature. However, it was quite possible in the operatic puppet theatre of the seventeenth century, since the acting of the human singers and actors at that time was fully schematic. The singers stood in a row by the proscenium opening and made schematic gestures. They were obliged to remain in that one place, since the candles which showed their faces while speaking, singing and expressing their feelings were at the front of the stage. To imitate such acting was easy for the puppet, especially since the light was not bright and the wire network hid the strings.

In general, the theatre managers trusted puppets and 'employed' puppets to perform instead of actors if, for some reason (social, political and so on), actors were not available.[39] Sometimes they used puppets to compete with the dramatic theatre as in the case of Charlotte Charke, an actress of the Drury Lane theatre. She left this theatre after a quarrel with the director, and made puppet shows performing the same repertory as in Drury Lane.[40]

There was a special situation in Paris because of the monopoly of the three official theatres (the Opéra, the Comédie Française, the Comédie Italienne). Other theatre troupes were not permitted to perform in Paris, with the exception of limited productions at the Saint Germain and Saint Laurent fairs, and with the exception of puppets. The theatre managers, then, were forced to perform with puppets. They reacted to this repression by trying to find some excuse to lead a live actor back on the stage. The famous theatre manager Bertrand, at the end of the seventeenth century, introduced children and made them act among the puppets in order to evoke the impression that all of the scenic characters were alive. When this practice was forbidden, he invented another solution: puppets performed the main play but the interludes were presented by actors.

The war between the theatre managers and the monopoly lasted more than half a century, but finally the managers won, and the result was the transformation of most puppet theatres into human theatre, with the puppets acting according to the principles of human theatre. However, the monopoly theatres wanted to destroy any resemblance of puppets to live acting. In 1722 it was forbidden for the puppets to speak with a clear voice. Puppets were obliged to distort their voice by means of the swazzle (French: *sifflet pratique*). So it was not the puppeteers who were fascinated by the swazzle, but the authorities who wanted them in order to keep puppets apart from the live theatre's acting. For similar reasons, the famous manager of the 1740s, Bienfait, whose theatre employed both children and puppets, called the children *petits comédiens pantomimes* and the puppets *comédiens praticiens*.[41]

The privileges of the actors' theatre provoked the puppeteers to parody their productions. The majority of performances in the Paris fairs were parodies of live theatre. One frequent method was to confront a serious subject with the comical approach of a popular character taken, for example, from *commedia dell'arte*. In France, it was Polichinelle; in England, Punch. Punch appeared in the Trojan War show 'The False Triumph', in which 'Signior Punchanella appeared in the role of Jupiter, descending from the clouds in a chariot drawn by eagles, and sang an aria to Paris'.[42]

It was seldom that the puppeteers or the artists cooperating with them wanted to stress the puppet's own characteristics in their productions. We might mistakenly see such a purpose in the comedy of Pier Jacopo Martello, *Lo Starnuto di Ercole*.[43] He suggested presenting Hercules as a man, while the Pygmies would be puppets. This division, however, was made for practical reasons, according to the proportions of the characters, and man and puppets were treated as homogeneous beings.

A strong feeling for the differences between human beings and puppets characterized English director and actor Samuel Foote. As manager of the Little Theatre in London, he produced live and puppet performances – the latter for economic reasons. As an interesting theatrical explanation for his activities he declared, in 1773, his interest in the primitive puppet show, which meant for him actors from antiquity with their masks and padded costumes. However, to have a complete puppet, Foote contended that it was necessary to sunder the character by the practice of one actor giving the gesture while another delivered the words, as introduced to the antique theatre by Livius Andronicus.[44] Leaving aside the historical aspect of Foote's statement, we must admit that he pointed at the essential feature of puppet theatre. He also made clever observations on the problem of the perception of puppet theatre, stressing the importance of the participation of the audience. He wrote:

> [A young country] girl being brought by her friends for the first time to a puppet show, she was so struck with the spirit and truth of the imitation, that it was scarce possible to convince her, but that all the puppets were players; being carried the succeeding night to one of the theatres, it became equally difficult to satisfy her, but that all the players were puppets.
>
> But the infinite difference that will be found between the different performances will, I flatter myself, make it impossible for any of my present hearers to commit that mistake; to which of us the superiority is due, your voices this night will determine.[45]

The feeling of the opposition of two systems (live theatre and puppets) led Foote to show a production as (puppet) theatre within the (live) theatre. Puppets performed *The Handsome Housemaid, or Piety in Pattens*, a burlesque of sentimental comedy:

> Just at the end of the play a constable (a human actor) entered, and took the troupe, with Foote as their manager, before a magistrate as common vagrants. At the trial it was proved that neither whippings nor a diet of bread and water would have any effect upon puppets, and as for Foote, he was three-quarters a man but one-quarter (his wooden leg) a puppet, so it would be impossible for the court to deal with him unless they could catch the body without the leg, or the leg without the body.[46]

This was the first time that the puppet was looked at as an independent actor with its own characteristics, which accounts for the historical significance of the performance. Foote's attitude was the starting point for the discovery of a separate sign system of the puppet theatre, which will be the subject of the next section.

Also belonging to the sign system of actors' theatre were the popular (or folk) marionette theatres, which were often copies of live theatre. Of course this kind of theatre is very different from the actors' theatre, but this is so more because it is a popular theatre (*Volkstümliches Theater*) than because it is a puppet one. I apply here the notion of 'popular theatre' after Hauser,[47] who understands popular art as an artistic or quasi-artistic production addressed to the uneducated urban public. Generally, this kind of production is not innovative, but instead repeats subjects and forms adapted from 'official' art. In the case of the popular puppet theatre, the live theatre model and live theatre repertory were adapted for two reasons (for the puppets and for their special public) and in two stages.

The first stage of adaptation covered the Baroque theatre model and repertory, including bible stories, myths, evangelical parables, hagiographic plays and two famous Renaissance subjects, *Don Juan* and *Doctor Faust*. Adaptation added a sort of folk flavour to the basic models. As a matter of fact, today we perceive the folk style as limited in theatrical skill and in the understanding of theatre.

The second stage of adaptation covered the Romantic repertory and theatre models. Puppet theatre in Germany, France, Belgium and Bohemia adapted the repertory, settings and costumes of melodrama. Managers of French puppet theatres stressed that their settings were taken from the Théâtre Porte Saint Martin in Paris. French puppet theatre was the most advanced in mimicking the live theatre and developed an imitative technique to a high level. When this technique reached its summit, the theatres turned to replacing the puppets with actors on the stage.[48]

The popular theatres in other countries were less imitative or, one could say, more limited in their abilities. They failed to achieve convincing imitation, instead developing individual folk stylization. There were big differences, for example, between the Belgian and Bohemian theatres, between the German and Sicilian ones. Each had its own sign sub-system. Nevertheless, there were common features: their origins, the popular resident characters, the common practice of introducing trick puppets and the efforts to emphasize the words. In almost all popular puppet theatre, the words were pronounced in a rather artificial way, as an emotional recitation. There is no doubt that this way of speaking was inherited from the actors' theatre. It was the Comédie Française that popularized chanting recitation in Europe, but when it was already forgotten in live theatre, the popular puppet theatre was still using and preserving it.

The comic characters (Kašparek, Tchantchès and others) were also taken from the live theatre, not immediately but over time. Such characters were known in live theatre from the beginning of the seventeenth century, and the last of them (Kasperle) appeared in Viennese comedy in the 1760s.

Trick puppets complemented the popular puppet productions. They included metamorphosis puppets and circus puppets, and were usually presented at the end of the performance. The metamorphosis puppets were technical accomplishments shown as such to astonish the public. In this they were successful, as were the circus puppets (jugglers, rope dancers, acrobats and others). These were not dramatic characters; rather, they skilfully imitated circus acts. However, in the nineteenth century some puppeteers (Brigaldi, Bullock) used trick puppets to create a special genre of theatre, the variety puppet show,[49] where trick puppets were complemented by many of the elements of live variety shows.

The sign system of the puppet theatre

We have already discussed the disposition of the hand puppet to fight and identified this as a special feature of this puppet. It can grasp and handle objects, too. Hand puppets are hands dressed in gloves, gloves that constitute theatre beings. Eichler contended that they are not real puppets because they prolong the human body.[50] They are expressions of human beings and thus they represent the mime tradition, not puppetry. He was right concerning the psychology of acting, but wrong concerning the perception of glove puppets. Since they are hand based, they are not fully able to imitate human beings. Yet for the public they are puppets because they are artificial creatures, they behave in their own typical way, and they are able to present different characters on the stage.

In the seventeenth and eighteenth centuries they served as advertisement puppets both for the charlatans and for theatres, although they also performed short stories. In the nineteenth century they appeared in street comedies such as Punch and Judy. Though this comedy seems to be the continuation of *commedia*, it was not a copy of it. The street comedy was a new stage in the development of the *commedia dell'arte*, performed only by puppets. The same origin is shared by the Guignol theatre in France, which developed its own means of expression and a special repertory of great social importance.

And what of the other kinds of puppets and their sign systems? Let us recall the Romantic writers in Germany, who wanted to describe the marionette as the ideal theatre actor: Kleist, Hoffman and Tieck. Ludwig Tieck's analysis related to the folk (popular) puppet theatre. He came to conclusions close to those reached by Zich a century later: puppets want to be perceived as important characters of Mystery plays and historical dramas, but they are limited, wooden figures, which is why Tieck found puppets to be grotesque and ironic creatures. From this starting point, Tieck suggested that we understand the marionette theatre as follows:

- as grotesque and ironic theatre that confronts the contradiction of great wishes and modest abilities, of refined and rude characters, of high social manners and their satirical, folk interpretation;
- as theatre that needs for its full expression the background of the live theatre – the puppet theatre expresses itself best when it exists within the frame of live theatre, which approaches theatricality;
- as theatre that is aware of its theatricality, which results in the fact that the puppet characters are conscious of their artificial and wooden existence;
- as a theatre of metaphor, based on the preceding three points.[51]

Some of these principles were applied by Franz Pocci and Josef Schmid in their activities in Munich. At the same time, French puppeteers applied a different kind of stylization. Maurice Sand founded a puppet theatre following the style of *commedia dell'arte*; Lemercier de Neuville introduced flat puppets which constituted a sort of graphic art; Henri Signoret used moveable statues, intended to revive the hieratic style of expression.

A similar, but somewhat different, tendency was born in Germany in the artistic theatre of Paul Brann in Munich. Brann, looking for a homogeneous theatre, chose puppetry because it appeared to him to be a material unity, in opposition to live theatre, which contrasts the actor's biological body with the material, artificial setting. Brann understood the puppet as an excellent actor belonging to the theatre, an actor whose material totality is the result of human creativity. The puppet is a creature of material, and to preserve its character it is necessary to develop its material features. That is why some of Brann's puppets were made as porcelain figures, and they moved as porcelain figures were imagined to move.

Almost all of the artistic puppet theatres of that time intended to be 'puppet-like', showing the puppet as scenic character and as material object at the same time. On this principle, the sign system of the puppet theatre was constituted. In the centre of this system was the puppet, which was to be perceived as the puppet, though in different theatrical functions. The most representative opinions on this subject were pronounced by Buschmeyer, Eichler and Obraztsov.[52]

Brann's homogeneous puppet theatre outlived its apogee in the 1930s. However, some puppeteers a few years earlier had looked for complements to such an understanding of the puppet theatre. They returned to the suggestions of Foote and Tieck to confront the puppet theatre with the actors' theatre, in order to intensify the puppet theatre's characteristics. The puppet seen alongside human beings is more 'puppet-like', and the human being seen alongside puppets seems more human-like.

So Vittorio Podrecca introduced actors to the stage and let them act among the puppets. Obraztsov did the same. The Polish director Jan Wilkowski applied this confrontation of actors and puppets by means of 'the puppet theatre within the live theatre'. These approaches demonstrated the basic relationship between two sign systems (live and puppet theatres) which then still existed as compact, self-contained totalities.

In this development of the puppet theatre sign system, solo puppet performers introduced to artistic practice two important subjects related to the problem of the puppets' existence: the opalescence (or opalization) of the puppet and the opposition of puppet versus human.

By 'opalescence of the puppet' I mean the double existence of the puppet, which is perceived (and demonstrated) both as puppet and as scenic character. Clown Gustav of Albrecht Roser is a clown character, but when his strings get entangled and he asks for help, he is a puppet; furthermore, he is a puppet playing on its awareness of being a puppet. Obraztsov operates quite differently. While singing a Mussorgsky lullaby, he stands in front of the public with his hand puppet called Tjapa. He shows the back of Tjapa's naked body (which may be recognized as Obraztsov's arm). These are typical and generally accepted sorts of opalescence.

Sometimes the opposition of puppet versus human being is based on the assumption that the puppet may be aware of its existence. Philippe Genty, Henk Boerwinkel and artists of the Hungarian State Puppet Theatre developed this reflectivity. The puppet, aware of the fact that it is manipulated by somebody, starts to fight that person in order to be free. In the case of Genty's Pierrot, conscious of being a marionette, this fight leads to the tragedy of its own destruction.

We should note that this expresses the opposition of two systems of signs. It has two functions. First, it serves to stress the artificiality of the puppet theatre. Second, it is the source of the metaphor of powerlessness and control by external forces, a metaphor applied as frequently to human existence as to puppet existence.

The atomization of all elements of the puppet theatre and its semiotic consequences

The puppet theatre is a less compact totality than the human theatre. As Kowzan observed:

> In the puppet theatre the characters are visually represented by puppets, while words are spoken by invisible artists. Certain movements of one or another puppet during a conversation make an impression that it is this particular puppet who is 'speaking', they point to the object of a particular utterance, make some kind of bridge between the source of the voice and the 'speaking' puppet character. It sometime happens that this mechanism of the puppet theatre is imitated in a live theatre performance; in such a case, however, the semiological function of the procedure is quite different.[53]

The separability of the speaking object and the physical source of the word is only an occasional practice of the live theatre, while it is the distinctive feature of the puppet theatre. Taking into consideration this separability, I tried to give a definition of the puppet theatre parallel to that given by Bogatyrev:

> The puppet theatre is a theatre art, the main and basic feature differentiating it from the live theatre being the fact that the speaking and performing object makes temporal use of the physical sources of the vocal and motor powers, which are present outside the object. The relations between the object (the puppet) and the power sources change all the time and their variations are of great semiological and aesthetical significance.[54]

This definition seems to be adequate to the present state of contemporary puppet theatre, because regardless of its form – be it substitution of live theatre or development of puppet-like features – puppet theatre avails itself of changing relations between the means of expression and the motivating powers. This definition also seems to be adequate to the present state of contemporary puppet theatre regardless of the means of expression it uses. It should be mentioned here that in the last 30 years, the puppet theatre has collected on its stage many different means of expression intended to complement and assist the puppets: actors, masks, props and other objects.

Puppets, props and objects have different kinds of existences and therefore they have different theatrical qualities and different connotations. Actors are human beings fulfilling theatrical functions; objects are things made by human beings not for theatrical use; props are things made for theatrical use; puppets are objects made to be theatre characters; masks are objects made for theatrical use in order to depersonalize an actor. All these things, including the actor, are present on the contemporary puppet stage. Their different basic functions and denotations create a sort of redundancy; order is created by establishing the relationships among them.

So contemporary puppet theatre may scarcely be called puppet theatre as such. It is a heterogeneous art form with an extremely abundant system of signs. We would call it 'impersonal theatre', as George Speaight suggests.[55] Nevertheless, today even this is not true, because regularly in this theatre, among puppets, props and objects, the live actor does his acting as a visible operator of puppets or a character of the play, or even both at the same time.

The tendency to multiply the means of expression resulted in the 1960s in the destruction of some elements of the theatre; that is, the destruction of the puppet stage, of the play character and of the puppet itself. All of these elements were fragmented:

- The booth and the screen were demolished to enable the operators of puppets and objects to perform in unlimited scenic space.
- The destruction of the booth and screens changed the mode of existence of the play's characters. They were no longer visually integrated. The operators became visible, but were not solely the visible vocal and motor powers. Sometimes they added their own facial mimicry and gestures to express the feeling of the puppet characters. The situation was more complicated when the puppet was simultaneously operated by two or three puppeteers. In other words, the puppet was no longer the complete depiction of the character; it was supported by complementary means. Although in theory this practice might enrich the theatre character, in reality the development of the complementary means led to the rising passivity of the puppet. This passivity in turn became a stimulus to experiment further.
- The first experiments were to introduce different techniques of operation. The second were to change the puppet's body as the representation of the character. Instead of a full puppet, we saw its elements

as *pars pro toto* (synecdoche). The same happened to the human actor on the puppet stage. By means of staging and composition, the actor's body was shown in pieces. We saw heads, feet, legs as symbols of characters, acting among puppets and objects.

This process of analysis fractured the entire puppet theatre, including the humans. It was Shpet who said in 1967 that puppeteers behaved like little children who wanted to discover what is inside the toy. Now when the puppet theatre is divided into fragments, there is no other way to proceed than by the reconstruction of the toy; that is, the puppet theatre.[56]

It is this process that I suggest we call the atomization of the puppet theatre. Fifteen years after Shpet's pronouncement, the situation was unchanged. The toy continues to be taken to pieces. Contemporary puppeteers have at their disposal a number of different pieces that might be used to reconstruct the puppet theatre, but this happens rather rarely. As was shown by Krofta's Don Quijote production that I discussed above, 'the pieces' are not used to recreate or refashion the classic puppet theatre. They are used to create productions with disintegrated characters, in order to stress their theatrical and metaphorical functions. In each production, 'the pieces' enter into new relationships with one another. The puppet theatre has become a theatre characterized by the constant pulsation of the means of expression and their relationships.

This last sentence, true of the contemporary puppet theatre, should be related as well to the history of puppetry as a whole. The puppet theatre throughout its history has been a theatre of the constant pulsation of the means of expression and their relationships.

First published in *Semiotica* 1983, 47.

Notes

1   Jurkowski H., 'The language of the contemporary puppet theatre', *UNIMA Informations*, Warsaw 1978, 2–10; also as Chapter 4 of this volume.

2   Bogatyrev, P., Lidové divadlo české a slovenské (Czech and Slovak folk theatre), *Stezky*, 1940, 136–7.

3   Zich O., *Loutkové divadlo. Drobne umeni – vytvarne snahy* (Puppet theatre. Small art – great endeavours) 1923, 4, 7–9, 56–60, 140–43.

4   Bogatyrev, 'Lidové divadlo české a slovenské' (Czech and Slovak folk theatre), 124.

5   Bogatyrev P., 'O vzaimosvjazi dvux blizkikh semioticheskikh sistem' (The interconnection of two similar semiotic systems), *Trudy po znakovym sistemam* (Studies on the system of signs), 1973, 6: 306–29.

6   Kott J., 'The icon and the absurd', *The Drama Review* 1969, 14: 17–24; Pavis, P., *Problèmes de semiologie théâtrale*. Québec 1976; Ubersfeld, A., *Lire le théâtre*. Paris 1977.
7   Peirce C.S., *Collected Papers*. Cambridge, MA 1931–58, vol. 2: 363.
8   Elam K., *The Semiotics of Theatre and Drama*. New York 1980, 21.
9   Peirce C.S., *Semiotic and Significs: The Correspondence between Charles Sanders Peirce and Victoria Lady Welby*, ed. Charles S. Hardwick, Bloomington, IN 1977, 80–81; Bense, M., *Świat przez pryzmat znaku* (World through the lens of the sign), Warsaw 1980, 39; Pelc, J., *Wstęp do semiotyki* (Introduction to semiotics), Warsaw 1982, 67–71.
10 Elam, op cit., 57–62.
11 Bogatyrev, op. cit., 306–29.
12 Kolar E., 'The puppet theatre: A form of visual or dramatic art?' In l'Union Internationale de la Marionnette and M. Niculescu (eds.), *The Puppet Theatre of the Modern World*, Boston 1965, 330.
13 Ando T., *Bunraku. The Puppet Theatre*. New York 1970, 33.
14 Adachi B., *The Voices and Hands of Bunraku*. New York 1978, 9.
15 Ortolani B., 'Das Japanische Theater', in H. Kindermann (ed.), *Fernöstliches Theater*, Stuttgart 1966, 440–47.
16 Ando, op. cit., 91.
17 Adachi, op. cit., 33.
18 Jurkowski H., 'Perspektywy rozwoju teatru lalek' (The perspectives of development of puppet theater), *Teatr Lalek* 1966, 37–8: 1–4.
19 Purschke H.R., *Die Anfänge der Puppenspielformen und ihre vermutlichen Ursprünge* (The beginnings of puppetry forms and their probable origins), Bochum, 1979.
20 Boehn M. von, *Dolls and Puppets*, trans. J. Nicoll, Boston 1956 [1932], 256–7.
21 Plato, *The Republic*, trans. Allan Bloom, New York 1968 [c.360 BCE], 358.
22 Xenophon, *Sympozjum oraz Wybór z pism* (Symposium and a selection of writings), trans. A. Rapaport, Kraków 1929, 121.
23 Athenaeus, *Les Deipnosophistes*, Paris 1956 [c.220].
24 Schmidt C., *Herrade de Landsberg*, Strasbourg 1897.
25 Varey J.E., *Historia de los títeres en España*, Madrid 1957, 82.
26 Pawiński A., *Młode lata Zygmunta Starego* (The early years of Sigismund the Old), Warsaw 1893, 256.
27 Speaight G., *The History of the English Puppet Theatre*, London 1955, 54.
28 Purschke, op. cit., 27.
29 Varey, op. cit., 12.
30 Leibrecht P., 'Zeugnisse und Nachweise zur Geschichte des Puppenspiels in Deutschland', Inaugural dissertation, Borna-Leipzig 1919, 72.
31 Purschke, op. cit., 37.
32 Sajkowski A. 'Kłokociana: Diariusz sejmowy z r. 1666' (Klokocki's patrimony: The Diet [Parliament] diary from 1666), *Pamietnik Teatralny* (Memories of Theatre), Warsaw: Instytut Sztuki PAN. 1964, 3: 273–4.
33 Speaight G., *Punch and Judy: A History*, London 1970, 18–19.

34   Serlio S., *Il secondo libro di perspettiva di Sebastian Serlio Bolognese* (The second book of perspectives by S. Serlio of Bologna), Venice 1560, vol. II: 26.

35   Ottonelli D., *Della Christiana moderatione del teatro* (On the Christian moderation of the theatre), Florence 1652, III: 463.

36   Magnin C., *Histoire des marionnettes en Europe depuis l'antiquité jusqu'à. nos jours* (History of puppets in Europe from antiquity to the present), Paris 1852, 144.

37   Speaight, *History of the English Puppet Theatre*, 92.

38   Ottonelli, op. cit., III: 463.

39   Creizenach W., *Die Schauspiele der Englischen Komödianten* (The performance of the English comedians), Berlin and Stuttgart 1873, XV.

40   Speaight, *History of the English Puppet Theatre*, 102–8.

41   Magnin, op. cit., 167.

42   Speaight, *History of the English Puppet Theatre*, 95.

43   Martello, P.J., *The Sneeze of Hercules*, 1723

44   *Biografia Dramatika or, a Companion to the Playhouse, containing Historical and Critical Memoirs, and original Anecdotes, of British and Irish Dramatic Writers ...* to the year 1764 by David Ershin Baker, to 1782 by Isaac Reed, to 1811 by Stephen Jones. London 1812, 150.

45   Ibid.

46   Speaight, *History of the English Puppet Theatre*, 113.

47   Hauser A., *Philosophie des Kunstgeschichte* (Philosophy of art history), Munich 1958, 307.

48   Baty G., *Trois petits tours et puis s'en vont ... Les théâtres forains de marionnettes à fils et leur repertoire de 1800–1890* (The fairground theatres of string marionettes and their repertoire), Paris 1942, 20.

49   Speaight, *History of the English Puppet Theatre*, 242–60.

50   Eichler F., 'Das Wesen des Handpuppen- und Marionetten-spiels', in C. Niessen (ed.), *Emsdetten: Die Schaubühne. Quellen und Forschungen zur Theatergeschichte* (Sources of research in theatre history), 1937, 17: 22.

51   Jurkowski H., *Dzieje teatru lalek. Od romantyzmu do wielkiej reformy teatru* (History of puppet theatre. From Romanticism to the great reform of theatre), Warsaw 1976, 22–30.

52   Buschmeyer L., *Die Kunst des Puppenspiels* (The art of puppet play), Erfurt 1931; Eichler, op. cit.; Obraztsov S., *Akter s kukloj* (Actor with puppet), Moscow 1938.

53   Kowzan T., 'Znak w teatrze' (Sign in theatre), in *Wprowadzenie do nauki o teatrze* (Introduction to theatre science), selected and compiled by J. Degler, Wrocław 1976, 308.

54   Jurkowski, 'The language of the contemporary puppet theatre', 8.

55   Speaight, *History of the English Puppet Theatre*, 11.

56   Shpet, L., 'Segodnia i zawtra w teatre kukoł' (Today and tomorrow in the puppet theater), in *Chto zhe takoe teatr kukol? Sbornik statei* (What is the puppet theater? Collection of articles), Moscow 1980, 31.

6
Puppets and the Power of the State

Puppetry is considered a marginal art form. Apart from some short specific periods, it was a form of theatre held in low esteem, a theatre for the folk who crowded around churches or at the fairs, for the idle passer-by on the street, for people who could not afford to go to the real theatre and, finally, for children.

Historians of theatre have not paid much attention to puppetry, since they have always been more interested in the main current of theatre art. It was only in the nineteenth century that the first history of puppet theatre in Europe was published, by Magnin in 1852. If it is true that the 'marginal' characteristic of puppetry discourages the interest of theatre researchers, it is also true that it has evoked the interest of other scientific researchers, for example folklorists. Puppetry is a field that also holds interest for sociologists, due to the special and diversified functions of puppets in human history. This is an attempt to show one perspective of such research, discussing the situation of the puppet theatre through the centuries *vis-à-vis* the state and the law.

Popular opinion has it that the puppet theatre is as ancient as the actors' theatre, and may perhaps be even older. One thing is sure: it was not born on the steps of altars like the Greek tragic theatre; it was born on the altar itself. Ancestors of the puppets were divine sculptures and figures used in religious ceremonies even as early as ancient Egyptian times.

Moveable religious figures could be considered as puppets. As images of divine powers they were not subject to the control or censorship of the civic powers. However, as soon as the puppet became a theatre performer the situation changed: it had to respond to the legal regulations of the land.

In the period of antiquity those regulations were commonly applied to the normal theatre – tragic or comic. We can guess that the famous puppeteer Potheinos, presenting his performances in the theatre where Euripides' tragedies were given, performed under the protection of the

115

archon (chief magistrate). We may suppose that the group of mimes playing at the Kallias home in Athens was accepted as legally permitted entertainers, even if their show was based on the erotic legends of Dionysus.

The decline of antique culture and the victory of Christianity brought about the destruction of the Roman theatre, except for the presentations of the mimes. They would have played with puppets as one of their multi-form means of expression. It is worth noting that the mime theatre was tolerated in Byzantium but was very much contested in the western Empire, where the Church Fathers, and especially Augustine, condemned the mime theatre as the remains of pagan culture.

Fortunately, the wandering comedians still found their protectors among kings, princes and feudal lords who needed them as entertainers at their courts and castles. These wandering entertainers were people of different skills and therefore of differing social positions. It was the Castilian King Alfonso who issued a special bill listing the *istriones* (stage players), *ioculatores* (jugglers), acrobats, *jongleurs* and troubadours according to their social status. The lowest class among them were trainers of monkeys and dogs – and puppet players (*cazurros*).

Some puppet players were protected by Church and cloister provided that they presented stories of the saints or of Christian chivalry, as evidenced in Germany. In Slavonic countries there were also groups of wandering players. They were musicians, dancers and puppeteers, but in time, as their profession grew increasingly hard to carry out, they became robbers and were called *skomorocky*, from the Greek *scomarcha*. In Bulgaria they were appreciated as much as the mimes were in old Byzantium; in Russia they served princes or were persecuted by the Church and civic authorities; in Poland they were the loyal subjects of kings and paid regular taxes.

In the late Middle Ages when the practice of liturgical drama and the Mystery Plays was established, the puppeteers followed the trend and tried to present these holy subjects with puppets. First they gave their shows in churchyards and later in the streets of the towns and even in theatres. They were still the wandering players, bringing their puppets in a box on their back, the box being the puppet stage. Their puppets were operated with the help of mechanical devices, and the puppeteer stood in front of the cabinet or booth to tell the story illustrated by the puppets. Very soon the civic authorities even managed to gain control over these performers, and puppeteers were obliged to apply for permission from the town hall to present their shows. Permission was frequently accompanied by many limitations and the enumeration of special conditions: the show could not be given on a Sunday during church service; the show could not be given after the setting of the sun; the show could not provoke noise or tumult. If the terms were not observed, permission was withdrawn and never given again.

In Spain, additional control of puppet productions was effected by the Inquisition, which was very sensitive to all disturbance to religious life caused by different kinds of performers.

However, the urban and church authorities were helpless in the face of permission or a permanent 'licence' granted by officials of the king (in England the Master of the Revels). They could hardly send a petition to Court to complain about the nuisance caused by these 'theatricals'. In seventeenth-century Norwich, however, some manu-facturing employers did just that, complaining to the king that their workers, attracted by a puppet performance, were abandoning their work.

There was one place where actors and puppeteers could perform without special permission, and that was in the fairgrounds. From the sixteenth to the eighteenth centuries fairs were privileged in being allowed to use different means of theatre to advertise different kinds of merchandise and services. Puppets appeared to be most useful for this purpose. They served to advertise pullers of teeth, the selling of optic instruments, drugs and other items. Very often the demonstration by the puppets was more profitable than the tooth pulling, thus many charlatans changed their profession and became puppeteers. It is worthy of note that the most famous puppeteers of Europe from the seventeenth to the beginning of the nineteenth century practised tooth pulling as their main profession. Such was the professional background of Jean Brioché, who brought to France the figure of Polichinelle; such it was of Johann Anton Stranitzky, the Austrian who popularized the German Hanswurst; and also of Laurent Mourguet, who created the famous figure of Guignol.

Privileges of the fairgrounds were an important help for all those theatre managers unable to perform in the town, due to the monopoly created by established theatres in many countries. In France this monopoly of the Paris Opera and the Comédie Française in the second half of the eighteenth century provoked the development of fairground theatre companies where puppet shows were involved. The monopo-lists, however, were very vigilant and selfishly did not even permit the puppet to speak with a clear voice, obliging the puppeteers to use an instrument called a swazzle which distorted their speech.

The theatre monopoly in England and especially the Licensing Act of 1737 caused much annoyance for all theatre managers. Nevertheless, the puppeteers tried to find an escape from its regulations, as when Madame de la Nash opened her 'Breakfast Room', pretending that the puppet show therein was only an accompaniment to the tea and refreshments.

At that time – the mid-eighteenth century – there were more and more efforts to found permanent theatres, and to win the coveted licence. The only way to obtain one was to seek the protection of a member of the upper classes who could exert his influence on the Master of the Revels. In Italy it was enough to win the protection of a cardinal or a prince, who could automatically bestow the right to perform. In Spain the common practice was to cooperate with a theatre monopoly association, such as the Cofradia de Novena, which extended permission to perform on condition that part of the income came back to its own coffers.

As we have already mentioned, puppeteers had easy access to royalty in their palaces and castles over the centuries. Foreign puppeteers always tried to present their show at Court to ensure a good reception throughout the rest of that country. If successful at Court, they were sure to find acclaim in countries such as England, France, Poland and Austria. From the seventeenth century there also existed a tradition of permanent Court puppet theatres, although it is true that these were not for kings so much as for princes. Among many, two were famous in the eighteenth century: the puppet theatre of the Esterházy family in Eisenstadt and that of Prince Radziwill in Biala in Poland. Both engaged true masters of their craft, invited from Italy, France and Austria.

The majority of puppeteers, however, were travellers, strongly resistant to control by police or any other authority. They did not care about licences. They travelled with their booths on their shoulders, giving short shows, collecting money from passers-by and using every means to avoid contact with the police. In Poland in 1793, the puppeteer occasionally known as 'Sheepskin' performed in front of the palace belonging to the head of the Russian army of occupation. The action included figures of collaborators with the Russians, traitors to Poland, being beheaded on the guillotine. Not surprisingly, the puppeteer was immediately arrested. In Italy at the beginning of the nineteenth century many wandering puppeteers – like the famous Ghetanaccio – mocked in their shows the Austrian invaders and the authority of the Pope. Arrested and then released from prison, they still continued their audacious protests.

This was one of the reasons for the low opinion of puppeteers held by the authorities. Another was their anarchic lifestyle, their 'immorality'. For instance, pairs of young puppeteers would live together without legal marriage, and their children escaped from school, preferring to go travelling with the company rather than attend classes.

The first state powers that tried to limit the activities of these puppeteers were those of Austria and Bavaria at the end of the eighteenth century. Their licences were withdrawn and their shows prohibited. This decision resulted in much poverty and distress for a large number of puppeteers and their families. The puppeteers were not able to do any other work, their families were starving, and so they looked for help to the local county authorities, appealing to them to free them from their new and heavy burden and to abolish the new laws.

In Bohemia the number of puppeteers increased after the Napoleonic Wars. The Austrian authorities wished to stop this rise, but were finally obliged to surrender. Some of the new players were former soldiers from the Austrian army, among them some who had been invalided out, some who had no profession, but for all of them it was very difficult to obtain a licence. Any widow of a puppeteer who had inherited her husband's licence found herself in a privileged position. Whatever her age, she found many men ready to propose to her, though to tell the truth they were really proposing to her licence!

Behind the social and economic problems of Bohemia there was an important political background. The Bohemian puppeteers performed only in Czech, in support of the renaissance of Czech nationalism. To fight against the puppeteers meant that the Austrian occupiers also found themselves fighting against the new national movement. Fortunately for the Czechs, they were not successful in their efforts.

In the eighteenth century the theatre licence was always granted to the theatre manager, in any country. However, he was obliged to state his repertory, and sometimes to give a short synopsis of each play. After he had been granted a licence he could perform without trouble, although there were a few cases when the state authorities intervened, as on the occasion when they stopped Titus Maas from presenting a show about the Russian Prince Menshikoff because it had 'a comical hunting scene in Siberia'. The German authorities were afraid of the intervention of the Russian ambassador.

The situation changed significantly at the beginning of the nineteenth century. It started in Prussia, where the Prussian king issued an edict of censorship that obliged puppeteers to present the script of their play to the police before its presentation in the theatre. This was a real

Figure 6.1   19th Century Punch figure, from the collection of John M. Blundall

shock for the puppeteers, most of whom were illiterate, performing their shows from memory. However, they had to obey the new law, otherwise they could not continue to perform.

The same happened in France after the coup d'état of Napoleon III. Censorship was imposed, and all puppeteers were obliged to stop improvising their shows and to present scripts to be censored, and later to play them without changing a word. It was hard for the puppet players, but paradoxically it is to these severe regulations that we owe the existence today of the scripts used by the wandering showmen of those times.

In spite of the regulations, there were always companies beyond the reach of the censors, especially where shows were not presented to a large audience. The most famous puppeteer of the Second Empire was Lemercier de Neuville, who was a 'parlour performer'. Though he presented political shows, he was never censored nor persecuted. Giving invited performances for small numbers, he was not considered a danger to the régime. In Poland, however, the *szopka* theatre that presented the patriotic Nativity play, though it was a family theatre, was not left undisturbed by the occupying powers. A similar patriotic play performed in one of the permanent theatres of Warsaw in 1912 provoked the intervention of the Russian censor and the theatre lost its licence.

The authorities were no more tolerant, even when the puppeteers wanted to establish a special permanent theatre for children. It is true that in the nineteenth century this was still something quite new, and when J.L. Schmid sent a petition to the Munich municipality, permission was refused. Fortunately, he found a patron and protector in the person of Count Franz Pocci who was close to the Bavarian Court, and the Schmid theatre for children opened in 1858.

Interest in the educational use of puppet theatre brought in a new partnership with the educationists. Now the puppet theatre could be developed under the patronage of educational associations, which increased greatly in number at the beginning of the twentieth century. At first the movement was an amateur one, but step by step it changed into a dynamic professional activity.

At the same time many other associations became interested in puppetry. The Bohemian Sokol promoted the art as an important factor in social life. In Poland the Association of Folk Theatre did the same. In Western Europe the first puppeteers' organizations were founded, some with their own performing companies. In such circumstances widespread social patronage was extended, much influencing the social position of the puppet theatre and helping in its relationship with state authorities.

In some cases the idea of raising puppetry to the level of a national organization was misused, as in the Fascist state of the Third Reich. It is worth noting that other totalitarian states like Spain and Italy paid little attention to puppets, though Mussolini's propaganda boasted in its own way of the successes of the Teatro dei Piccoli of Rome.

In Germany the situation under Hitler was different: a special organization was founded, Kraft durch Freude, which took control of the German puppet theatre. Kraft durch Freude (Strength through joy) monopolized the administration of puppet shows and no company could present a performance unless it consented to cooperate with the organization. Of course it was a Fascist organization; nevertheless, many puppeteers managed to keep faith with their own concept of the puppet art, and did not serve the propaganda machine. More engaged with the Fascists was the amateur puppet movement and the Puppetry Institute founded in Berlin.

In Russia the postrevolutionary establishment formed a new kind of puppet theatre patronage – that of the Communist state. According to the Leninist concept, puppetry should be 'an art of the Party' to serve the revolution. Puppet theatre, due to its folk origins, was considered a very appropriate instrument of propaganda. During and after the revolution itinerant puppet groups still existed – with the help of state and social bodies – working to compromise the enemies of the revolution and to propagate its ideas. This kind of theatre was very active, but only for a short time. The complete Soviet patronage of the art was accomplished much later. The programme of the Soviet state was to make all theatre state theatre: that meant founding a 'universal' system that would realize the policies of the government. This system was intended to include the puppet theatre, but the first attempts to take it over were not satisfactory.

Those theatres first supported by the state, in Moscow and Leningrad, were not considered revolutionary enough. So at the beginning of the 1930s, the famous Central State Puppet Theatre, headed by Sergei Obraztsov, was founded in Moscow. It brought together the most experienced artists with the task of elaborating the new (revolutionary) repertory through modern means of expression, which they were to share with all other state puppet theatres. Obraztsov's theatre soon became the model for the others, with many of them repeating his experiments and his repertory. However, in the 1960s, due to increasing contacts with world puppetry, the Soviet puppet theatre began to find more diversified and original artistic tendencies, especially in those theatre centres where there was already a strong national tradition, for example the Baltic republics.

The Soviet state system indeed became a model for puppet theatre in all the so-called People's Republics after the Second World War ended in 1945. However, a Central Puppet Theatre was founded in only two other countries, Czechoslovakia and Bulgaria, and these never became as influential in their countries as did Obraztsov's in the Soviet Union. Naturally numerous state puppet theatres were founded, and in some countries the new system completely replaced the old one, as in Poland.

In Poland in the 1930s, the Workers' Association of the Friends of Children was already developing cultural activities, including the promotion of puppetry. After the war the association founded several puppet and youth theatres, which can be seen as belonging to the category of 'social patronage'. The political changes in 1948 established a new cultural policy and after that priority was given to state patronage. After some changes of name and programme, the Association was dissolved in 1952.

The puppet theatre in Communist-ruled countries is an integral part of the state monetary planning system, so that finance and different kinds of supplies are assured in advance for each theatre. The theatre is able to plan the number of performances it will give, and virtually the number of spectators. It also plans its repertory according to the cultural policy of the state. The puppet theatre is not merely an artistic institution; it is also a social unit in the system of employment. It means a definite number of 'working posts', which of course varies from theatre to theatre, but is in fact a very large number if taken all together. The Central (today the Academic) State Puppet Theatre in Moscow employs over 300 people; the Budapest State Puppet Theatre over 200. The average Polish puppet theatre has 60 to 80 employees. Considering that in Poland there are 26 state puppet theatres, the number of more than 1500 'working posts' is considerable. In the Soviet Union, where there are more than 200 theatres, this number would be even more significant. In the DDR (East Germany) a slightly different system exists. In addition to the state theatres there are a number of freelance puppeteers working alone or in small groups.

In Western European countries almost all puppeteers may be called freelance artists. In recent years, however, it is to be noted that increasing support is being given by state and social organizations. The biggest financial involvement is offered by municipal and other local authorities. Some funds are given by social organizations wishing to preserve national or local traditions, as in Belgium and Sicily. Support is sometimes obtained from educational institutions on condition that the performance accords fully with the national programme of education. In some countries the state delivers money to some social bodies serving the development of the puppet theatre, such as the Centre National de la Marionnette in Paris or the Puppet Centre Trust in London.

Most puppeteers feel that this patronage is not yet enough. Nevertheless, it is possible to consider that the puppet theatre today has gained a higher social position than it had at the beginning of the twentieth century and is now acknowledged as a part of theatre art. The current system of state and social patronage provides the proof.

First published in *Animations* 1984, 10(1).

7
Eroticism and Puppetry

Eroticism pervades all human culture. The statement is obvious: love and sex have always been essential elements of life. Eroticism marks human manners in many respects. It influences art: painting and sculpture, literature and theatre. Who does not know about Romeo and Juliet? Who has not heard of Boccaccio or the Marquis de Sade? Between them the main span of erotic presentation is approached, from the innocent sexuality of young lovers to lust without feeling, often perverse and unnatural.

The threads of love are woven into theatre as much as literature. They are as common and their presence as generally accepted as that of other social or political subjects. Normally they evoke no physical sensation; however, when they slide towards undisguised sex, when the physical act is extolled over the feelings, when the image of this act is designed to excite the spectators or, at its extreme, when eroticism is exposed without veils, then the audience is drawn towards the spectacle in a manner which has little to do with artistry. In all such cases the notion of erotic literature and erotic theatre is introduced. The term is reserved for those phenomena beyond the borders of love which transgress society's adopted moral codes. This essay will deal with such phenomena.

The choice of the subject – eroticism and puppetry – arose from scientific curiosity. The history of puppets has often dealt with erotic representations. They vary in character, proving that erotic puppetry has fulfilled different functions. This fact in itself is worthy of interest.

Today the general feeling about the puppet is that, being an artificial figure, a simulacrum, it does not imitate life but represents it. The same is valid for erotic puppets, which bring to all erotic images, even the most audacious, a sort of alienation effect. Perceived as the 'artificial lover', the puppet contests the truth of the sexual act, emphasizing its 'representative' aspect, which sometimes becomes a parody with little to do with corporal experience. In the puppet theatre eroticism has another dimension, compared with actors' theatre. This too will be a matter of interest in this study.

In order to review erotic phenomena in the theatre, we have to go back to the culture of primitive societies, not of course to discover theatre but its antecedents; that is, rituals containing para-theatrical elements. Some rituals incorporate erotic motifs; they are mainly linked with the cults of procreation and fecundity. Much evidence exists which tells of the erotic participation in many of these rituals of men and puppets. James George Fraser tells that Papils from Central America ordered a young, specially selected couple to execute, in the open, a coition to coincide exactly with the moment when the first seeds were to be planted in the soil. It was an act of magic based on the principle of analogy: the sexual act was intended to provoke the fertility of the soil. Thus the spectators were witnesses to a 'sacred marriage'.[1] A similar act, this time using puppets, was to be found at the rituals of the Yoruba tribes (Dahomey and Nigeria in Africa) dedicated to the cult of Sapata, the deity of fertility. The previous, real coition of a man and a woman – or even in some cases of a man with the soil – was here replaced by the artificial coition of two primitive puppets.[2]

Sex fulfilled an important function in boys' initiation into maturity, a ritual of the Marind-anim tribe of New Guinea, as described by Joseph Campbell, who ended with the words:

> In front of their bodies the dancers hold large phalluses made of bast [bark] and testicles made of the red cones of a certain tree. First they dance in a line, one behind the other, in quick time, their bodies bent forward, stamping their right feet on the ground and singing ... suddenly they spring forward with vigorous coital movements and loud groans, and finally halt in an irregular group. They stroke the phalluses gently with their right hands, tap them with their fingers, making loud clicking sounds, and blow upon them, making wafting movements with their hands as scattering something in the air. They carry the spurting semen everywhere, to every corner of the house, to the edge of the forest and to the adjoining cultivated area, and leap in among the women and girls, who scatter, screaming and laughing ... Nevertheless this is a serious, and, as it represents a natural process, a perfectly decent dance in the eyes of people in a state of nature.[3]

Sometimes the eroticism of primitive peoples exploded into orgy, which had little to do with the cult of fertility. Orgies were an attempt at the deprecation of cosmic or social crisis like drought and epidemic, or a reaction to strange meteorological apparitions. Sometimes they were staged in the hope of bringing benediction on a marriage or to the newborn child of a ruling family, as suggested by Mircea Eliade. However, according to Irving Goldman there were some other aspects:

> Erotic ritual is commonly presented as fertility rites, but this cliché of 19th-century anthropology should not obscure for us the significance of erotic excitement as a value in itself.[4]

This would explain why this ritual was enacted so frequently. Orgies in primitive societies excluded puppets for obvious reasons. They were real and no replacement was needed.

Returning to the cult of fecundity, we should mention different kinds of figures (some of them animated) spread throughout Asia, Europe and Africa. In Japan, statues in the form of a phallus were very popular, as were female Dogu figures with enlarged sexual organs. It is certain that these had sacred functions. They were not animated, but this says only that they represented the earliest stage in the development of erotic puppets. European antiquity has left much evidence of the use of human or divine figures with the mobile phallus. These figures were often carried on a large platform in ritual processions, and the custom has been preserved up to our own time. In Spain and Portugal it can still be regularly seen. In Mohacs, Hungary, at the folk festival known as Buscho, women carried the puppet of Jancsi in procession only 30 years ago. Jancsi was a male figure whose penis was moved by the pulling of a string.

In Africa, especially Zaire, this kind of erotic puppet was even more developed. Here one could witness the sexual junction of a puppet man and woman. The manipulator, seated on the ground, used for this purpose the technique known as *marionnette á la planchette*; that is, puppets hung on the string stretched between the feet of the puppeteer. The movement of his toes on a small plank sets the puppets in motion, and they approach each other until, having large sexual organs, they are able to join up as though copulating. No doubt they belonged to some ritual of procreation. Today there are places where these puppets can be bought and are given as toys to children. When performed by children their actions provoke much laughter, from adults as much as children. This is a good example of the change in the function of the puppets. Dispossessed of their sacred function, the puppets become comic toys, even while imitating the sexual act.

Figure 7.1   Killekyatha, comic figure in Karnataka, courtesy of Mel Helstien

Sex and coition had yet another function in the religions of the Far East, as in Hinduism and Shinto. It resulted from the conviction that sex helps communication with supernatural forces. The desire to join with deity or demon was often accomplished in the temples with the help of priest-prostitutes. Traces of such beliefs are still to be met in Europe in the rites of the 'witches' sabbath', so much deplored by Christianity. We possess some evidence of the use of such puppets in eleventh-century Japan, in the performance of *kugutsu mawashi*. As reported by Donald Keene, a show like this took place in a Shinto temple. An old man had a voluptuous dialogue with a young girl before copulating with her. However, sex was apparently an intimate affair even then, because the 'spectators tried to separate the puppets, slapping their faces, although they also liked such games'.[5]

Sexual themes fulfilled strange magic functions in the Indian puppet theatre. These have nothing in common with the ritual of fecundity, nor with the desire to achieve union with the deity. In this case they served to ward off the evil eye from the puppeteer. Mel Helstien mentions it when describing the comic figures of Killekyatha and Bangarakka from the theatre of small leather shadows of Karnataka state:

> Bruce Tapper tells us that one of the most important functions [the South Indian] jesters reserve for the shadow players is the deflection of the evil eye ... they [the shadow figures] not infrequently [have] exaggerated genitals. This enhances [their] ability to attract attention and thereby to lure away injurious glances from elsewhere ... Bangarakka [the female comic] serves to protect the shadow players by absorbing the injurious glances of the audience ... and thus harm-lessly fulfilling the misfortune caused by the evil eye.[6]

Proceeding from magic to rational thought, we have to refer once again to European antiquity. It is widely known that the Greek comedy actors carried on their abdomen an artificial phallus, a visible symbol of the phallic cult which in turn emphasized the links with the mythological Satyr figures. Aristophanes, in his *Lysistrata*, used the visual motif of the phallus in a state of erection; this arose from the story and in prin-ciple did not offer any erotic provocation. On the contrary, it mocked sexuality.

A different approach to eroticism was to be found in the perform-ances of mime groups where erotic scenes were often presented in a naturalistic way. Xenophon mentioned it in his 'Symposium', at the Feast of Kalias to be precise, describing the event as follows:

> So all watched with solemn emotion, observing that Dionis was truly beautiful and Ariadne charming in her youthfulness, and that their kissing was no joke, but in truth lips fastened on lips ... It did not appear that anyone had taught them their roles but as if they had at last been permitted to do what they had been wanting to do for a long time. Finally the banqueters saw them withdraw to bed entan-gled in embraces. Then did the bachelors promise to marry, and the already-married mounted on horseback to return to their wives as soon as possible.[7]

This group of mimes also possessed puppets. Socrates, who was also present, asked the manager of the troupe whom he most appreciated among his company. The manager stated, 'My puppets, which help to earn my living.' He said nothing about the puppets' repertory, but we may reasonably guess that they too appeared in erotic scenes, although it is hard to tell whether the puppet shows were serious or parodies.

The first complete 'eroticization' of theatre was accomplished in the period of the Roman Empire. It took place on two levels: the subjects of the performances were as lewd as the behaviour of the actresses, who were frequently treated as prostitutes. All this followed changes in Roman social customs, when the public of every social class demanded more and more erotic scenes in theatre performances:

> Naked naiads swam in the artificial lakes of pantomime perform-
> ances, unclothed nymphs bustled about in the forests, and during
> the farces the garments of actresses were left in the brute clutches of
> some clumsy man. In the guise of mythological events scenes of
> copulation and seduction were presented. They were as piquant as
> the pantomime farces were vulgar. The theatre knew no other
> subject, and its actors were able to give their audiences the pleasure
> of sensual delight through refined depravity or heavy sensuality.[8]

Even if this picture is a little exaggerated, it is hardly surprising that Christianity rose up against the theatre, regarding it as an instrument of wickedness, leading to the destruction of the human soul. Europe waited several centuries after this for the foundation of a new Christianized theatre. From antiquity only mime survived to the new era.

In Western Europe, the mimes mixed with troubadours and *jongleurs* to entertain feudal lords during their feasts. In the East, the mimes survived in Byzantium until its fall. They also spread to other lands: in Slavonic countries they were known as *skomorokhi*. Their presence was recorded in Bulgaria, the Ukraine, Poland and Russia. They were musicians, acrobats, actors and puppet-players. We may guess that, according to the mime tradition, their 'art' reflected life with some degree of realism.

A description of a *skomorokhi* erotic performance has been left to us by Adam Olearius. He travelled to Persia in 1634 as a member of the Holstein envoys, visiting Moscow on the way. He carefully observed the habits and behaviour of the peoples through whose countries he passed and he wrote a report of the journey. On the Russians and their entertainments he wrote:

They are so devoted to carnal games and debauchery that some of them disgrace themselves with the ignominious transgression called sodomy in our country; they exploit not only pueros muliebria assuentos (as Curtius says) but men and horses. The occasion subsequently supplies them as a subject of conversation at their feasts. People accused of such a crime are not seriously punished. Similar ignominies are sung of by the inn musicians in the crowded streets or shown with the use of puppets to the youth and children for money. Their acrobats and bear tamers also have with them such players who – among others – produce shows with the use of puppets (Dutchmen call them Klucht). These comedians tie around their body a cover which they pull up around themselves, making in this way a portable stage with which they can run around the streets and at the same time perform the puppet games.[9]

Although the *skomorokhi* were described in the seventeenth century, they were representative of a sort of wandering player typical of the Middle Ages. This form of theatre survived longest in eastern Europe.

In the west of Europe during the Middle Ages, puppet productions were differentiated in their functions, but there was little in the way of erotic puppetry. However, such might be considered the puppets referred to by Thomas Murner in his poetic work *Narrenbeschworung* (Exorcism of the fool), written in 1512, in which he describes a puppet show. One scene presents a prioress wishing to seduce a monk, but for this sinful desire she is punished, so in fact this satirical image of the cloistered life was intended as an opposition to licentiousness.

The development of Renaissance literature, including the plays of Rojas (*Celestine*), Machiavelli (*Mandragora*) and Aretino (*The Court Dandy*), did not directly influence the development of erotic theatre in spite of their subject matter. Because of its parodic function, puppet theatre of the time seemed in this respect to be well in advance of the actors' theatre. Puppets mocked the solemnity of the Renaissance repertory and its admiration for themes of antiquity, wherein erotic persiflage was frequently used. This is illustrated by the puppet play *The Ancient Modern History of Hero and Leander or the Story of the Sincere Love and within the Sincere and Honest Test of Friendship of Damon and Pythias, the two faithful friends from the seashore,* inserted into Ben Jonson's *Bartholomew Fair* of 1614.

Jonson here vulgarized two particularly noble themes, that of Hero and Leander and of Damon and Pythias. The subtle and delicate sentiments of the characters were reduced to the level of life in a brothel. He strengthened the friendship of Damon and Pythias by making them buy favours from the same whore, Hero. However she betrays them both in favour of her new lover, Leander:

> This while young Leander with fair Hero is drinking
> And Hero grown drunk to any man's thinking
> Yet was it not three pints of sherry could flaw her,
> Till Cupid, distinguished like Jonas the drawer,
> From under his apron, where his lechery lurks,
> Put love in her sack. Now mark how it works.[10]

These are the words of the puppeteer Lanthorne Leatherhead, so it can be assumed that the onstage action was to be played realistically.

Some years later, the parody and burlesque of the puppet stage became popular in the theatre of actors, when eroticism became an entertainment, the entertainment consisting of the provocation of sexual excitement. This is easily discerned in England and France at the end of the seventeenth and the beginning of the eighteenth centuries. In England it was a period of triumph in the restoration of the monarchy. Theatre was the main source of court entertainment but was deprived of any superior aims: enjoyment and sensual pleasure were its chief purposes. Historian Leo Schridowitz wrote:

> To what extent it was deprived of moral restraint and to what extent it allowed itself to become a theatre of debauchery in the King's circle is proved by a quotation from Prosper Marchand's 'Dictionnaire Historique' namely that Lord Rochester's 'Sodome', a work that has a special position in pornographic-erotic literature, was produced before the Royal court and before an audience among which ladies were present. This performance was, strictly speaking, an orgy, staged by the highest command, in the frame of dramatic action. It would not be so remarkable were it not for the fact that it was an example of the offerings of many private theatres of the time to their sponsors and guests, that is, a luxurious brothel. The whole of the theatre of this epoch only differed from this performance by nuances. And if there was no display of actual physical coition, the theatre action was so full of allusion that even the decent scenes provoked genuine carnal delight, accomplished with the participation of the actresses. In 'Sodome', however, after the introductory scene in which Bolloxymion, the king of Sodom, proclaims the complete abolition of any restriction in sexual relations, the ensuing four acts served to

illustrate all possible conjunctions of human bodies that fantasy could invent. At the end of the fifth act, when the sinful city became destroyed by fire and sulphur, the rather pompous allegory in the style of the later opera's final scene was given as the author's moral.[11]

The situation of the French theatre at the Regency period was no different. Acts of love-making were presented onstage and the actresses had to satisfy the caprices of the aristocratic libertines after the performance. Pierre Boudin mentioned two plays as examples of licentiousness:

> In 'Juno and Ganymede' the unprecedented scene was presented in which the cup-bearer of the gods, after a passionate kiss, divests Juno of her tunic, covers her body with ardent kisses and in the throes of ecstasy removes the last veils. Later Juno, successfully liberated from emotion, notices that she is stark naked; she rises and escapes to her boudoir, not however forgetting to leave the door open.
>
> 'Heloise and Abelard' opens with the scene in which the Master undertakes a surprising study of the breasts of his female student and after places blazing kisses on those corporal hemispheres. All finishes with the Master's desire to experience flagellant pleasure on his own hemispheres.[12]

It is necessary to state that puppet theatre, performing as it did for another kind of public (the poorer and the middle classes), avoided similar dissoluteness. It did not stay away from erotic subject matter, but treated it in another way. The licentious scenes presented in the inn in the puppet version of the *Prodigal Son* were hardly an exposé, and the whorehouse scenes in Fielding's *The Covent Garden Tragedy*, although piquant, refrained – in the writing and the playing – from presenting a picture of carnal relations or even of nudity. Fielding even inserted a moral in which he preceded the French by about 100 years in defending the dignity of a prostitute. He compared her situation with that of a marriageable young lady:

> Kissinda: To be mistress kept, the Strumpet strives
> And all the modest Virgins to be Wives.
> For Prudes may cant of Virtues and Vices
> But faith! we differ only in our Prices.[13]

Less moral and rather more in the spirit of the court entertainments was the comedy *La Cendre Chaude* (The hot cinder) by Carolet, produced in

Paris in 1718 and including the wild fantasies of the protagonist brought back from the dead.

In the same category belongs the production of the *Temptation of St. Anthony* produced in Warsaw in the second half of the eighteenth century, probably by a painter, Alexander Orlowski. The show was visited by the Polish king Stanislaw Poniatowski:

> The King heard by chance that a young man from the school of Norblin had made an optical theatre at his home in which small people presented the temptation of St. Anthony in the desert. The show was reported to be well executed in the storyline, the colour and the movement of the little people in this licentious subject, imitating the 'Metamorphosis' of Ovid. The King wished to see it and so at night in order not to be recognised he walked with some courtiers to this house in the Market of the old town, some distance from the castle, and there climbed to the second floor to satisfy his curiosity.[14]

More evidence of this kind exists. As a rule, puppet theatre as folk art was a moral art. The sultry and over-refined emotions of the court circle were absolutely alien to it. If an erotic subject was produced for the commoners, it was treated in the most natural way or the public openly derided it.

In the nineteenth century there were erotic themes in many folk performances, especially in the plays featuring Petrushka and Karagöz. Petrushka is one of the rare examples of a perennial character of the puppet stage who is unmarried, unlike Guignol who has his 'Madeleine, Punch who has Judy or Kasperle who has Greta. Petrushka is a bachelor, although he dearly wants to marry his Verushka. First he examines her body like a mare before buying. He counts her teeth and feels her all over – it could be regarded as one way of wooing – and finally he decides he will marry her. Playing before a suitable audience, for example the soldiery, Petrushka would 'consummate' his passion without concealing any detail of the action.

In contrast to this comic naturalism of Petrushka was the grotesque eroticism of Karagöz, the principal character of the Turkish shadow theatre. In some productions he came equipped with a mobile protruding phallus, which was to be the symbol of his virility but often the source of all his troubles and sometimes the central subject of the play.

Gerald de Nerval inserted in his book *Journey to the East* the description of a Karagöz show in which Karagöz falls victim to both his shyness and his phallus.[15] His Neighbour asks him to take care of his wife, because he has to set out on a journey. Karagöz is in trouble: on the one hand he cannot reject the request of his friend; on the other hand he is convinced of his own obvious and virile charms. He is afraid that the Neighbour's wife will fall in love with him. So he decides to attend on her from a distance, and the first thing is to hide his protuberance. He pretends that he is a bridge, bending forwards to make an arch of his back. People, dogs, even a patrol of soldiers pass over him without trouble, but he collapses when a cart – *arba* – appears, especially as it is heavily loaded. In another scene he lies on his back, pretending that his phallus is a big post. Passers-by are surprised and wonder where the post has come from. Women make use of it for fastening their clotheslines, riders to tie up their horses. A sudden nervousness among the horses forces Karagöz to uncover his disguise, and he escapes, shouting for help.

Entertaining play on the subject of the phallus was characteristic for folk puppetry in many countries. It is still to be found in the Brazilian Mamulengo theatre, in which the main character regards his phallus as a club, sometimes even throwing it at the audience for everyone's enjoyment.

The function of erotic puppets differed in the hands of French artists. It would seem that they were first used for the amusement of a smart and exclusive group of people; in reality, however, their purpose was to express opposition to the hypocrisy of middle-class morality. The Erotikon Teatron was founded in Paris in 1862 through the initiative of young artists – writers, poets, designers, caricaturists – who were friends of the writer Amédée Rolland. Rolland allowed his lodgings to be used for the construction of a small stage on his large verandah, with the spectators seated in the adjacent living room. The audiences were excellently amused by the artists, who used texts written either by themselves or other poets. The enterprise lasted a year, until Rolland moved to another apartment.

Five erotic plays survive from the repertory of Erotikon.[16] Their action mainly takes place in whorehouses, a realistic introduction to the 'brothel sub-culture'. The revelations of this shameful area of life were certainly directed against bourgeois hypocrisy, although of course much pleasure was extracted from the shows' producers, authors and audiences. It was an amusement for an artistic Bohemia, where no taboos existed.

The opening performance was *Signe d'Argent* (Sign of money) by Jean du Boys. It was about the problems of a Marquis in his attempts to perpetuate the family line. Finally it was the butler, Germain, who provided the offspring for the Marquis and his lady, demonstrating – onstage – that the Marquise liked 'it' in the butler's special way.

Louis Lemercier de Neuville, journalist and puppeteer, wrote two plays: *Les Jeux de l'Amour et du Bazar* (Games of love and the marketplace) and *Un Caprice* (A caprice). The first presented the adventure of Sylvia, procuress and proprietor of a brothel, who decides to try out her own seductive charms. On the street she meets Durant and takes him to her brothel to fulfil his every wish. However, she is not paid: Durant turns out to be a procurer himself and discovers that they are both of the same profession. In future they decide to work together.

Caprice was a play with a moral for errant husbands. Before leaving home to visit his mistress, Urinette, Florestan makes love to his wife, a deed to which he confesses on arrival at Urinette's. The remainder of the action consists of the efforts to revive Florestan's virility – in vain. Therein lies the moral of the play.

Scapin Maquereau (Scapin the procurer) by Albert Glatigny discusses the problems of hygiene. A young and slovenly girl from a middle-class family learns about hygienic customs within a brothel and, more importantly, manages not to lose her virginity there. This is an obvious satire on bourgeois habits.

The play *La Grisette et l'Etudiant* (The shopgirl and the student) by Henri Monnier was about eroticism of a non-brothel provenance. The famous character Monsieur Prudhomme takes part in the action, although he is not involved in the love affair. In fact the lovers – and the audience – only hear his voice, which provides a sort of alienation effect, also heightening the drama and the comedy. The *grisette* visits the student and immediately arouses him, but when he is ready to take the initiative she refuses to cooperate, lengthening the game of love and dictating her conditions for surrender. Eventually they get to bed and she dominates the rhythm of the action. When she finally, in a moment of ecstasy, shouts to the student 'Ah yes! ... kill me! ... ah! kill me! ... ah! kill me!' the voice of M. Prudhomme sounds from above: 'No assassinations in this house if you please! ... You ... over there!, have you now finished your acts of moral depravity?' It appears that it is Prudhomme who is actually in charge of the situation. When the student chooses a form of caress that the girl dislikes and protests against, Prudhomme switches on once more, saying: 'Hippolyte, take your hand off it!'

Further on, the action develops according to a typical scenario: the student, having satisfied his desires, tries to get rid of the girl, even offering her money. This causes the girl to protest and to weep, thus demonstrating her respectability. The student proves to be a sensitive young man and the play ends with a sentimental scene in which the lovers re-discover their tender feelings for each other.

It is worth noting here that Erotikon Teatron expressed the current tendency towards realism in both French literature and theatre, of which *La Grisette et l'Etudiant* is an important example. The same subject interested Henri Monnier for some time, and Daniel Gerould wrote of it:

> 'Les Grisettes' is the title of a series of lithographs produced by Monnier in the period 1827–1829, and in the first edition of 'Scènes Populaires' of 1830 there is a short dialogue between the artist Charles and his mistress, the shop girl Fanny, which tells exactly the same story as 'The Grisette and the Student' even to the inclusion of many of the same lines, but without the sexual episodes or the inter-ruptions of M. Prudhomme. Freed from all constraints of propriety and censorship, Monnier was able for the first time to develop with total honesty a sketch which he had begun some 30 years earlier, now showing it as it actually would have occurred and in the language the characters would really have used.[17]

At the beginning of the twentieth century nakedness onstage was frequent and popular, although the nudity was limited to dance, cabaret and revue. In the later part of the century nudity entered into other forms of the performing arts, for example *Paradise Now* in the live theatre. It was firmly planted in the commercial theatre (*Oh Calcutta*) and it served a new metaphorical function in modern poetic drama (*Operette* by W. Gombrowicz).

Puppet theatre also presented erotic subjects, no longer as an amuse-ment for a small group of artists but as a regular performance for a wide public. The world of sexual chimera was a frequent subject for the play-writing of the German modernists. It drew protests and demands for censorship, as well as the exasperation of the bourgeois critics. The most extreme dramas of Schnitzler and Wedekind were little performed and often withdrawn after the first performance. Some artists thought to produce them with puppets, since the materiality of the puppet dimin-ished the violence of the portrayal, lending it distance and transform-ing the realism into something comic. The puppet was both the poet and the caricature of eroticism.

Ivo Puhonny, founder of the Artistic Marionette Theatre in Baden-Baden, was conscious of this aspect of the puppet's expression, and adopted Wedekind's *Totentanz* (Dance of death) into his repertory. He re-named it *Tod und Teufel* (Death and devil), the story about a degenerate aristocrat who tries to take advantage of a number of women of easy virtue. The play was well received by the critics, one of whom wrote:

> Wedekind's drama stands interpretation by marionettes, and, even more important, seems even to demand it, because the grotesque rigidity and terrible eccentricity of the marionette produces a strong impression, an ability to portray phenomena which are otherwise difficult to represent.[18]

In 1920, during the same period, Ernst Toller wrote an erotic play for puppets while in prison, to which he had been sentenced for revolutionary activities. The play was actually produced as much in the actors' theatre as in the puppet theatre and was called *Die Rahe des verhonten Liebhabers* (The revenge of the derided lover). Elena exposes her lover to the danger of death at the hands of her husband, and her lover Lorenzo takes his revenge by displaying her naked body with covered face to his guests gathered in her bedroom. No one recognizes her, not even her husband. Later the lovers re-discover their mutual attachment and the quarrel is forgotten.

Toller was here dramatizing a story by the Renaissance writer Cardinal Bandello, and in this way became a forerunner of the numerous interpretations of the *Decameron* for the puppet stage. Today his play is regarded as an amusing adventure faithful to the style of Boccaccio.

There is not a large number of examples of modern eroticism. Here and there the *Decameron* is performed, for example in Sofia, Bulgaria, or Bialystok, Poland. Sometimes *Celestina* appears, as in Torun or Wroclaw (Poland). Typical examples of modern erotic performance include the item played by Yves Joly in his cabaret programme *On the Beach* when he was still only 30, and another short scene from the programme of Spanish theatre produced in the 1970s by La Claca of Barcelona.

Yves Joly's story was produced with the use of hands. Two hands, wearing gloves and representing a man and a woman, arrive at an empty beach. Here as an expression of their mutual interest they begin an amusing striptease, which consists in the removal of several layers of gloves, each representing an elegant item of human attire. After a while the hands, now naked, 'lie' on the beach and start to draw nearer together, offering mutual caresses. The scene is interrupted by the arrival of two black-gloved hands – policemen, the tiresome guardians of middle-class morality. The piece was of a poetic eroticism spiced with satire but without vulgarity.

The scene from the La Claca show bordered on the vulgar in a somewhat perverse fashion. At first the staging seemed to represent a colourful abstract composition, which some minutes later turned out to be the entrance to a grotto protected by a curtain. During the development of the action which concerns the destruction of the curtain, it became clear that the grotto represented a vagina and the action its deflowering.

The artistic idea behind this demonstration was not clear. It was understandable only as a confrontation, an attempt to shock a middle-class and clerical public. The political and social situation in Spain at the time contributed some explanation: the programme was mounted after the dissolution of the Franco republic, when Spain had just returned to a democratic government, and the artists were manifesting their opposition to any continuing social censorship.

In the most recent period the erotic current in puppet theatre remains rather weak, especially in that puppetry is now mainly a children's form of theatre. It seems too that the sources of inspiration have dried up.

Folk parodies by artists displaying their alternative attitudes to sex cannot often attract the public, for the good reason that the majority of sexual taboos have been liquidated. There remain opportunities for the grotesque or poetic portrayals of sex, but few have availed themselves of these. The Wroclaw Puppet Theatre tried both styles. In *Celestina* a long phallus served as a wrap for the main character, but due to its lack of any other function this became monotonous; it was merely a pictorial sign. However, in Kafka's *The Trial* the company discovered a poetic equivalent of the coition scene, which consisted in the vertical opening of the whole female figure to meet her partner.

During this same period there has come into being the surprising phenomenon of the drawing of cartoons with erotic puppet themes, which has spread all over Europe, to the extent that some puppeteers have recently organized special exhibitions on the subject in the Netherlands and Italy.

I hope that this review demonstrates convincingly the rich and differentiated functions of erotic puppetry. First, the puppets appeared as ritual figures linked with the cult of fecundity and similar rituals. Later on they gave erotic theatre an alternative aspect with naturalistic presentations (the mimes), grotesque parody (folk art), social protest (artists of the nineteenth and twentieth centuries) and, finally, poetic signs of desire and fulfilment in a modern, artistic theatre.

It is not important that erotic puppets are not in frequent use. It is enough that they have proved applicable to erotic subjects, bringing with them a special social and aesthetic value. For this is only one more aspect which confirms the puppet as the universal actor.

First published as 'Erotyka i teatr lalek' (Erotica in the puppet theatre), *Teatr Lalek*, 1988, 1–2: 2–9.

Notes

1   Kirby E.T., 'Ritual sex: Anarchies and absolute', *The Drama Review* 1981, 25(1): 3 et seq.
2   Darkowska-Nidzgorski O., 'Théâtre populaire de marionnettes en Afrique Noire', Paris 1976 (typescript).
3   Kirby, op. cit., 5.
4   Ibid., 6.
5   Keene D., *Bunraku. The Art of the Japanese Puppet Theatre*, Tokyo 1968, 27.
6   Helstien M., '*Killekyatha and Bangarakka*, Mischievous Imp and Golden Sister, two comic figures in Karnataka, India leather shadow play', USA 1988 (typescript).
7   Xenophon, *Sympozjum oraz wybór z pism* (The Symposium and selected works), Krakow 1929, 27, 29.
8   Schidrowitz L., *Sittengeschichte des Theaters* (History of customs of the theatre), Vienna and Leipzig n.d., 48.
9   Olearius A., *Podrobnoje opisanije putieszestwija Golsztinskogo posolstwa* (Detailed description of the journey of the Holstein envoys), St Petersburg 1906, 189.
10   Jonson B., *Bartholomew Fair*, London 1614.
11   Schidrowitz, op. cit., 138.
12   Ibid., 181.
13   Fielding, H., *The Covent Garden Tragedy*, London 1732, 19.
14   Magier A., *Estetyka miasta stolecznego Warzawy* (Aesthetic of the capital city, Warsaw), Wrocław 1963, 100.
15   Chesnais, J., *Histoire générale des marionnettes*, Paris 1947, 64.
16   Brisacier, J., *Le Théâtre Erotique de la Rue de la Santé*, Paris 1866.
17   Gerould, D., 'Henri Monnier and the Erotikon Teatron: The pornography of realism', *The Drama Review*, 1981, 25(1): 19.
18   Critic from *Frankfurter Zeitung* in *Der Puppenspieler*, Bochum 1949, 12: 185.

8
The Human among Things and Objects

Imagine the first moment when man became aware of the existence of the world. He looked around and saw other people, animals, trees, sky, sun and so on. This was the world. In fact what he was seeing were – things. Things, objects, are in opposition to subjects, to myself, to ourselves. Thus early man saw things. His first problem was to use things for his advantage, to exploit them, to make them a help not an obstacle. The first human invention was the transformation of things into objects and thus into tools, into instruments which might serve him to achieve his objectives. (I am saying 'thing' as opposed to 'object' with some backing in current philosophical terminology. In fact I needed a more popular notion for the word 'matter'.)

Certain experiments were made some time ago with monkeys. A caged monkey was offered a banana, but out of its normal reach. Being humanitarian, the human put down a stick next to the monkey, a testing stick. The question was, would the monkey use the stick or not? It did. It took the stick in its hands and used it successfully to reach the banana. This was a typical example of making a tool from a thing. Unfortunately for the monkey, it was not able to go beyond using the stick to help itself to reach the banana. Man, as we know, went further.

The stick which served to reach a piece of fruit or the stick which served to defend the tribe or the stone which served as a primitive weapon to kill an animal – these were the first tools which started the development of human civilization. There is no need to make a list of tools which came later, from the first knife to the first cutting machine or the first hammer to the first mechanical forge. We know about the different stages of their development and we are deeply conscious that we live in the midst of objects, and that some of them serve for our comfort. The number of objects that came into existence became so great that the question of their consumption became the centre of our present preoccupations.

141

From the beginning of civilization humans, surrounded by various objects, have tried to defend their identity by making those objects more personal. They added to them some magic or ornamental signs, unimportant perhaps for their practical efficiency, but fundamental as a sign of their emotional and artistic expression. Of course, this practice was more visible in handcrafts than in contemporary capitalist industrial production.

Objects were submitted to scientific research and to philosophical reflection, as we may see in the works of Brentano or Kotarbinski. Sociologists are fascinated by objects of consumption and by their currently dominant social role. My aim here is to present some aspects of artistic objects, which also include instruments of theatrical expression, mainly in the puppet theatre.

Psychoanalysts say that works of art originated from fear of an unknown destiny, a fear which urged humans to look for forms of consolation. This resulted in the creation of a fictional world which humans could dominate according to their imagination. Certainly early man was not conscious of his search for consolation: he was too busy ensuring his own survival and that of his tribe, and perhaps had no time for psychological deliberation. In the process of focusing his energy on survival, he established some essential and for him most important truths, the first being that the world is dominated by either hostile or friendly powers. Man tried to imagine how he might have some contact with them, in this case visual contact.

The first objects invented by early man, recognized in modern times as works of art, served mimetic, magic and religious purposes. Mimetic objects helped to create a model of the world in order to understand it and if possible to improve it. Magic objects seemed to dominate the world, the religious ones to honour deities and sometimes to negotiate a better life for people. The mimetic tendency of early man, who created the first religious system based on the powers of nature, led him directly to animism and idolatry. Modern religious systems such as Judaism, Christianity and Islam, based on revelations, fought idolatry energetically to assure the spiritual dimension of their faith.

Idolatry concerns the visual presentation of gods and saints. Ancient Greeks and Romans were not concerned with the sin of idolatry, because they never considered it a sin, but for the first Christians idolatry was the sign of paganism. That was why they allowed only a symbolic presentation of their faith. On the way it was also possible to apply a syncretic treatment of the problem such as we find in Islamic Indonesia, where the figures of *wayang* have the shape of ornaments rather than real people.

However, human instinct also led Christianity into producing icons which represented Christ and his Saints, a practice which ended in the famous war between the iconophiles (lovers of icons) and iconoclasts (enemies of icons) in the eighth century. Fortunately the iconophiles won, and Christian authorities allowed mediaeval artists to present their icons and figurative sculptures, even accepting them as church decorations, enabling the future development of the liturgical theatre. This was transformed later into the Mystery plays, which maintained the theatrical tradition in Europe. It is true that the art of the Middle Ages dealt mainly with religious subjects, and that the coming centuries turned to ancient and secular themes, escaping from Church control, but I believe that the victory of the iconophiles of the eighth century was essential for the development of European art, including puppetry, in its secular form.

I have been trying to identify some factors influencing artistic activities in order to emphasize that the puppet theatre is not somehow an invented genre of theatre, but the result of a long historical process embracing the general development of art and theatre. While speaking about puppetry, we have to take into consideration many other circumstances and especially the psychic imperative discussed by Freud and Kerényi which, according to their ideas, impels humans to imitate the act of creation, and especially the creation of artificial human beings.

In the course of history puppetry, like the other arts, tried to present a picture of the world. Puppets changed their expression according to the artistic fashions dominating sculpture, painting and live theatre, and puppets followed their manner of the imitation of life. In the nineteenth century and the beginning of the twentieth, when the wave of naturalism was at its peak, puppets were three-dimensional representations of various beings including gods, humans, animals, fairies and other fantastic figures. The principal group was always human and that is the reason to consider the puppet as a human simulacrum. This concept has led us into a rich world of human representation.

A human simulacrum is specifically a three-dimensional icon or representation. In the course of history it fulfilled different functions, among which we may consider their practical use, their ritualistic employment, their mythological participation, their appearance in literary fiction and also their theatrical presence. Of course some of these functions overlap, which tells us that each classification has some weak points.

Any use of human simulacra is marked by a practical purpose, but some are used more pragmatically than others. Take for example fashion dolls, all kinds of shop window mannequins, tin soldiers and children's dolls. Their use is simply practical. Only children's dolls provoke some difficulties in their classification because the child's fantasy gives them special psychological functions, thus placing them on the ritualistic and especially animistic level. Children use dolls in their play, which consists in giving them life or, if you prefer, in giving them roles, which recalls the theatrical employment of puppets. This form of playing, like all the games of children, serves also as an exercise before children undertake social, adult roles in real life. This procedure, the child's endowment of life to a dead thing, one day became an inspiration for the theatre and especially for puppet players.

The ritualistic employment of human simulacra is spread all over the world. We can recall Roman funeral puppets, and funeral figures such as the recently discovered clay army of the Chinese Emperor buried with their lord. Puppets also participated in various rituals from which the most theatrical seems to be the Niombo, which consists in using a huge puppet which serves at the same time as a coffin. The puppet carried on the platform performs the last spectacle of the recently deceased chief of the tribe. We wonder whether the Egyptian mummies also had this privilege.

There are occasions when the corpse has served as a sort of puppet in an endeavour to placate the dead person immediately after death. We know about the replacement of the corpse by a wax copy, identical to the original, and the famous museums of wax figures founded by Madame Tussaud, which probably owed their origins to the existence of a large number of wax funeral figures. These were used in the seventeenth century in the ceremony of displaying the coffin of the deceased person in church to avoid any possible profanity. When the body was buried the wax figures were no longer necessary and remained in store. One such figure was in a story, *The Kidnapp'd Earl* (as told by James Boswell, June–July 1763) by Lillian de la Torre, who presented Dr. Samuel Johnson in the role of predecessor to the famous Sherlock Holmes. To prove the identity of James Aslay, the 'kidnapped Earl' of the title, Dr. Johnson brought to court a wax funeral figure, the only existing portrait of the second Duke of Bredingham. When the barrister announced the arrival of the dead Duke as a witness, Dr. Johnson took the matter into his own hands, demonstrating a fine sense of theatricality:

Instantly pandemonium burst forth, everyone shouting at once. In the din Dr. Sam Johnson came marching up the aisle and the wax-work Duke seemed to march with him, supported on one side by Dr. Johnson and on the other by Frank Barber, who rolled his dark eyes in terror, yet strode manfully forward.

In the terms of our enquiry, I feel that each idol as well as each simulacrum may be, and often is, animated by means of suggestion. Dr. Johnson behaved as if the wax figure of the Duke were alive and this suggestion had theatrical value – it served to produce the illusion that the wax figure was able to participate in the unfolding action, which it finally did. We will find a similar procedure in using suggestion for the purpose of puppet animation in the modern puppet theatre.

Animation and especially the animation of human simulacra is a mental process, with regard to the manipulator who intends to bring life to his simulacra and with regard to the spectator who comes to the theatre in the expectation of a fictional experience. Before we can see the scenic fact of animation, we have to pass through the preparatory psychic process of allowing our imagination to work.

It is worth noting that some people were indifferent to the material (in our case theatrical) accomplishment of the life of the simulacra. They were happy simply to imagine that the simulacra were alive, and they limited themselves to fixing their imagined world as a story belonging to the oral tradition, as all myths are, or as a literary fiction, which is an extension of our mythical thinking.

It would be possible to collect enough mythological stories which include puppet themes to make a whole book. Some of these stories tell of puppet demonstrations which appear to be a model of human dependence on destiny or on the gods. Other stories emphasize the possibility of the transformation of an artificial being, such as a sculpture, into a living person. The first group of stories refers to the puppet theatre as a source of metaphor. The second one touches the very important problem of the human instinct to re-create life, beyond the limits of the order established by God or by nature. In other words, it touches the problem of the creation of an artificial life.

Two of these stories are worth discussing: the story of Pygmalion and Galatea and the story of the Golem. Each of them approaches the problem from a different point of view. Pygmalion created Galatea, the most beautiful woman he could conceive, in the imagined image of the goddess Aphrodite. In love with his sculpture, he urgently asked the Goddess to bring her to life. Aphrodite granted his wish, gave life to the statue, and Pygmalion and Galatea lived happily ever after – as any fairy tale should end. The story presented and confirmed the traditional role of humans in relationship to gods. Humans are limited in their creative acts: they cannot go beyond fictional artistic expression. On the other hand, gods have unlimited power and can create living beings. The transformation of Galatea into a living person, later the mother of Paphos, was a divine affair. Pygmalion was made happy because he accepted his modest existence and addressed his humble requests to the proper divine authority. The story is full of light, beauty and optimism.

It is quite different in the case of the Golem, a story of darkness, sin and imperfection, because man dared to oppose his creator. A rabbi, in imitation of God, made a being of clay and tried to bring it to life, using a magic Cabbalistic formula. He was almost successful – the clay was fashioned into a moving being, the Golem, but it was without the power of speech. Its end was tragic because all its magic powers were helpless in the face of human faith and human rationalism. However, the Golem provokes our special interest because it makes a new comment on the muteness of puppets.

Gradually the power of gods and the power of magic were replaced by the power of human fantasy. We know well that human fantasy takes impulses from real life and that without the engineers who create the mechanical beings known as automata or androids, the writer's fantasy could not cross into the regions of mythology. We needed the mechanistic genius of Philo from Byzantium, Torriani, Kempelen and Droz in order to have Jean Paul, E.T.A. Hoffmann and Villiers de l'Isle-Adam. These engineers took their work seriously, trying to combine the beauty of sculpture with mechanical perfection. Especially in the century of the Enlightenment, their belief in the unlimited possibility of human technical skill led them to surprising results, their works enchanting both Court and popular audiences, even if each was obliged to pay the entrance fee proper to its respective social standing. There is a strong analogy between automata and puppet shows if we consider them as market activities appealing to the same human instinct; that is, the human fascination for the creation of artificial life.

Passing through different periods in human history, especially in Europe, we note that both forms of show – puppets and automata – existed in parallel, although their social functions were different. Androids were made for cardinals to satisfy their pride, mechanical figures were produced for princesses and kings to ennoble the entrances to their lands or towns and demanded a large financial investment, unattainable by wandering puppet-players who had very limited resources. On the other hand, the automata presented first to the French courtiers were later offered to all kinds of audiences through public exhibitions, like the proceedings of puppeteers who often performed in palaces before returning to fairgrounds and town squares.

Automata (mechanical puppets) were valuable and expensive objects which were kept in palaces or the houses of the rich. Puppets were available for almost everybody and in this sense they belonged to the so-called poor art popularized not long ago by Peter Schumann. Puppets did not lose in the competition with automata. After the first period of surprises the automata, with their repetitive mechanical movements, disappeared into oblivion. On the other hand puppets, due to their complicity with the human performer, have always been more flexible and versatile than the best automata. Finally they attained the honour of their own theatre genre, at the moment when their participation in the art of spectacle started to be called 'puppet theatre'.

In the period of Romanticism especially, writers fell under the spell of puppets and androids, and both served as a source of metaphor. If writers included puppets in their stories they always stressed their theatrical character, treating them, as did Kleist, Hoffmann and Andersen, as the perfect theatrical instrument. Andersen, in his famous tale *The Director of the Puppet Theatre*, followed Kleist and Hoffmann in giving to the puppet, as artificial actor, superiority over an actor of flesh and blood.

If they included androids they were often used as a misogynistic metaphor. Poor, sensitive, neurasthenic poets could only solve their psychic problems by placing the burden of responsibility on the other sex, presenting the horror of sudden discovery that a woman's beauty hid a soulless mechanical life, as presented by Jean Paul in his novel *The Wooden Lady* or by E.T.A. Hoffmann in *The Sandman* through the character of Olympia. They also tried to prove that a female android may bring more pleasure to a lover than a real woman. The hero of the novel *Tomorrow's Eve* by Villiers de l'Isle-Adam ordered the construction of a mechanical being that was to be the 'ideal woman'.

Human simulacra have been present in the art of spectacle as long as the art of spectacle has existed. Different kinds of mechanized sculptures, figures and manikins peopled fairground tents and fit-up stages. They were objects of curiosity, but sometimes they were the actor's double, as in the mediaeval miracles, where a manikin of human size might be tortured instead of the actor playing a saint or martyr. In the twentieth century the subject of manikins attracted writers, sometimes as their main character, as in *El Señor de Pigmalion*, a play by Jacinto Grau, and *The Manikins' Ball* by Bruno Jasienski.

Of course the puppet was the main representative of human simu-lacra in the art of spectacle. Puppets fulfilled numerous functions, start-ing from the rituals which always had a spectacular value. The mediaeval fairgrounds knew puppets as an advertising medium and vagrant storytellers took puppets all over the world as an illustration of the narratives they presented. In present times we see storytelling coming back into practice under the banner of so-called epic theatre, but in fact I doubt if these two notions mean the same thing.

It is curious that even if we in Europe have seen puppetry go from storytelling through a period of practising 'real theatre' and then return-ing to the same storytelling formula, in the Asian theatre the practice of storytelling has hardly changed in centuries. All types of *wayang* as well as *ningyo joruri* have remained on the same level: stories illustrated by puppets.

The storytelling formula has given an important privilege to the performer: he or she is the central point, speaking directly to the audi-ence, in effect a visible creator, a sort of demiurge of the show. On the other hand the puppet theatre, according to its classical concept which obtained from the seventeenth to the nineteenth centuries, demanded some sacrifice from the player, who was obliged to hide himself in the booth, giving all the glory to the puppet. For this reason this kind of theatre could not be called other than 'puppet theatre'. Puppets were given the function of characters and as such the function of the scenic subjects (of course *apparent* subjects, but in fact in the theatre every-thing is apparent).

Modernism and the avant-garde attacked this 'classical' model of theatre: they accepted only one subject in art, that is the creative human being. Thus they emphasized the artificial nature of art, and artificial creations of art are equal to artefacts. Again humans confronted different things and objects (and also living beings), aiming to use them as materials of their own creation. In treating things, objects and living beings as elements of a possible composition, it was decided to mix them up. Different means of expression were combined, including masks, puppets, objects, acrobats, clowns and actors. The way was opened to heterogeneity.

Under the pressure of these ideas, the puppet-player was able to abandon the booth to become the visible demiurge of his show. He (or she) could face the audience, talking directly to the spectators without the intermediary of the puppet. Many things changed and the puppets received new functions, including that of an object involved in the process of creation.

Figure 8.1 From the Hungarian State Puppet Theatre production of *Aventures* by Gyorgy Ligeti, Designed by Ivan Koos, 1972

It is interesting that in previous centuries puppeteers never spoke of puppets as objects. The popular player in particular believed that his puppets inherited a part of his own life, often asserting 'my puppets are alive'. In such words we sense the remote belief in the puppets' magic life. Contemporary puppet actors seem to forget about the puppet's magic life when they say: 'I am the player, the puppet is only my instrument'. Perhaps that is right: it seems that few yearn for the lost illusion of the living puppet. For this there are many reasons, the first being that the 'theatre of illusion' still exists and it is strong enough to give new impulses to contemporary artists endowed with some curiosity as to the expressive potential of puppets. Second, the new situation of puppetry has some advantages: the consideration of the puppet as an object has given puppetry a closer connection with fine art.

It is a fact that some time ago Andersen in his search for enchantment showed much sympathy for common objects, giving them personalities and the gift of speech. He pretended to accept the old animistic proceedings, which unfortunately in his time belonged only to a child's world. Perhaps that is why he is chiefly recognized as a writer of children's stories. He also used objects as allegories, a continuation of an old tradition from antiquity, the Middle Ages and the Baroque period.

However, surrealist painters and sculptors penetrating new fields of life discovered the attractions of objects and found that they not only have their functions and their biography, but also that they generate some special meanings, especially in the context of other objects. This discovery has given birth to the fashion for various kinds of collages, which helped the attainment of new poetic expression in the field of fine art and theatre, above all puppet theatre.

Waste materials were in themselves another source of inspiration. The enormous accumulation of junk produced by our present civilization has obliged people to think of ways for its re-use. In art, junk is considered cheap and inspirational. On the other hand, its use in some works may be understood as a manifestation of sympathy for matter in general, in opposition to its senseless and exaggerated consumption, especially the elimination of worn-out objects. Artists are convinced that nothing is so used that it has completely lost its value. It is not difficult to discover in this attitude the remote reflection of animism bowing respectfully before even the smallest piece of material.

The interest in objects is balanced by a high level of subjectivity in contemporary art. The modern player trusts completely the force of the imagination and believes that he can project all his feeling and intention

Figure 8.2   From the Voronezh Puppet Theatre production of *The Lake Boy* by Pavel Vezhinov, 1987

by using any means of expression. The modern puppet-player believes that the actor's presence is essential for the transformation of any material vehicle used as a character. Sometimes figurative puppets are still employed, but they are very often replaced by simple common objects. Is this curiosity for a new means of expression or a more serious phenomenon emerging from general trends in the art of the present?

One answer may be found on the level of theatrical language. By 'theatrical language' I understand all means of expression in the process of their use. It means that I am interested both in their characteristics and their function. According to my analysis the use of puppets demands less linguistic operation than the use of objects. The puppet is a more or less simple three-dimensional icon manufactured to be manipulated on stage. It is the icon of a potential character which becomes real if the puppet brought on stage is endowed with movement and perhaps a voice. Distinct from puppets, common objects are manufactured for some practical use. Naturally, each has its own iconicity, which allows people to recognize it. If a performer produces an object in order to turn it into a stage character, the task is more complex than that of presenting a puppet character. By means of acting and manipulation he has to transform the object (for example an umbrella) into a character (for example a woman), first by contradicting the iconic and practical value of the object and next by endowing it with new functions and a new appearance to make it recognizable as the intended character.

Objects as characters circulate in a world of hints, allusions, suggestion and metaphor. Objects are not able to give a full and complete iconic equivalent of a character in the manner of the classical puppet, bringing information about the visual qualities of a character which can be exhaustive. The opposition between common objects and puppets as characters may be translated into the opposition between the suggestion of an image and its realization.

Should we accept that the process of communication in art has changed so much that we have now entered into a world of hints and allusions? Should we think that in this context the puppet has become a medium that generates too much information? Should we think that this is one of the reasons for the intense interest in the theatrical use of ordinary objects? It is possible. However, I believe that the abundance or paucity of theatrical information does not depend on the shape and assignment of icons, but on the style of their expression.

Think about figurative painting: after a period of crisis it is coming back into fashion, even if changed and bringing new values. The same

may be true of figurative theatrical puppets. Figurative puppets, especially human simulacra, have had to find their way into a new age of
artistic expression, sharing their situation with many other objects.
Some of them have disappeared from use and have entered museums,
some have successfully attracted managers of new markets and new
technology.

This has been a long journey in time among objects produced by
human civilization. First I laid emphasis on these special objects in the
form of gods or human simulacra, which appeared in the dawn of art
and theatre, including puppetry, all of them belonging to a figurative
presentation of the world. Next I pointed to the crisis in this kind of
presentation. The modern imagination and modern concepts of art
have questioned the value of the figurative, provoking new tendencies
in art which are believed to be more intellectual, more analytical and
also more subjective.

Certainly there are no puppets or simulacra which dominate any
artistic expression. In the centre of modern artistic creativity we see the
human, an artist, a performer, a puppeteer who decides on the means
of expression, choosing those which best articulate his emotions. No
matter how much the philosophy of art and its practice may change, to
be a theatre artist or puppet-player is a joy connected with a great
responsibility to the spectators, trusting the theatre to lead them into a
world of uplifting emotion and essential human values.

October 1994. Presented at Brighton University and published in book-
let form by the British Centre of UNIMA.

9
Craig and Puppets

We normally associate Edward Gordon Craig's notion of the Über-marionette with the theatrical puppet, an association that is both right and wrong. It is right because both have the same origins; but it is wrong because, over the course of time, the puppet has moved a long away from its sacred origins. Craig himself was quite aware of this when he wrote: 'He [the marionette] is a descendant of the stone images of the old temples – he is today a rather degenerate form of a god.'[1]

This explains why Craig did not at first appreciate the puppets of his own time. Indeed, his judgement was quite severe:

> The marionette appears to me to be the last echo of some noble and beautiful art of a past civilization. But as with all art which has passed into fat or vulgar hands, the puppet has become a reproach. All puppets are now but low comedians. They imitate the comedians of the larger and fuller-blooded stage. They enter only to fall on their back. They drink only to reel, and make love only to raise a laugh. They have forgotten the counsel of their mother the Sphinx.[2]

Nevertheless, Craig's dreams of a new kind of actor made him think about the marionette as a descendant of 'the stone images of the old temples'. At first he wanted to hold to the original presentation of gods:

> And who knows whether the puppet shall not once again become the faithful medium for the beautiful thoughts of the artist. May we not look forward with hope to that day which shall bring back to us once more the figure, or symbolic creature, made also by the cunning of the artist, so that we can gain once more the 'noble artificiality' which the old writer speaks of? Then shall we no longer be under the cruel influence of the emotional confessions of weakness which are nightly witnessed by the people and which in their turn create in the beholders the very weaknesses which are exhibited. To that end we

must study to remake these images – no longer content with a puppet, we must create an über-marionette.[3]

This was not a new idea. Maeterlinck too had dreamt about a new actor in the shape of sculptures and statues. Craig, however, was consistent in his demands over many years. His essay 'The Actor and the Über-Marionette' (published in 1908 in an issue of *The Mask*, and later in a collection of articles published as a book, *On the Art of the Theatre*, in 1911) provoked a long-lasting discussion, dividing theatre practitioners into partisans for and against. Today, it seems that most contemporary researchers do not believe in Craig's famous proposition about replacing the actor by the über-marionette, or 'super-puppet', which they say was only vaguely defined and really no more than a metaphor. They consider it to be a mere provocation to the actor, intended simply to persuade actors to change their egocentric attitudes for the better realization of an authorial vision in theatre.

Although Craig's writings after 1924 give some grounds for this belief, it is not really the case. Craig had clear and concrete ideas about the über-marionette and its use, but he did not at that time envisage a complete ban on the actor. In 1905, Craig was in Berlin where it seems that Count Harry Kessler promised him financial support to allow the foundation of Craig's own theatre in Dresden. It is probable that all the ideas he entertained at that time about puppetry were related to this project.

In 1992, the French researcher Didier Plassard, investigating Craig's theories on the über-marionette, was the first to quote from three of Craig's daybooks dated 1905–06, now in the Bibliothèque Nationale in Paris. He discovered that Craig in fact entertained doubts as to whether the puppet could ever be accepted as an actor for the whole duration of a play. On June 15, 1905, Craig listed the 'participants' of his productions in which he proposed mixing the über-marionette with other performers:

> The Über-marionette will average in height from 4 and a half to 5 feet. The Heroes and other distinguished characters will measure from 5 to 5 and a half feet – or even 6 feet. The Gods 6 and a half feet, or more if necessary, [with human] athletes and dancers, gymnasts and models.[4]

Craig also projected a repertory for this new theatre, which would include plays he had already staged, such as *Dido and Aeneas*, while adding dramas by Maeterlinck, *Faust*, *Macbeth*, Flaubert's *Temptation of St. Anthony*, and others. Among these would be a 'Duse Play' in which 'Only Duse will speak. The rest move around her as in a dream. Masks and Über-marionettes.'[5] Evidently Craig was not yet proposing to eliminate the actor, and we may be sure that Eleonora Duse would have been allowed into his productions anyway, judging by Craig's esteem for this famous actress.

The Dresden project was never realized, however, and Craig transferred his concept to essay form, in which he took his controversial theories even further. It was at this time, in 1908, that Craig embarked on his celebrated, fundamental attack on the actor, claiming that no actor could be considered an artist. However, it is clear that Craig did not appreciate the puppet theatre of his time, and simply had in mind a great idea of the puppet's potential, derived from its first sacred functions. What Craig really meant by his notion of the über-marionette was still not really comprehensible.

Nonetheless, he became gradually more sympathetic towards the primitive popular puppets of his day and even considered the possibility of using them. While getting his school ready for actors in the Arena Goldoni in Florence, he commissioned some Italians to manufacture a special figure for him. As Craig's son, Edward, described it:

> An experimental marionette, eight feet high, was made by the carvers, and attempts were made to manipulate it. Typically for Italian craftsmen, on the day it was finished they hurriedly rigged it, suspending it from a platform twenty feet up and, as Craig arrived, the giant figure bowed, and with slow gestures, addressed him in Italian, wishing him good luck in all his enterprises.[6]

The Arena Goldoni school, founded in 1913, was closed the following year, when it was requisitioned for military use at the outbreak of the First World War. Craig's disappointment did not put a stop to his reflections on puppetry; on the contrary, he began to make a more intimate study of it. In fact Craig was under the spell of his puppets and he enthused about their expressiveness:

> By the way, I have a Puppet which (if I only knew how to let him move) does really move as to cause delight. I had him with me in Roma, and some of my friends who came to see me will forget me but I am sure they will never forget him.[7]

Indeed, Craig still dreamt of puppets as performers and began to write short plays for them: his *Drama for Fools,* under the pseudonym of Tom Fool. He also referred to them as 'motions' and the first of these was published in his magazine *The Marionnette* in 1918. This was an opportunity for Craig to demonstrate his belief in the importance of the puppets' role in theatre:

> Future – Today – these words defining time are clumsy and do not fulfil their task. Because you could judge that, speaking of the Future, I think of five or ten years ... while all the time I mean what will come after the victory of the puppets. You may consider, that when I say Today I am thinking – this year, but this is not true. I mean the time of the victory of the puppets. The Über-marionette comes later.[8]

Here the puppet becomes a precursor of the über-marionette. It was supposed to influence actors in theatre, as Craig considered the puppet to be a model for actors, claiming:

> The puppet is the ABC of the actor. The Puppet is the Actor's Primer. Architects have Vitruvius, Palladio and a dozen others: musicians have Rameau and a dozen others: painters have Leonardo, Cennini and a dozen others: writers have the Dictionary, and actors have the Puppet.[9]

According to Craig, only the puppet can realize the ideal of human movement, which is why he wanted actors to consider the puppet as their tutor. Craig advised the actor:

> to renew his acquaintance with the Puppets. Never travel without one. Have one made; let it be three feet high. See that it's well balanced and carved by some really good wood-carver; have it carefully strung and put on a cunning stick. For the stick is the soul of the Puppet. Then practise with this in front of a glass. Hold it easily, letting the feet just touch the carpet. Do this a dozen times every morning and every afternoon before your other exercises.[10]

The purpose of this advice seems clear. Craig demanded from an actor a stylized, 'artificial' gesture and he hoped that this would be obtained by the example or intermediary of the puppet:

> But once you have made a Puppet and taught yourself to allow it to
> move (and it's that and nothing else; I mean you don't move it; you
> let it move itself; that's the art) ... once you have done these two
> things I promise you, if you are a born artist, the world is in for a very
> great treat. The Idea of man in motion, in perfect motion, will be
> seen for the first time in a generation.[11]

Craig does not speak here about replacing the actor with super-mari-
onettes. He wants to show the puppet to the actor as an interesting partner, a partner who *offers an idea of man in motion*. Thus we can see that
Craig's point of view changed considerably. Perhaps he lost his enthusiasm for the super-marionette after his first experiments in Florence, but
in any case he withdrew from his initial ideas of introducing 'the stone-
like images of gods' on stage.

It is not surprising, then, that after such an evolution in his thinking
Craig changed his attitude towards actors' theatre and in 1924 offered it
an olive branch. For the fourth edition of *On the Art of the Theatre* he
wrote a new preface, stating that his intention had not been to replace
actors by puppets. 'Is it not true,' he wrote, 'that when we cry "Oh, go
to the Devil!" we never really want that to happen? What we mean is,
"get a little of his fire and come back cured".'[12] At the same time he gave
a new definition of the über-marionette:

> The Über-marionette is the actor plus fire minus egoism; the fire of
> the gods and demons without the smoke and steam of mortality. The
> literal ones took me to mean pieces of wood one foot in height; that
> infuriated them; they talked of it for ten years as a mad, a wrong, an
> insulting idea. The point was gained by them, and I think I owe them
> here a word of thanks.[13]

We should not think, however, that Craig was interested in puppets
simply in terms of his über-marionette theory. It seems that, especially
during the period of his life in Florence, he was indeed under the spell
of puppets: he admired the richness of the puppet's forms of expression;
he bought for the Arena Goldoni a collection of Asian puppets from
Burma and Java; he was in contact with the English puppeteer Walter
Wilkinson; he saw productions of the famous Italian puppeteers, such
as the Colla and Lupi families, as well as Vittorio Podrecca's company.

That nearly all of these Italian companies' directors employed
members of their own family might be the origin of Craig's idea for
founding a 'family theatre'. Craig's son, Edward, tells us that his father

envisaged a domestic theatre for his own children. Craig ignored the tradition of toy theatres that were already available and decided to write his own plays, which are however hard to think of as being really 'plays for children'. Rather than theatre for children, Craig was thinking about an intimate theatre in which he might accomplish his own idea of a modern art. His project must be analysed as an original theatrical project in miniature.

After his experiences in Moscow and elsewhere, he was aware that he would not be able to change existing theatre practice. He therefore imagined his own (puppet) theatre in order to present the history of humanity in miniature dramas. Craig planned to have 365 of these dramas – one each for every day of the year. In calling them *The Drama for Fools* he was referring to the tradition of the Fool, from which puppet theatre derives much of its inspiration.

Craig never fully realized this fantastic project of 365 plays. He published a few of them – *The End of Mr. Fish and Mrs. Bones, The Tune the Old Cow died of,* and *The Gordian Knot* – in his magazine *The Marionnette* in 1918; *School* and *Blue Sky* in the *English Review* in 1918 and 1921; *Romeo and Juliet* and *The Three Men of Gotham* in separate editions of *The Marionnette*. However, we know that Craig wrote far more than these few published plays. Among the documents that he left after his death there was a mass of material concerning the *Drama for Fools*.

The first scholar to look at this material, and later to publish a commentary on it, was Marina Siniscalchi. The most interesting of the documents she discovered was Craig's 'Sketch Plan to Drama for Fools', which gives the most detailed information on his project. Although we do not find the whole cycle of 365 dramas presented there, the 119 that are mentioned are surprising not only for their quantity but also for their range of themes. It seems that Craig followed the model of the mediaeval cycles of Mystery plays. The list includes themes from the creation of the world up to Craig's own time. Two characters are leading, recurring figures, Cockatrice and Blind Boy, appearing in most of the projected plays, representing opposed moral values. To quote Marina Siniscalchi:

> The first three scenes within the Sketch Plan take place in Hell at the beginning of the world. Blind Boy meets the Parrot, a crafty and rich parrot, who brings in his bag a huge egg as a gift for Pluto. From this egg Cockatrice will be born. Pluto, being aware of this, sentences Parrot to death. Parrot however plays a trick. As his last request before

execution he asks for his bag, opens it and breaks the egg. Cockatrice is born while the bells of Bow toll – the old tale says that anyone born in Cheapside in earshot of the church in Bow is an authentic cockney. Cockatrice's gaze terrorizes the hellish court and Blind Boy and Parrot escape in the general confusion. From this episode onwards Craig introduces motifs of travel and searching – travel along unknown roads and searches for hidden treasures – according to the archetype so dear to mythology and popular tales. Blind Boy, bored by his hellish adventures, wishes to see the wonders of the world and suggests to Cockatrice that they set off. Parrot joins them.

Gradually Cockatrice demonstrates his vulgar nature provoking man to commit sin. This is the beginning of a succession of scenes following Genesis: episodes such as the Flood and comic discussions inside and outside Noah's Ark remind us of the York Mystery cycles. Some scenes refer to oriental motifs such as 'Divano', which probably refers to Hafiz' magic carpet. The birth of Jupiter in the thirtieth scene starts another group of 'motions' inspired by mythology and illustrated with charming drawings. In one scene, Jupiter tries to avoid a meeting with the Blind Woman, transformed into the Sphinx. He boards a ship but because it is wrecked he visits an island inhabited by wild people ...[14]

Craig opened the way to a new, ironic interpretation of the history of humanity in the puppet style. With the 50th scene, the cycle of plays which includes Looney, the Magic Idiot, begins. Craig gives him many themes to play, from the *Pentamerone* and from Grimms' Tales. Scenes 101–118 present the history of Rome, showing the influence of Pliny, Apuleius and others. In some of the plays the Magic Ass appears, its origins drawn from mythological and Fool traditions (for example the mediaeval *Processio Asinorum*).

The plays published during 1918–21 are given a 'preface' by Craig: 'The Marionnette Drama. Some Notes for an Introduction to 'The Drama for Fools' by Tom Fool', published in *The Marionnette* (1918). This introduction is a eulogy of the puppet at the expense of the live actor. Craig wrote:

What are marionettes? Men without egoism. What are men? – Egoists. They walk, sleep, read, play, visit, eat and drink and work as egoists. And more – they think, feel through egoism, see through it, hear through it. They soak it up like sponges. Once well filled in every pore, and we have what we call a man.

A marionette walks, sleeps, prays, visits, eats, drinks, seems to do all these things exactly as men do, and what makes him so fresh, so free from something detestable, something which haunts us when we see real men, is that this awful thing Egoism is not with him.

He seems to think and feel, to see and to hear without egoism ... and without that pose of altruism ... egoism's top-notch.

All this makes the marionettes so refreshing, and gives us a sense of surprise and gaiety when they appear. Who could quarrel with one of them? Why, they are even unaware that we see them.[15]

And what is the puppet drama? It is quite different from the 'proper drama'. In Craig's comparison:

Perhaps one of the chief distinctions between a Drama for Marionnettes and a Proper Drama is this ... that whereas a Proper Drama has to be vague and roundabout in its movements, a Marionnette Drama had always better be direct and rapid and even obvious.

With the Proper Drama so much can be helped along by the actor; for example, if its author wishes to draw a subtle character like Iago he can do so, making him seem to be quite a pleasant personage; for the actor who completes the work will explain, by additional exercise of subtlety, that he is not as pleasant a personage as the audience might suppose.

Now a Marionnette cannot do that. A Marionnette is not at all clever, not subtle. He must fit the character like a hand fits a glove, or all is undone. Therefore, when we make a character in one of our Dramas we make the Marionnette to fit it. And so it comes about that a Marionnette does not play a number of parts, he plays only one ... that is himself. This is different from the actor who plays many parts and must therefore pretend. The Marionnette never pretends ... therefore the Marionnette can save the Theatre.

Neither in character nor in appearance must the Marionnette be 'subtle'. There must be no shilly-shallying about either his looks or his actions. He is or he is not 'Hamlet' ... whereas in the Proper Drama, 'Hamlet' is sometimes one thing, sometimes another, and seldom is he 'Hamlet'.

Thus the cunning of the playwright, of the actor and of the audience is properly exercised, while this directness of the Marionnette Theatre curbs our fancy; and though, when writing, we must deny ourselves very many excursions, still, we may range pretty freely so long as we keep on the high road.

For example, we may if we wish give life and movement and even a voice to inanimate objects. A clock of course already has its life, so that we should not be doing well to give it any additional powers. We would not cause it to talk other than it does in ticks, and in striking the hours, and in its cuckoo notes. But to a cushion we can give life.[16]

The contemporary reader may be a little confused by all this exhortation. On the one hand, we see here the traditional (albeit artistic) view of the puppet and its drama, a view held by such artists and puppet players as Meyerhold, Tairov, Brann and Obraztsov: that the live actor may deal with psychology, while the puppet must present schematic characters; that puppets demand clear, direct images and situations; that they cannot enter into any exercise of subtlety. And on the other hand, we read about the use of inanimate objects, which was a novelty in the world of puppet theatre at this time. As we discover from his *Drama for Fools*, however, Craig did not make use of this novelty himself. Although he developed the idea of puppet theatre in a prophetic way, in practice he remained bound by its traditional forms.

To make this clear, we should remember that at the beginning of the twentieth century the puppet theatre which Craig knew was the 'true' puppet theatre, using figures that imitated live beings. Sometimes their expression was stylized according to new tendencies in the fine arts, such as could be seen in the productions of Brann, Podrecca, Teschner and the Swiss artists. But in general the world the puppet theatre represented was ruled by the same conventions wherever it was played.

Craig's innovations consist in the fact that he proposed, in some of his 'motions', a new approach to puppets. First, he suggested the use of a dynamic visual metaphor as the vehicle for a message. For example, at the beginning of his *Romeo and Juliet*, Romeo is a complete figure while Juliet is only a bust. In the course of the action Romeo loses his limbs, while Juliet receives new ones. By the end of the play, Juliet is a complete woman while Romeo is a broken invalid. It is up to the audience (or the reader) to discern the signification of this transformation of the figures.

Secondly, Craig suggested connecting the presentation of the story to a revelation of the mechanisms of puppet theatre. He proposed showing the presence of the manipulators, as well as the theatrical god – the director of the show. In the final scene of *Mr. Fish and Mrs. Bones*, for example, Mrs. Bones (the puppet) is banished from the theatre, but finds support in the arms of her faithful manipulator (a human actor), 'Miss Nellie Smith'.

Eighty years after Craig's motions were published, we can say that contemporary puppet theatre has developed in accord with Craig's suggestions, although it is hard to say that puppeteers were consciously following Craig's ideas. They went their own way, unaware of his writings. It is a coincidence that Craig's imagining of the future has been confirmed by theatre practitioners. This is why I consider Craig to be a prophet. For the puppeteers of our day Craig's plays sound like an old tune, but one which reminds us of the well-known tunes of our youth. His short dramas are appreciated but only as material for analysis within theatre schools – they are hardly ever performed.

There is still research to be done. Marina Siniscalchi did not have access to all the documents relating to *The Drama for Fools* project. As often occurs with the legacy of great artists and writers, the documents aroused the interest of too many people and were dispersed. Today they are in the possession of an American collector.[17] Thanks to the kindness of Mischa Twitchin, I have a list of the unpublished plays from the American collector's section of the *Drama for Fools*. On this list there are interesting titles such as *The Rape of Unicorn, Jupiter and the Sphinx, Uplifted Petticoats*, and *The Gate of Hell*. Also on the list are those plays already published (seven in all), so that all together there are thirty plays. Until now no one has written on the content and structure of these plays and we can look forward to new discoveries concerning Craig's innovations for the future of puppet theatre.

Craig's idea of writing an ironic interpretation of the history of humanity in the marionette style was a great project, such as only occurs once in a thousand years, but he did not live long enough to accomplish the project himself. Even with the available collections we still have only 30 of his projected year-long cycle. There remains a possible total of 335 missing plays. During his lifetime nobody wanted to share his consideration of puppetry as an ironic mirror of humanity. Now, 80 years later, his project may become public property in order to fulfil his testimony.

My dream is to found a '*Drama for Fools* Club'. Any scholar or writer may become a member if he or she writes a short drama in the spirit and style of Edward Gordon Craig. This Club might even offer a special award of 'Fools in Drama' as a mark of recognition for all those who think that the twentieth century was significantly influenced by Craig's ideas and imagination.

First published in *Dialog*, Warsaw 1988, 5. Edited by Mischa Twitchin and Penny Francis 2013.

Notes

1　Craig E.G. *On the Art of the Theatre*, London 1911, 82.
2　Ibid., 82–3.
3　Ibid., 84.
4　Craig E.G., *Über-Marions*, cahier A, p.13a. Coll. E.G.Craig, nr. 272, Bibliothèque Nationale, fonds Arts du Spectacle. Quoted by Didier Plassard, *L'acteur en effigie*, 'Lausanne 1992, 50. Also see Plassard, D. et al. (eds.) *The Drama for Fools/Le Théâtre des Fous* (in English and French), Montpellier 2012.
5　Ibid., 51.
6　Craig E., *Gordon Craig: The Story of his Life*, London 1968, 292.
7　Craig E.G., 'Puppets and poets', *The Chapbook* 1921, Feb.: 18.
8　Craig E.G., 'The marionnette drama: Some notes for an introduction to *The Drama for Fools* by Tom Fool,' *The Marionnette*, Florence 1918, 1. (Tom Fool was one of many pseudonyms of Gordon Craig, used in *The Mask* and in *The Marionnette*.)
9　Craig, Puppets and Poets, op. cit. 13.
10　Ibid., 14.
11　Ibid., 18.
12　Craig, *On the Art of the Theatre*, vii.
13　Ibid.
14　Siniscalchi M.M., 'E.G.Craig: Il dramma per marionette' (The drama for marionettes), *English Miscellany, Theatre Research International*, 5, 2. 1980 122–37.
15　Craig, 'The Marionnette Drama'.
16　Craig E.G., *The Marionnette*, 1918, 2: 38.
17　Since this essay was written, the American collection of the 'motions' has been acquired by the Institut International de la Marionnette in Charleville-Mézières, France, which has published it (see note 4).

10
Among Deities, Priests and Shamans

In this essay, I will focus on the first stage of the ritualistic use of puppets and on their presence in proto-theatre. Although I may look back to some ancient periods of the past, my intention is to write about contemporary puppetry, or at least puppetry from the recent past. I will also avoid any geographical ordering, assuming that humanity is a single whole. The history of puppetry's cultural transformation will be reflected within the 'world of puppets' and its changing functions. This will be a reflection on their specificity, which has become a subject of my interest.

Puppets belong to both ritual and theatre. We can guess that they were born as a visible representation of deities within ritual. Thanks to the work of Charles Magnin[1] we have learnt about rituals from Egypt, Greece and Rome, in which large moveable sculptures (puppets of great size), and later smaller puppets, participated. These were idols – inanimate figurative sculptures – representing a divinity or deified ancestors or their acolytes (for example spirits of the hearth), some fixed on a plinth or other manufactured base (such as we know from Christian churches, providing a stand for altar figures). Probably at some point in their development the necessity arose (perhaps dictated by magic) to make the idols' limbs moveable. African figures offer us proof of this, where some of them, though fixed on their base, have mobile heads and hands.

Egyptian, Greek or Roman puppets were huge statues, like the one of Jupiter-Ammon fixed in a golden gondola, and carried in procession by 24 priests. The head moved to point the route that the procession should follow, until the priests arrived at the place where the deity indicated it would deliver its prophecies. In Christian churches too, sacred, sometimes mobile figures were included in the religious service. The fifteenth-century *mitouries* in Dieppe, for example, became very famous.

These were in fact a mechanical representation of the Virgin Mary's Assumption by human-like figures.

Though ritualistic religious puppets in Europe have been well catalogued by researchers, they almost do not exist in contemporary life, with the exception of the mechanical Nativity, shown at Christmas in many churches. There are more which remain in African and Asian rituals, where they too have their histories.

It is widely assumed that puppets with moveable limbs originated directly from cult figures, such as fetishes, talismans and idols. In the complicated relations between divinities and humans it became necessary, perhaps dictated by sympathetic magic, to make idols' limbs moveable. This looks like a transitional stage from statues to mobile puppets. But in many cultures even unfixed moveable puppets were considered gods, as we can surmise from the evidence of the Spanish monk Sahagún, from the time of the conquest of Mexico:

> then (the conjurer) stood up, moved his sack, shook it and summoned those in the sack … Immediately figures as small as children started to come out. Some of them were disguised as women – it was a very good disguise: as women they wore a skirt and blouse; they were as well disguised as the men; they wore a band, a pelerine and a necklace of precious stones. They danced, sang, and expressed that which is the essence of the heart. When they had accomplished all this, he again shook the sack and they hid and found places inside it. 'The one who makes this happen, that gods appear, move and act' should get his reward.[2]

One might question this description and especially whether the designation of 'gods' corresponded to the indigenous belief in the divinity of puppets as such, or whether it was meant only as a metaphor, which pointed to the divine functions of the puppets. Claude Levi-Strauss has shown that early man understood the symbolic functions of art. He shows that art's early creators and recipients were conscious of the difference between someone 'presenting' and someone 'presented', as proved by the temporary incorporation, in successive rituals, of either ancestors or gods.[3]

The privilege of manufacturing puppets, given equally to men and women in Africa, seems to be from a period when competition between the sexes in some tribes had diminished. It was different at Blazing Island, where Mircea Eliade tells us that the ritual of initiation into maturity among Selknams was an exclusively masculine secret ceremony, for which there were special reasons:

The myth of genesis tells that women, under the leadership of the Woman-Moon, the powerful witch Kra, started to terrorise men, as they had the power to transform themselves into 'spirits', that is, they could manufacture masks and they could use them. But one day, Kra's husband, Kran, the Man-Sun, discovered the secret of women and informed all the other men about it. The men in their madness massacred all the women with the exception of little girls, and since then they have organised secret ceremonies with masks and dramatic rituals intending to terrorise women.[4]

Thus puppets and masks possessed a special magical power, which allowed for domination over distinct groups of people. This was a by-product of the sacred derivation of puppets and there is no interest here in the conflict between the sexes. For me, what is important is that the puppet has its origins in the other world; that is, in the sacred realm, which authorized men to use it in various religious rituals. This is also the right moment to note that the use of the word 'puppet' for the material presentations of divinities in non-European cultures is not exact. They were not considered by native people to be puppets in the European meaning of the word (although, of course, there are exceptions). Especially in Africa, their designations were differentiated and the names of figures responded to their functions in ritual. In general no attention was paid to their function as a substitute figure, which became so important in European theatre. When puppets entered various rituals, the participants (believers) had no sense of what would become their theatrical character in the future.

It seems that among the earliest rituals employing puppets two were the most important: funeral rites, connected with the cult of ancestors, and fertility rites. The first addressed the end of life, the second its beginning. According to the Dutch researcher W.H. Rassers,[5] the cult of ancestors and funeral ritual gave the first impulse for the creation of puppet theatre. Rinnie Tang expressed a similar thought while discussing funeral rituals in China:

> The burial procession of important persons is accompanied by decorated wagons on which musicians play, and by straw dummies wearing masks, which symbolize the keepers of the tomb. Toward the end of the Tchou Dynasty (770–256 B.C.), these dummies were replaced by articulated wooden puppets. The masks worn by the dummies were burned or buried, according to the customs of various regions, whereas the puppets were returned to the people who made them.

Figure 10.1   Sainte Trinite figurines from Ethiopia, 1977. Photograph by David Denis

Specialized craftsmen made these puppets, to be rented especially for funeral ceremonies, and they also managed their manipulation and musical accompaniment. These rich burial processions became true spectacles. Such funerary ceremonies may be considered the origin of the Chinese puppet show, and of the masked dances performed by actors. These manifestations gradually departed from their ritual character to become pagan entertainments.[6]

Jacques Pimpaneau came to the same conclusion in offering several examples of the use of puppets in funeral rituals.[7] It is worth noting that in Africa too the cult of ancestors was considered as giving the first impulse for the creation of a manipulated puppet. We can suppose that among the images of divinities (whether totemic animals or fantastic allegories of forces of nature), the first humanoid model was given by puppets representing dead ancestors. These were recognized as taking care of a tribe, as its 'guardian angels', and as such they might be a stimulus for using human forms in sculpted representations of gods.

Akpan Etuk Vyo discovered puppets in the land of the dead, giving rise to the later use of puppets by the Akpans and other humans, and holding a symbolic meaning as the repetition of sacred acts. Puppets were therefore suitable instruments for worshipping dead ancestors.

The Fangs from Cameroon and Gabon employ puppets in an initiation ritual called *melane*, which symbolizes the first contact of the initiated with the dead ancestors. The climax of the ritual is carefully prepared: the young boys, subjects of the initiation, must stay for some time in seclusion while they meditate, receive instruction, and eat special food. After taking drugs they are taken by night to another hut, where they see a demonstration of rod puppets, which they are supposed to identify as their ancestors. In Gabon the same Fang association used a kind of bust on a rod, with moveable arms, which appeared over a primitive screen made of kerchiefs, for the same purpose. The village dignitaries manipulated them and the ritual helped to contact the dead ancestors, while also fulfilling a purifying function. These 'puppets' are considered as sacred objects; they are placed on cylindrical bark boxes with skulls inside.

On the Ivory Coast, in initiation rituals the young initiates carry *déblé* figures on plinths about 95 cm high. (The *déblé* may probably be identified with the image of death.) They hold the *déblé* and hit the ground with its base. *Déblé* and *déguélé* (similar to *déblé*, but can only be touched by the initiated) are used in funeral processions, accompanied by drums, wooden rattles, trumpets and songs. This ceremony is meant to help a dead person take leave of the living community. Many other tribes and associations use puppets for the same purpose. For example, within the Ibibo tribe of Nigeria, there is a spectacular ritual called *Akan*, which is performed over several nights after the end of a war, to worship their dead.

In some regions Africans employ puppets in funeral ceremonies, giving them – as it seems – a symbolic form. Such was the case in Zaire, in the Bwende tribe, where figurative wooden participants in the funeral receive a stylized form of a musical instrument. The Bwendes also organize a special ritual called *niombo*, which allows the dead to leave the village community peacefully. *Niombo* signifies a coffin in the shape of a large manikin, normally offered to the chief of the tribe.

The preparation of the *niombo* may take place while the tribe's chief is still alive. He himself orders a special craftsman to make an effigy, starting with its head, which should have all the characteristics of the future deceased. In general, the head is made of a red cloth and stuffed with grass and cotton. Its hair is fashioned after the chief's crop of hair. Beard and ears are also similar. Eyes are opened and surrounded with a make-up of black and white lines. Cheeks are rounded and lips display teeth filed according to the local fashion. Sometimes the manikin's lips hold a pipe. Thus prepared, the *niombo* waits for the death of its master. When the tribe's chief dies, his subjects must do many things, such as dry the corpse over a fire, which lasts about six weeks; wrap the corpse in cloth, which is done by women, after the state of the body has been made stable; transform the shapeless lump of cloth by use of needles and scissors into a recognizable manikin, and then cover it with a protective plate.

The huge 'corpse' is covered with tattooing, copying that of the deceased, also with symbolic signs and blue ornaments. The left arm is bent diagonally forward, the right one is raised up and fixed. Thick legs are shaped in a dancing position. The *niombo* is three metres high and four metres wide and is usually made for a single dead body, but sometimes it has two heads and contains two corpses.

The Bwendes take the *niombo* ritual lightly and even make of it a joyful occasion. Some days before the funeral ceremony they start to dance. On the day of the funeral the *niombo*, at first without its head, is placed in front of the funeral house. The women surround it, weeping together with the widow. A band composed of six or seven musicians, mainly drummers moving in a circle, plays. Other people join them clapping rhythmically and making various leaps and occasional obscene gestures. After some hours of dancing, the host offers food for the makers of the *niombo* and for the musicians. Now the *niombo* gets its head attached and is fastened to a special platform. The band continues to play. The children and grandchildren of the dead lift up the *niombo* many times. The women also jump, imitating this movement.

At about four o'clock in the afternoon, the pageant of the *niombo's* farewell begins. The women mourn. A rifle shot is the starting sign to form the procession, in which the whole village participates. The young people lift the platform onto their shoulders. They perform a little comedy, pretending that the *niombo* does not want to go to the grave-yard but wishes to visit all the places that the chief saw often while alive, especially the huts of his loved ones. By accident they also carry him into the courtyard of the Christian mission, but the *niombo* shows its disapproval and finally lets itself be carried to the grave. After a short dialogue about what is the best way to bury the *niombo*, the participants in the ceremony lower it into the grave, shout triumphantly and joyfully, and continue their dances and games.

We cannot say much about the origins of this ritual, although we can see its clear analogy with the mummification of the dead in Egypt. It is possible that the *niombo* is a derivation from Egypt as a folkloric form of rituals appointed for the pharaohs. We find its mutation in Togo, in the *unil* ritual, and in Ghana in a custom called *ga*. The interpretation of these rituals is based on the need to satisfy the deceased before he starts on his journey to another world. Sometimes it takes a naturalistic or even macabre form. Darkowska-Nidzgorsky[8] reports that in this respect some tribes animate the dead person using a special but hidden (and still unknown) means of manipulation. It seems to observers that the dead makes its own way to the grave. The Mitsogo tribe shows its dead moving through fields in full splendour. The Mofu-Gudur tribe in Cameroon is famous for an operation on the bones of the corpses that allows them to manipulate the dead body and suggest life.

We should not be surprised by these customs in Africa. Not so long ago similar customs were known in Europe too. The fishermen of the Catalonian village of Leucate were famous for their attachment to play-ing cards. When one of them died, his fellows organized a last card game for him. Someone took the place of the corpse in its bed and the other companions carried the corpse to the inn, where they propped it up at the table and manipulated its hands as if it were playing cards. The contemporary puppet player would call this endeavour of animating the dead body an 'exterior manipulation'. We know of a similar custom of animating a corpse from the Ukraine, although in a different situa-tion. Due to a clever mechanization of the dead body with the use of strings, the family gathers around the deceased for the night vigil and is suddenly surprised by movements in its legs, arms and hands. This is considered to be a sign of sympathy with, and a final farewell to, the living.[9]

It is worth noting that similar customs were the basis of more developed rituals (considering their theatrical aspects), as, for example, in Iran, which might be a surprise given the Islamic interdiction on figural presentations of God and persons. However, the acceptance of some elements from pre-Islamic culture, even if dealing with the faith of the Prophet, is a typical exception. Here I have in mind the Tazîe mystery procession that commemorates the death of Hussein, the grandson of Muhammad.

In the course of a fight for power in the state (caliphate) left by Muhammad, the Shi'ite insurrection, led by his grandson Hussein, was defeated and the leaders killed in battle by the army of the usurper Yazid. The most brave and dramatic figure was Abbas who fought fiercely, defending his brother Hussein. When his enemies cut off his right hand, he took his sword in his left hand; when they did the same to the left one, he took his sword in his mouth, fighting until the moment of being killed.

When Islam conquered Iran in the sixteenth century, the mourning over Hussein's death became one of the most popular religious customs. After the story's recitation by a dervish, the procession of mourners began to include some theatrical elements with puppets. As the mystery was not allowed to be observed by non-believers, the first descriptions originate only from the nineteenth century. According to the theatre historian Medzhid Rezvani:

> On the tenth day of the month of Mokharrem people carried the martyrs of Kerbela (the site of the battle) on handbarrows. These are manikins made of straw, covered with red stains and riddled with kindzhals (daggers) ... On the big barrows or mobile platforms ... they perform entire scenes ...[10]

This description brings to mind parallels with other ancient mysteries such as the Passion of Dionysus or the Christian Mystery Plays from the Middle Ages. In some cases manikins were replaced by puppets, as has been proved by D.I. Longo, a Russian travelling circus artist, who secretly bought three puppets after having seen them in a Mystery Play at the beginning of the twentieth century. They can now be seen, albeit without legs and arms, in the Puppet Museum of the Central Puppet Theatre in Moscow.[11]

Information from Africa, from Dahomey and Nigeria, offers new aspects of the cult of the dead. In its funeral ceremonies the *Gelede* association in the Yoruba tribe uses puppets on bases, with limbs manipulated by strings. Puppet-players hold the base with one hand and manipulate the puppets with the other, performing an erotic dance, which ends with the display of the puppets' sexual organs, after which they have 'intercourse'.

Another example is the *Nevimbur* initiation ritual from the New Hebrides, observed at the beginning of the twentieth century, which was fully dramatized. It took place in the square in front of the house reserved for men, which was surrounded by a palisade, allowing women and children to see only the part that happened in front of the palisade. *Nevimbur* was divided into two parts performed within a few weeks of each other. The main figures (Mansip, his wives and his enemies) were lifesize manikins surrounded by more or less elaborated puppets (made of bamboo, leaves and cloth). In the first part, four puppets were destroyed by an elder, to allow the birth of the new spirits. In the second part, the Mansip figure was destroyed and all the other manikins burnt. Scholars explain the meaning of *Nevimbur* by referring to the myth of Ambat (Butwanabaghap or Kabat), the ancestor and creator-god of the tribe.[12]

This mixture of funeral ceremony with the sexual act resulted naturally from beliefs in the union of death and life. In many countries the initiation of youth into adult life (and thus sexual life also) includes an experience of initiation through symbolic death. One must die to be reborn.[13] Very often the state of being dead is expressed by the 'puppetized' movements of initiates:

> In the initiation ritual, young people often take on a mortal appearance or more exactly an appearance of those who have been brought back to life. After staying in some secret place, where they were considered dead, they are reborn. This birth finds its essential meaning in the final ceremonial acts, when the initiates are brought to life and allowed to rejoin the living. Initiates from the Kissi tribe in the Guinea forests, as well as in other African societies, have whitened bodies like phantoms and they move as automata or puppets. Their steps, their smallest gestures are mechanised and completely submitted to the rhythm of a drum, beaten by the master of ceremonies. In spite of the importance of the ceremony, there is also a place for satire and buffoonery, and even a sudden display of hostility: the 'puppets' abandon their environment and make threatening approaches to the spectators, who step back ...[14]

We can suppose that this twofold rite of passage, linking death with birth, gradually split into two separate rituals. If the rite of passage had, principally, a symbolic character, fertility rites were aimed at real effects, vital for assuring the whole tribe of its future existence. Probably for this reason we see in these rites elements of sympathetic (analogic) magic, through which human beings propitiated nature and supernatural powers, to grant the richest harvests possible. By its very nature, the ritual of fertility lets its participants see two aspects of the sexual act – the sacred and the instrumental:

> Often, especially in Africa and Oceania, the young initiates after circumcision enjoy great sexual license. However, we should not see this as debauchery, because the situation has nothing in common with sexual freedom in its contemporary, desacralised meaning. As with all the other biological functions, so sexuality in early societies is marked by sanctity. It is a means of participation in the fundamental mystery of life and of fecundity.[15]

A majority of early tribes were convinced that the copulation of people had an influence on the rate of growth of crops. The Pipiles from Central America appointed a special couple to accomplish the sexual act at the moment that the first seed was thrown in the soil, to be understood as an example of a 'sacred marriage'.[16] Puppets in Africa often participated in rituals of fecundity. Some of these were large-scale, long-lasting ceremonies. *Gelede* puppets from the Yoruba tribe took part in fertility rites, worshipping the Sapata divinity, which took place at the time of the first sowing. The ceremony consisted of several dances during which the initiated could have sex and some young men even acted out sexual intercourse with the earth.

Normally puppet-players demonstrated the sexual act in its most simple version. Fixed to the big toes of the seated manipulators, two puppets, suspended on one horizontal string, danced and were conjoined through their large sexual organs. Such puppets were very popular in Cameroon, Gabon, Congo and many other countries. They were made from various materials, mainly wood and raffia, with a special accent on sex and its pilosity [hairiness]. Nowadays these puppets have lost their sacred functions and are given to youngsters, who take them simply as piquant toys. We also find traces of this forgotten sacred sexuality in Brazil, where the former African slaves have developed their own industry of figural toys presenting sexual intercourse; for instance, in the form of a pistol which shows two people making love when the trigger is pulled.

Sexual motifs appeared in many rituals, not necessarily connected with the cult of fertility. Hausa puppet-players from Nigeria place several puppets with huge, erect phalluses around a square shadow screen, standing like guards of the show to be performed, or indicating the boundaries of a sacred territory. The show itself is composed of scenes of manners, including copulation, but this has no connection with the vigilant figures around the screen. These guards, whose main weapon is their phallus, remind us of the use of sex in the shadow theatre in Karnataka, India, as reported by B. Tapper, who researched the function of the Fool in Indian theatre:

> One of the most important functions served by the south Indian guards for the shadow players is the deflection of the evil eye. They not infrequently have exaggerated genitals. This enhances their ability to attract attention and thereby lure away harmful glances from elsewhere. Bangarakka the female comic also serves to protect the shadow players, by absorbing the harmful glances of the audience and thus harmlessly deflecting the misfortune caused by the evil eye.[17]

Independently of these sacred or protective functions, we can assume that the spectators of these shows experienced much erotic excitement in the demonstration of the sexual games. This was thought a good reason to preserve these, as part of a ritualistic and spectacular repertory, despite the protests of all kinds of moralist.

There are also fertility rituals in which the sexual elements have been forgotten, probably initiated at a later period, when any explication of life-giving energy became much more complicated. The Anand tribe, in Nigeria, focuses the attention of spectators on a huge figure (manipulated from inside) called Mother-eka, in water. She appears among audiences in the grip of a python and presents the dance of life, representing feminine reproductive energy. The presence of the serpent might remind us of the scene of temptation in Paradise. However, if the Bible considers the serpent to be a symbol of the Devil-Tempter, the source of original sin, the folkloric mythologies, practising 'natural' religions, consider the serpent to be a symbol of life and encourage their believers to solicit its goodwill.

The same motif of the serpent was found in the Congo in the Djo initiation ceremony of the Koyo tribe. The participants of the ritual saw the serpent as the creator Elongo, five to six metres high, with its head covered with raffia and hen's feathers, on a long rod. The puppets, *ifya* (also on rods), surrounded him and danced with him. This ritual is almost forgotten, although some traces may be found in the popular puppet dance *kyebe-kyebe*.

Serpents represent the energy of nature and life among the Hopi American Indians of Arizona, in a ritual called *Palölöqangw*, which is performed in the presence of *kachina* dancers. From a big screen (a kind of booth) in the centre of the ritual space emerge the heads of serpents, which receive offerings from the worshippers:

> One of the tableaux introduced was a cotton cloth [screen], upon which were depicted in bright colours seven blazing suns, through which issued seven serpents wriggling over miniature fields of growing corn.
>
> Then came two images of young virgins, bowing to each other and lifting their hands to and from their heads. Finally, a living maiden came out from behind the screen and presented to one of the dignitaries in charge of the ceremony a basket-platter of their sacred corn-meal. The snakes were made of small hoops covered with skins, and were moved in a life-like way by medicine men stationed behind the canvas.[18]

The Hopis also use puppets for more pragmatic purposes, with miniature *kachina* figures. There are more than 40 of these which help these Indians in their troubles. The story goes that each of them can be useful in a specific situation and a full set of miniature *kachinas* may manage every human problem. In Africa there are also local magicians who possess numerous figures of magic energy, allowing the solution of all kinds of everyday troubles. Among these are a detector of thieves, a discoverer of lost money, a night watchman, the agent of a cast spell and many others.

Another group of figurines and puppets serve the medicine men and the fortune tellers. The use of puppets in cures was widespread in many countries, especially in Mexico and other parts of North America. The best-known examples are of the medicine men from the Iroquois tribe, who demonstrate the power of their drugs through a small puppet show. The medicine man arranges things so that at first a puppet representing a dead squirrel seems to regain its life force after the application of certain herbs, which serve as a recommendation for his powers. This testimony from the seventeenth century was one of the first examples of many cases where a shaman or a medicine man has used puppets for curing people.[19] One may find many such cases in Africa. In Gabon, puppets help a medicine man to claim that his diagnosis has magic origins, saying that it is the puppet which sees, diagnoses, and prescribes the medicine: 'Bwiti points at ... so I see ... Bitwie says ... so I know ...'

In Africa there are relatively large numbers of divining puppets; that is, puppets which predict the future or ones which solve the topical problems of individuals. In the Pende tribe, in Zaire, the divining puppet – *galukoshi* – which is placed by the knees of the secret-teller, gives signs with its head when the name of a guilty person, a thief or other criminal, is mentioned. On the Ivory Coast, members of the feminine soothsaying association Sandogo carry their puppets on their heads. When necessary they lay them on the ground, dance around them and pronounce their verdict. In the Upper Volta another association used the *kafiguélédio* puppets. They have no face and their entire body is covered with traces of sacred blood. They were probably used to cast spells.

Soothsayers from the Upper Volta present their divination sessions as an unusual show. Using hematite or caolit, a square is demarcated, which is divided into four sections, and then a circle is drawn, linked to the square by the sinusoid lines. In the centre of this design, the soothsayer places a bottle made of bull hide, containing *kauri* shells, and an iron bell. Having done this, the 'teller of the hidden facts and things' ties a string to his big toes, from which are suspended two wooden figures on wheels, eight centimetres high. These figures are placed near the intersecting lines in the middle of the square. Once the stage is prepared and the first customer appears, the operator (the 'teller') rings the bell summoning one after another all the tellers of hidden truth, both living and dead, as well as his own ancestors – including the Python, Hyena, Earth, Sky God, Owl, Caiman, Hippopotamus, River, the fish Tetrodon, the sacred hill Koumbou, the hills Nawo and Sangoe, the hill Tiolo, the sacred pool and sacred tree from Oussourou.

Next he turns to the two wooden figures, representing the man Sié and the woman Yeli, and exhorts and admonishes them to be obedient, to avoid laughing and to perform their task. Then he throws two shells on the ground, summoning his father and requesting protection against the possible bad influence of the divination session to be undertaken. At this point the shells should lie in the appropriate position. If this does not happen the soothsayer starts his summoning once again. Next he turns to the puppets, asking them about the nature of an issue. Normally the customer does not ask questions and does not reveal the aim of his visit. This purpose should be discovered by the soothsayer with the aid of the wooden puppets. It is generally assumed that, under the influence of gods and other protectors summoned at the beginning of the session, the puppets move on the string, greet each other, bow to each other and fall on the ground. It is believed that there is a special god who allows for the interpretation of their movements. The sooth-sayer watches the whole show. Now and then he throws shells on the ground, which is his way of controlling the puppets' response. When the session ends, the customer appears satisfied and pays the agreed fee as if he has understood the puppets' response.[20]

Where these Africans believe in the magic power of their puppets, they do not think of it as a negative force in the way that the ancient Chinese did. The Chinese believed that puppets with open eyes are vulnerable to the evil influence of demons, which might even enter into and inhabit them. Numerous stories told of the independent life of possessed puppets, especially during the night. For this reason a puppet player should protect his puppets, keeping them in a special box, protected by charms, and should also cover the puppets' eyes by a cloth with magic incantations written on it. The Tao priests were experts in the composition of such charms and the puppet players cooperated with them. As they dealt with magic objects and puppets, puppeteers were considered dangerous, making the ancient Chinese suspicious of them. On the other hand, people needed their help in situations involv-ing the evil influence of malicious demons, especially if installed in their houses. So they invited and engaged puppeteers, because they were thought capable of dealing with this kind of situation.[21]

In spite of the continued presence of ritual puppets and their use in magical activities in Africa, the process of transition from the primary, sacred puppets to theatrical puppets, intended to entertain participants in village festivities, has been long underway. These 'entertaining' productions do not necessarily have a unified, fictional dramatic struc-ture. They are compositions of many episodes, presenting topical scenes, animals and also such mythical figures as Une Meven with a caiman head, the water god Fanro, or a divinity like Yankadi with its double face and four breasts. Despite the presence of these mythical characters, such shows seem to be exclusively for entertainment. We may surmise that this is an example of the transition stage from ritual to theatrical puppets, with their cognitive and amusement functions. This process has been accelerated due to the numerous contacts of African puppeteers with the European theatre. In many cases Africans puppeteers themselves classify ritual puppets as belonging to folk culture and endeavour to make their puppets comparable to interna-

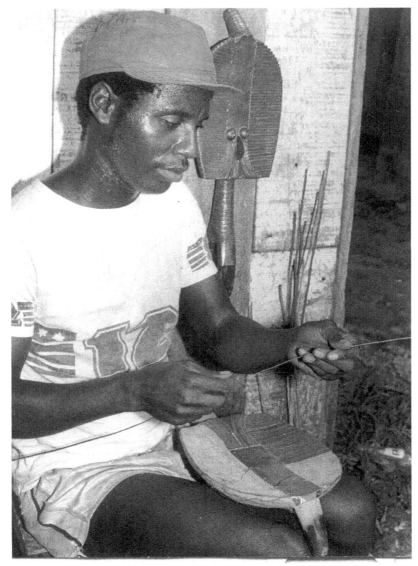

Figure 10.2 The sculptor Victor Bazibadi sculpting an ancestor figure, Lilieville, 1977. Photograph by Denis Nidzgorski

Figure 10.3   Folk group with Musicians and Hand Puppets from Uzbeckistan, 1928

tional models. Rightly or wrongly, they are cutting themselves off from their roots and the chance to create their own theatre, based on an enduring culture of magic.

In general, Asian puppet shows present well-developed stories. It seems that they broke their links with ritual structures many centuries ago, creating such performing genres as the Indian shadow theatre, Indonesian and Malay *wayang* theatre, Japanese *ningyo joruri*, sometimes called *bunraku*, and the puppet opera in China. However, when we analyse the functions of most of these theatres we see that they remain in the arena of the *sacrum*. A typical feature of most of these theatres is its narrative character, which is distinct from the Aristotelian dramatic structure. In many of these theatres there are visible narrators, such as the *tayu* in Bunraku, the *pulavar* in the Kerala shadow theatre, the *dalang* in *wayang purwa*, *wayang kulit* or *golek*. Among these theatres only Bunraku distinguishes itself by the profane subjects of its repertory, although the preparation of the performances includes many ritualistic elements. The other theatres mentioned here not only continue with sacred themes in their shows, but they also fulfil sacred functions in society. Many of them remain within the domain of Hindu culture, presenting on a stage or a screen subjects drawn from the two famous Sanskrit epics, the *Mahabharata* and the *Ramayana*.

How, then, to distinguish ritual from theatre? In other words, is it correct even to call these Asian theatres (especially the shadow theatres) 'theatre'? Richard Schechner proposed the following differentiation of ritual and theatrical elements (Table 10.1), according to his idea of opposing efficacy [usefulness] to entertainment.[22]

Table 10.1   Differentiation of ritual and theatrical elements.

Efficacy	*Entertainment*
(the ritual)	(the drama)
results	fun
link to the absent Other	only for those present
abolishes time, symbolic time	emphasizes 'now'
brings Other here	audience is the Other
performer possessed, in trance	performer knows what he's doing
audience participates	audience watches
audience believes	audience appreciates
criticism is forbidden	criticism is encouraged
collective creativity	individual creativity

The application of this model to Asian performances may help to clarify many of our doubts. However, we must remember that between pure ritual and pure theatrical phenomena there also exist hybrids, which are difficult to classify but are much more common in real life.

Many shadow performances in India are shown on the occasion of a festival held to worship a particular divinity (in Indonesia similar customs concern the rice deity, Sri Devi), or are used for more pragmatic reasons such as provoking rain, staving off an epidemic and so on. In Indonesia, the *wayang* performances accompany human beings in all important moments of their lives, starting at the seventh month of pregnancy, continuing at the birth of a child and the severing of the umbilical cord, on occasions when important social and official recognitions are received (where, similarly, in China a short play called *Reconciliation* is performed) and at marriages and funerals. Some performances also help to exorcise evil spirits or to avert a dangerous disease. There are some national differences between Indonesian and Chinese practices in their dealings with demons. Indonesians use *wayang* to exorcise a man possessed by an evil spirit, while the Chinese use puppet theatre to purify buildings (private houses, offices, cinemas). Certainly, Chinese demons need some material basis (such as a house) in order to torment people, whereas Indonesian demons can attack people directly within the psychic realm.

The Indonesian tradition gives priority to themes from the *Mahabharata* and *Ramayana*, where the show is meant to assure some benefit to individuals or families. There is a general conviction that at the seventh month of pregnancy it is good to perform the birth of Arjuna, and that on the occasion of a marriage it is positive to show the wedding of a rajah. In other situations, especially in cases of exorcism or avoidance of dangerous diseases, different special subjects would be chosen for performance.

Closest to ritual are performances shown in India during the temple festivities in honour of the goddess Bhagavati, where non-transparent shadow puppets are used, with a restricted repertoire of movement. Normally these are presented near the temple in a dedicated space called *Kuttu Madam* (unless ordered by a private sponsor). The show is run by a *pulavar*, who is an expert in old scriptures and poems (*vedas, puranas*) and who has his own short version of the *Ramayana*, which is known as *Kamba-Ramayana*. The *pulavar* is a kind of priest, delivering prophecies. His assistants say prayers to the goddess before the show and convey her blessings upon it.

The tradition of these performances derives from the following legend about Hanuman, king of the monkeys. Hurrying to Lanka to help Rama in his struggle with the demon Ravana, he liberated Mahamaya from a spell. She wanted to join Hanuman, to witness the final encounter with Ravana; however, the goddess Parashakti summoned her to help in her fight with the demon Daruka. In the first instance, Mahamaya rejected this summons, but then Parashakti repeated her request and promised to make Mahamaya a goddess, with the name of Bhagawati, at the same time assuring her that every year she would be able to see the events she was now missing (the battle of Rama and Ravana) in special performances. Thus the shadow shows presented near the temple of Bhagavati are a recompense for the goddess who helped Parashakti in her fight with the demon Daruka. This is then a votive performance, with the difference that it is not a gift of the worshippers but a privilege given by another goddess. In any case, we remain in the domain of the sacred. Similar performances take place in other temples.[23]

In Indonesia, as well as in many other countries dependent on a rice culture, the mythology of rice and the rituals associated with it are important. In these countries rice is treated as a living being, as a person or, more exactly, an animal. This is not so surprising if we recall the customs of totemic, hunter societies, which owed their food to the hunted animal. After each successful hunt, people organized special ceremonies in order to appease the spirit of the killed animal, the provider of the food. Where the provider is rice, its animalization or anthropomorphization is not then surprising.

Shadow performances (in general *wayang purwa*) supplemented the rice rituals on traditional occasions, such as the purification of a village before the coming sowing of the rice crop, or to evoke rain, or for the harvest and so on. These are opportunities to perform the play *Sri Machapunggung*, which tells of the adventures of Sri Devi, the goddess of rice, and her wish to avoid an unwanted marriage. In the repertory, there was also the play *Mengukuchon*, which presented evidence of the divine origins of rice.

The *dalang*, a priest, an expert on the old texts which he recites, the sole manipulator of the puppets and also the conductor of a group of musicians (the *gamelan*), is responsible for the preparation of the show. He invites participants to make a presentation of gifts for the dead ancestors, to whom he prays for their approval for the performance. The place where it is to be held is filled with incense and he demonstrates his respect to the shadow figure called *gunungan*, a symbol of the cosmic tree of the world. The *dalang* is the guarantor of the religious character of the whole show and his priestly functions cover not only those offered to the rice goddess but all of his performances.

The show with the greatest religious power and, as some would say, with the strongest magic energy is *wayang ruwatan*. This is performed to avert the bad effects of such negative events as overturning the rice kettle on the fire, or overturning the *dalang*'s screen. It also helps a family disappointed at having only a small number of children, or when a man possessed by a spirit becomes a taboo and needs spiritual help. European and American researchers have given a great deal of attention to the exorcist functions of *ruwatan*. Generally, for this occasion, the *dalang* performs the play called *Murwakala* (The Birth of Kala):

> In this story the gods descend to the earth to perform in a wayang (shadow theatre) play in order to halt the murderous assault of the ogre-god Kala (son of the high god Siwa) who is symbolically pursuing the child or adult being exorcised. The represented victim hides in one of the instruments being used in the play within the ruwatan show and, as the puppeteer reads the powerful mantra, Kala is appeased, the victim is exorcised, and order returns for a time to the world.[24]

The *ruwatan* performances normally take place during the day, starting at 10 a.m. and ending at 4 p.m. The audience generally sits to either side of the *dalang*, thus watching the puppets and not their shadows. The performance gathers such magic force that only the experienced *dalang* (whose father is already dead) may sustain it. The show is understandable only to the initiated because gods appear onstage in the guise of traditional heroes and elements drawn from life are woven into it. In fact, a 'theatre within the theatre' is created which develops on many levels:

> It is when the gods descend to the earth to take part in the wayang performance in the *Murwakala* play that the ruwatan becomes texturally rich and dense. The gods must disguise themselves and take on the forms of other characters, *malihan* in Javanese. Visnu, a high god, becomes the puppeteer but takes on the form of Arjuna, the noble warrior; Brama, another god, becomes the gender player and takes the form of Arjuna's wife Sumbadra; and Narada, a funny misshapen god, takes the form of Semar, clown servant to the hero Arjuna and older brother of the high god Siwa, and becomes the *pendendang*, or

drummer. In this way, two wayang performances intersect – the one that is being held and the play within the performance.

Because the performance I am describing was an offering to the ancestors as well as an attempt to address the problems of the family holding the ritual, the ancestors appeared in the story. Coincidentally, this particular family happened to be a family of puppeteers and musicians. After the ancestors had been on the screen for a while, fiercely pursued by Kala, the present living family members, who were holding the performances, appeared as puppets on the screen.[25]

It was even more complicated than this, but I think that the quoted material is sufficient to make us understand the possibility of multiple levels of fiction and life in the *wayang* performance. Of course, in this case, as in many others, Kala was subjugated and the family problems given a positive outcome.

Dealing with demons in China has also been complicated, but the Chinese developed another treatment. The story goes back to the structure of ancient Chinese society. Since the time of Confucius the social group of food producers, thus the peasants, was the most respected. In winter the peasants gave their free time to manual and craft work, considered a good change from a year of farming work, and also a recreation. If somebody from the group of farmers gave all his time to craftsmanship, he was treated as a parasite, which explains the repugnance of farmers to craftsmen, with a special aversion towards the builders of houses. The latter were considered renegades, committing the terrible sin of applying magic in their work. The builders adopted this 'game' and themselves enclosed their profession with many secrets. Therefore the general belief grew up that a builder might insert into a house he was constructing a hidden, magic formula, which would influence the life of the house's inhabitants and encourage the presence of demons.

This has led to the practice of purifying new houses, a task only to be done by the puppet-players and their magic puppet shows. It is true that they were as much disdained for their 'parasitic' life as were the builders; nevertheless, since the most remote times puppeteers have been engaged to play in haunted houses. Normally they performed a play named *Zhao Xuantan Tames the Tiger* in the empty house, only to be seen by the invisible demon. The play was thought so frightening that the demon would leave the house voluntarily and for ever. The puppet-players were paid a double fee for such a horrifying performance, full of magic force.

First the Tiger enters an empty stage, where pieces of raw pork are fixed. The Tiger finds the meat and starts to devour it. Zhao Xuantan then enters, leaping onto the little table in the centre of the stage. He looks at the Tiger eating the meat and makes another very dangerous leap onto the back of the Tiger, as if riding a horse. He puts a curb into its snout or a red string around his neck and, still astride it, easily leads it off the stage. Normally the player throws away the rest of the pork, but if dogs do not want to eat it or, as happened many times, the grass under the meat changes colour, it is a sign of approaching misfortune.[26]

A show of greater power was necessary in the case of the exorcism of a temple or a new theatre. Normally this would be the play *The King of Phantoms Takes Away the Bad Influence*. The invited puppeteers construct in the interior of the building an altar for the worship of the god Huangang, the patron of theatre arts in the province of Guangdong. They put on the altar a wooden bucket full of rice, adding on top a mirror, scissors and string. On the side of the box is a sheet of paper where is written the year, month and day with the hour of birth of each puppet-player and a prayer for the help of the god in their coming fight with the evil spirit. There were also many other useful and symbolic instruments which the puppeteers used in their magic activity, and when this was ended they performed the play about the 'King of phantoms' who in the course of the performance transforms into Guanyin, the goddess of charity. After the space has been purified, the audience was invited to see another show named *Guan Gong Surrounded by Daughters-in-Law*.

Puppetry from the Guangdong area strongly influenced the ritual practice in Taiwan, where it has survived uninterrupted till today. The usual aim of the Taiwan ritual is to gain the blessing of the Jade Emperor or other divinities bestowed on the community or the family. The puppeteers use string puppets 60 cm tall and moved by 14 strings attached to a wooden control, with a handle and a hook to hang up the puppet behind the performance area. The company is composed of 18 puppets, 66 heads, 1 puppet player and 2 musicians. The puppet participation is only a small part of the bigger ritual, which is run by the Taoist priest. In the nineteenth century puppets were also used in funeral rituals and for exorcism, but recently puppeteers have limited themselves to participation in the marriage ceremony.

Normally the performing area is arranged in front of the bridegroom's house, since it is the bridegroom's father and his family who have invited the ceremony. Only the members of the bridegroom's family are present and the reason is clear – because the main purpose of the ritual is to assure the prolongation of the family through the male line. In front of the performance area there are paper altars consecrated to the family gods or ancestors; in the same place the actual family is seated in the role of participants and spectators. On their right is a bamboo pole struck horizontally through the top rung of the ladder. On the pole the puppeteer hangs his puppets in a particular order. The central place is given to the puppet Chief Marshall Tiandu.

As is often stressed by the puppeteers, there is a significant similarity between Marshall Tiandu and another figure known as Zhong Kui. The latter was famous for his performances in funeral and exorcism rituals, thought much more dangerous than the marital ritual. Marshall Tiandu became a crucial figure in this more peaceful wedding ritual due to his capacity to communicate with the Jade Emperor, one of the important gods. Legend explains his capacities as follows:

> Tiandu came into contact with the Tang court because the empress was ill and he was said to be able to cure her. In one case, he cured her with his medical skills, and in another case the empress was so amused by his comic performance that she was cured after bursting out laughing … This version would explain the good relationship between the Jade Emperor and Tiandu Yuanshuai.[27]

Tiandu belongs to the category of the *chou*, the characters who play the clowns in Chinese opera. As a small boy Tiandu was always joking and dancing; what is more he was very ugly, even as an adult, and was thus included in this category. This is not a surprise: clowns or comical characters were believed to be effective intermediaries between people and gods, as is well known in the Southeast Asian region.

Returning to the wedding ritual and the participation of puppets, it is reported that at a sign given by the Taoist priest the puppeteer starts to manipulate the puppet of Tiandu, which, in kneeling and prostrating itself, emphasizes the importance of prayer. Next the puppeteer performs a short part of the story of Xue Rengui, a loyal general of the Tang dynasty. A conversation between Xue and emperor Li Shimin is accompanied by arias, and at the end of the scene Xue prostrates himself before the emperor. The next scene is called 'Reunion' and illustrates marital happiness. Then Marshall Tiandu re-appears and the puppeteer whispers prayers to the Lord of the Three Realms and the Lord of the Dippers asking for their blessing on the family. This is where the brief participation of the puppeteers ends, although they could be engaged for further purely ritualistic acts, without puppets, up to the end of the ceremony.

All the performances included here took place on sacred territory: they served to contact divinities and were intended to obtain a definite result. Considering the differentiation between ritual and theatre mentioned above, it is difficult to classify these performances either as entertainment or as theatre. In addition, we cannot prove that the players were possessed, or in some kind of trance or ecstasy, or that these performances were produced as a collective work: we are witnessing a phenomenon in its transitory stage – between ritual and theatre. Ritual serves to recall the story and deeds of the gods. In some cases the function of worship is completed or replaced by the supplicatory function, such as requests to avert a danger menacing the whole society, or a request for help to one of its members (diseased or possessed by evil spirits). The presence of these supplicatory functions suggests the influence of another ancient tradition and religious practice, namely shamanism. It is tempting to examine this possibility if we bear in mind the fact that in most Asian performances, as in shamanist sessions, we have only one coryphaeus, one sage, who decides on the impressions of the show's participants. The matter is complicated, as observed by Levi-Strauss:

[The Shaman] before starting the drama has two kinds of data. On one side his own conviction that the psychological state to be reached has a definite reason; on the other there is his own system of interpretation and his own invention which fulfils an important role and which sorts out the different stages of pain, from diagnosis to cure. The transformation of reality into fairy tale, which in fact remains unknown, can be realised due to three kinds of experience: first, the experience of the shaman himself, who, if he is a vocational shaman (and if not, then as a result of his practice), experiences some psychosomatic states; second, the experience of the invalid, who either feels some relief or not; third, the experience of the spectators, who participate in the process of the cure, feeling by the way some enslavement and some intellectual and emotional satisfaction, which is the basis of the collective accord, regarding the validity of the cure and leading to its next stage.[28]

The essence of the shamanist operations consists of the following stages:

- The summons of a shaman in a situation of collective or individual misfortune.

- The summons by the approaching shaman of the helping spirits – setting off on the journey to meet these deities, who support the fight against the antagonists of the victim and who allow the primary negative state to be averted.
- The shaman's return from the journey, the transmission of the spiritual values and prophecies he has collected and the liberation of the helping spirits.

In terms of theatrical categories we are dealing with a solo theatre performer, who often includes narration as well as dance and states of ecstasy.

Herein lies the essential difference between the ritual and the shamanist session. The first (ritual) gradually retires from the function of coryphaeus and replaces it with seemingly autonomous scenic characters; the second (shamanist) preserves the function of the coryphaeus and entrusts to him the new function of the solo actor and narrator. From this we can easily recognize the ancient shaman in the new narrators of the Asian theatres, such as the *dalang* and the *pulavar*. They are intermediaries between audience and deity. They undertake actions intended to help people coming to them with their life and spiritual problems. They are possessed by the text of the sacred scripts and they act within a tradition which should be respected and followed. The structural and functional differences between the ritual and the shamanist session may be seen easily if we use the diagram of A.J. Greimas, normally applied to the analysis of various stories. Let us first recall our starting point (Figure 10.4).[29]

Figure 10.4   Diagram by A. J. Greimas

An appropriate interpretation of the ritual and the shamanist session might be presented as in Figure 10.5.

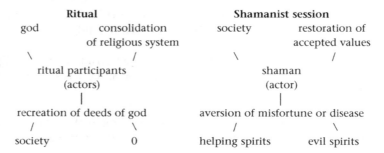

Figure 10.5   Comparative diagram of the ritual and shamanistic session

The structural differences, which had some importance in the development of theatre (either from ritual or from shamanism), are quite clear and convincing. The ritual structure responds to the religious beliefs of each human society and for this reason it will change according to changes in the religious faith. The shaman session's structure resulted from the relations within human society. The shaman is society's representative in relation to the gods. Here lies the importance of the shaman and the solidity of his position. The participants of ritual have been transformed into theatre actors, the servants of various characters and various stories. The shaman, even while changing his function (priest-medicine man, actor, reciter, psychoanalyst), has preserved his complete independence from a story, which only serves him for his narration. He uses it as his own weapon in order to achieve his religious (magic) and profane aims.

Due to this structural difference ritual gave birth to the dramatic spectacle in the Aristotelian form, while the shamanist session gave the impulse for shows directed by the narrator. Naturally, this conclusion proposes only a certain orientation in theatre research, which needs to be confirmed by further studies.

In spite of the specific structure and character of theatre forms, their characteristic features depend on the rich context of many different cultural impulses. Many of these are intertwined, especially nowadays as we observe the linking of dramatic and narrative elements in a new unity, against which nobody protests, at least for the insignificant reason of a defence of 'generic purity'. For this reason *wayang*, in spite of its ritualistic or shamanist essence, retains for many the status of 'theatre'.

The presence of dramatic and epic elements in contemporary puppet theatre means that the dynamic character and the mutual relationship between drama and narrative structures change constantly. We see it distinctly in countries whose tradition is strongly rooted in sacred culture and where new puppet players are promoting the development of a modern and profane puppet theatre. On the other hand, in countries rich in modern puppetry there are artists trying to re-discover ritual, to find within it some new inspiration for their art. This is, however, a separate subject. Let us end by saying that the history of ritual seems to be similar to the history of myth. Human society has preserved the energy to create new, contemporary myths, and we can say the same of rituals. Ritual as a method to evoke and to realize myth has been renewing itself constantly, adopting new forms according to new conditions of life.

First published in '*Konteksty*', 1998, no ", 35–45. Edited by Penny Francis and Mischa Twitchin 2013.

Notes

1   Magnin Charles, *Histoire de Marionnettes en Europe depuis l'Antiquité jusqu'à nos jours* (History of puppets in Europe from the time of Antiquity to our days), Paris 1852.
2   Sten Maria, *Teatr – którego nie było* (The theatre, which did not exist), Kraków 1982, 22.
3   Lévi-Strauss Claude, *Anthropologie structurale (Structural anthology)*, Paris 1958.
4   Eliade Mircea, *Inicjacja. Obrzędy. Stowarzyszenia tajemne. Narodziny mistyczne* (Initiation. Rituals. Secret associations. Mystic birth), Kraków 1997, 50.
5   Rassers W.H., *Pandji, the Cultural Hero*, The Hague 1959.
6   Tang Rinnie, 'From the funeral mask to the painted face of the Chinese theatre', *The Drama Review*, 1982, T96: 59–60.
7   Pimpaneau Jacques, *Des Poupées à l'Ombre: Le théâtre d'ombres et de poupées en Chine* (From dolls to shadows: The shadow theatre and dolls in China), Paris 1977, 9.
8   Darkowska-Nidzgorski Olenka, 'Le chant de l'oiseau: Théâtre de marionnettes racines africaines' (Birdsong: Puppet theatre with African roots), Paris 1997 (typescript).
9   Badiou Maryse, *L'ombra i la marioneta o les figures dels deus* (Shadows and puppet or figures of the gods), Barcelona 1988, 21.
10 Resvani Medzhid, *Le Théâtre et la Danse en Iran*, Paris 1962, 92.
11 Solomonik Inna, *Traditsionniy Teatr Kukol Vostoka* (Traditional puppet theatre of the east), Moscow 1992, 223.

12   Girard Françoise, 'Un théâtre de marionnettes aux Nouvelles-Hébrides: Son importance religieuse' (Journal of ethnology and its neighbouring science), *Zeitschrift für Ethnologie und ihre Nachbarwissenschaften*, Stuttgart 1957, 11.

13   Eliade, op. cit., 30, 52, 78.

14   Schaeffner André, 'Rituel et préthéâtre', in *Histoires des spectacles*, Paris 1966, 51–2.

15   Eliade, op. cit., 45.

16   Kirby E.T., 'Ritual sex: Anarchic and absolute', *The Drama Review*, 1981, T89: 4.

17   Helstien Mel, 'Killekyatha i Bangarakka', *Teatr Lalek*, 1988, 10: 21–2, after B.E. Tapper, 'Andra shadow play jesters: Meaning, iconography and history', Conference on Asian Puppet Theatre, London 1979, 26–8.

18   Geertz Armin W. and Lomatuway'ma Michael, *Children of Cottonwood: Piety and Ceremonialism in Hopi Indian Puppetry*, Lincoln, NE, 1987, 218.

19   McPharlin Paul, *The Puppet Theatre in America. A History: 1524 to 1948*. Boston 1969, 9.

20   Darkowska-Nidzgorski, Olenka, *Théâtre populaire de marionnettes en Afrique noire* (Popular puppet theatre in black Africa), Paris 1976, 40–41.

21   Pimpaneau, op. cit., 19.

22   Ashley Wayne and Holloman Regina, 'From ritual to theatre in Kerala', *The Drama Review*, 1982, T94: 68.

23   Seltmann Friedrich, *Schattenspiel in Kerala: Sakrales Theater in Süd-Indien* (Shadowplay in Kerala: sacred theatre in south India), Stuttgart 1986, 87–90.

24   Sears Laurie Lobell, 'Aesthetic displacement in Javanese shadow theatre: Three contemporary performance styles', *The Drama Review*, 1989, T123: 125.

25   Ibid., 126.

26   Pimpaneau, op. cit., 21.

27   Ruizendaal Robin, 'Performance as ritual: The performance practice of the marionette theatre of Southern Taiwan', in Aijmer G. and Boholm A. (eds.) *Images and Enactments*, Göteborg 1994.

28   Levi-Strauss, op. cit., 197.

29   I have taken this diagram from a study by Elena S.Novik, *Obriad i folklor w sibirskom szamanizmie* (Customs and folklore in Siberian shamanism), Moscow 1984.

11
The Acting Puppet as a Figure of Speech

As long as theatre has existed, spectators have been aware of the metaphorical meaning of scenic materials, images, or even of performances taken as a whole. The use of such terms as metonymy, metaphor or synecdoche has been widely accepted in theatre, although they derive from literary criticism.

Recent semiotic studies have justified even more the application of these terms to theatre studies on the basis of a generally accepted principle that theatrical performance itself may be treated as a text; that is, as a distinct whole, independent of the sign system in which it is perceptibly manifested. To quote Grzegorz Sinko, 'The distinctive characteristic of theatrical performance treated as a text is its high degree of semiotic polyphony.'[1]

This theoretical approach opens the way to research into theatrical figures of speech. To quote Sinko again:

> The process of metaphorization has thus far been investigated in natural languages only, but since it is a property of semantic relations, the results of this research might also apply to texts in other sign systems as well, and thus provide a key to the investigation of the so-called poésie du théâtre.[2]

It is clear that the model of visual metaphor in theatre is taken from the structure of linguistic tropes in natural language. Furthermore, the technique of their generation is similar, if not the same, and consists in the influence of the paradigmatic (substitutive) axis on the syntagmatic (combinatorial) axis of the ensemble of signs, following the linguistic theory of Ferdinand de Saussure. We also find important directions for research in the views of Charles S. Peirce, especially in his concept of signs, according to which a sign does not exist separately but in a chain of other signs, each one generated by its antecedent and producing its consequent.

The generation of new figurative meanings depends on the context and relationships of some particular sign. Thus a single sign by itself, extracted and separated, is not able to produce a new semantic effect until it is associated with other signifiers. Naturally, the engagement in a simple syntagmatic order does not change the semantic content of the sign. To achieve this change we need to refer to the paradigmatic (substitutive) order and combine it in a linear juxtaposition of specifically selected signs likely to produce new meanings owing to their mutual interaction at the semantic level.

If we keep this perspective in mind, the question then arises: is the puppet a single separated sign, or the effect of interaction between metaphor-generating elements? An answer cannot be given immediately. To begin to clarify the question, we must think, for instance, of the distinction between a 'resting puppet' and an 'acting puppet', between the puppet as a possible signifier and as an actual scenic sign. It does not require lengthy analysis to see that these are not equivalent. The 'resting puppet' is an object made for theatrical use; it is meant to represent a stage character but is not able to fulfill this task by itself. As a sign, the 'resting puppet' is the passive icon of a stage character, with a latent capacity for movement. To represent the value of a complete stage character, the 'resting puppet' needs the help of a manipulator as its motor power and generator of gestures, and also to give it a speaking voice. It is only when these helpers (sometimes one and the same person) come into action that the 'resting puppet' starts to be the 'acting puppet' and at the same time the signifier of a stage character. Thus the acting puppet is not a single separated sign but an effect of cooperation between three elements: iconic value, movement and gesture, and verbal action.

This image of the puppet accords with the 'classic' understanding of puppet theatre. However, the modern idea of the puppet goes far beyond this concept and identifies the puppet with an object, considered in its broadest meaning. In 1953, Gerard Marinier proposed the most classical definition of the puppet:

In fact the puppet is the reproduction of a living being, more or less truthful, more or less interpreted, varying in proportion and more or less capable of determined movements, which can generate all sorts of feelings, states of soul and attitudes, in short, which have dramatic capacities and which are animated either visibly or invisibly by any means invented by its 'manipulator'.[3]

The ambiguity of Marinier's utterance does not obscure the clear idea of a puppet as a figural representation of a living being and its involvement in dramatic action. These two notions of 'figural representation' and 'involvement in dramatic action' are essential for any 'phenomenological' definition of the puppet, which assumes the harmonious coexistence of these components, and where any infraction of their balance changes the virtual function of the puppet.

In the past some artists over-estimated the figural function of the puppet, which led to the concept of 'living sculpture' by Jefimova, for example. In our time greater emphasis is put on 'involvement in dramatic action'. The puppet master Alain Recoing gave us this definition in 1963:

> The puppet is a movable object of dramatic interpretation in opposition to the automaton, and different also from the doll, and moved intentionally by the manipulator. In opposition to the automaton, and different also from the doll, the puppet is a movable object of dramatic interpretation moved intentionally by the manipulator.

The dramatic involvement of the puppet here is pre-eminent; its properties as an object are defined only negatively and its iconic value is not even mentioned. The pre-eminence of 'acting' in puppetry has received an extreme formulation in some recently published papers. In 1990 Roman Paska wrote:

> Like a fish out of water, the puppet out of the performance is a dead thing, a potential signifier only. As demonstrated most recently by the theatre of objects, the signifying properties of the puppet as a passive formal object or sculpture are ultimately unnecessary to the object's kinetic signifying activity as a puppet actor in a performance context. The puppetness of an object is determined by use, not latency, and is a renewable, not a permanent quality.[4]

I appreciate Paska's eagerness to emphasize the subjective aspect of theatre creation, which belongs to the role of the performer. In the theatre the most important factor is the human being or, as I prefer to say, human beings. It is rather seldom that a theatre production has one creator. Normally there are many, from the writer through to the director, designer, different sorts of technician and maker (including of puppets), and the actor or performer. In puppet theatre all these skills may be incorporated in one person, which imposes some limits and certainly reduces the number of sign systems employed. However, the principle of interaction between signs remains the same. Even a single artist as the source of all theatrical signs cannot neglect the manipulation of his or her puppets. It is this juxtaposition of the puppet icon with the movement and the voice given to it by the player that is of interest to us.

The iconic value of the puppet is usually manifested on two levels. The first includes all the iconic signs (material, hair, facial expression or the lack thereof, costume and so on). The second has a virtual character, which is the capacity for movement, defined by the puppet's material and construction, as it is to be exploited by the manipulator.

We could call this its theatrical predestination, which is the distinctive nature of the puppet in opposition to the simple object, often used nowadays for the representation of a stage character. The simple object was made for non-theatrical use, which is why its iconic quality refers to the class of objects, while the iconicity of the puppet refers to the definite, unique representation of its stage role.

I doubt if we can or would even wish to neglect the fact of the puppet's pre-existence and its iconic value. Normally these have been carefully projected as an essential element of the artist's vision. Bunraku, *wayang* and other kinds of puppet may serve as convincing examples. On the other hand, it is really the manipulator and the voice donor who supply the puppet with its apparent life. The iconic value of the puppet as a representation of a live being is enriched by a new set of signs, particularly important because of their dynamic qualities. The puppet becomes more than a three-dimensional passive icon. It becomes an icon in motion and even something more: a speaking icon in motion. Due to this dynamic complement, the puppet becomes more credible and recognizable as the substitute of a living being.

As a substitution the puppet belongs to the paradigmatic axis of the ensemble of signs. The puppet producing movement and gesture enters into a syntagmatic relationship with other signs. In this case, however, this relationship seems to be unusual, as it juxtaposes contradictory notions: the puppet as a dead thing and as a thing of dynamic motion. It thus gave birth to a new figurative meaning – as the image of a dynamic human being.

According to Obraztsov, the puppet is a metaphor of the human because it is not itself a human being. And this accords with the substitutional principle of metaphor already formulated by Aristotle. If anyone is surprised by this conclusion, I would suggest treating the acting puppet as a petrified metaphor. We are so familiar with the acting puppet that we hardly perceive it as a metaphor. Nevertheless, from the historical point of view the acting puppet is a metaphor, especially if we consider it as a special kind of metaphor; that is, as an oxymoron.

Oxymoron is the figure of speech by means of which contradictory terms are combined so as to form an expressive epithet such as 'black sun', 'cruel kindness' and, last but not least, 'living object'. When combined with the appearance of life, supplied by movement and voice, the material puppet is an oxymoron.

Beginning in the seventeenth century, artists and particularly playwrights were extremely sensitive to the oxymoronic character of the puppet. Ben Jonson, Lesage, Foote and Tieck were all fully conscious of the double, self-contradictory nature of the puppet and they exploited it in various ways. In most cases they emphasized the artificiality of the puppet in order to entertain the public through the interaction of reality and illusion. Some of them appreciated its lifelessness and materiality as a basis for mechanical performance, which they claimed to be the highest form of theatrical art.

It is not my aim to present a review of various approaches to the oxymoronic quality of the puppet. However, it is worth noting that the oxymoron was the starting point for Otakar Zich in his study in 1923 of the psychology of the puppet theater.[5] His basic observation was that puppets are usually perceived from two opposing points of view: as a live figure or as a lifeless doll. In the first case puppets seem to the public to be magical creatures, while in the second, comic and grotesque, because of their uncanny imitation of human movement.

The perception of the puppet as 'magic' obviously suppresses the oxymoronic effect. It is preserved, however, in the 'grotesque and comic' model of reception. The grotesque, oxymoronic understanding of the puppet fascinated German writers and researchers. The first was Ludwig Tieck, who demonstrated the grotesqueness of the puppet resulting from the contradiction between the puppet's ambition to perform important roles and its limited capacity to fulfill its aspirations. Another German, Paul Brann, was a puppet theatre artist opposed to this theory as he exploited the materiality (texture) of puppets in his musical productions at the beginning of the last century. He proved that playing with the oxymoronic effect might generate other aesthetic effects of high value, different from those of the grotesque and the comic.

In spite of Brann, two German researchers continued with Tieck's concept of the grotesque puppet. First, Lothar Buschmeyer in 1931 decided that puppets are dead things pretending to be living beings, and since they are not successful in their endeavours they become comic.[6] He came to the conclusion that the comic nature of the puppet lies in the contrast of its mechanism with its pretended vitality: puppets are comical due to their schematism and primitivism. That is their natural style and so they continue to be comical unless the efforts of the puppeteer can create some special expression or style. With this idea he predicted a new era of puppet theatre.

Fritz Eichler in 1937 did not go so far.[7] Speaking about string puppets, he stated that they are passive as stage characters; their performance is indirect and objectified, as a result of their particular mechanical life: the string puppet becomes comic while imitating an active character and is thus capable, at most, of being a grotesque and eccentric performer. There is little to be gained in elaborating the studies of Buschmeyer and Eichler, but in their time these were serious and complete. Their deliberations on the potential of the puppet were based on philosophical criteria; they looked for the characteristic features of the puppet and they believed that they had found them in the puppet form as it then existed. They limited their eidetic research to the expressive power of the puppet as such, without giving credit to the creative ability of the puppet artist. That is why they interpreted the oxymoronic value of the puppet rather mechanically. Kleist's concept of the puppet as an unconscious mechanism, and thus an excellent performer, still prevailed in European puppet theatre.

In the 1950s and 1960s a new approach to the acting puppet was the result of experiments which increased the puppet's means of expression, tested the tradition of the puppet and put an emphasis on the performing subject as manipulator, puppeteer, actor (or whatever he or she might be called). From that time on the performer has appeared on stage as a visible operator of the puppet, and in some cases as the actual creator of the production presented onstage. As a result, the puppet has entered into a new relationship with its manipulator. This relationship has been known since the beginnings of puppetry, but for many centuries it was latent. Now it has become part of the modern understanding of the art form.

The manipulator as subject and motor power is nowadays the visible cause of the puppet's presence and of its acting. Between the manipulator and the puppet, the cause-and-effect relationship has been established and displayed to the public. The puppet has become an indexical sort of sign. As such, the puppet has changed into metonymy, which accords with Keir Elam's observation:

It is clear that if metaphoric substitution is allied to the iconic sign-function (both are based on the principle of supposed similarity), then metonymic substitution is closely related to the index (each being founded on physical contiguity).[8]

The metonymical character of the puppet is confirmed by the frequent presence of synecdoche (*pars pro toto*) in its performances. The most obvious synecdoche is the hand or glove puppet, which in fact is a disguised part of the human body. The Polish romantic writer Juliusz Słowacki humorously observed that some puppets were the two dressed hands of a street puppet player who was sitting within the booth, giving rise to the thought: 'I guess that none of these heroes will hit the other very hard.'[9] In the twentieth century, hand puppets were undressed and the public often saw the bare hands, as in the productions of Sergei Obraztsov or Yves Joly. Synecdoche bloomed, encouraging a broader use of figurative language.

The transfer of the puppet's application from metaphor to metonymy has greatly changed the style of puppet theatre. According to Roman Jakobson: 'Realism ... is largely metonymic in mode while symbolism is primarily metaphoric.'[10]This seems to be quite true in puppet theatre.

The puppet, understood as an autonomous stage character, was a symbolic substitute for an actor or human being, and opened to the public a mysterious world of fiction, strong enough to absorb such disturbances of illusion as the play within a play, paradox or oxymoron.

The puppet as metonymy is a real thing. It does not deceive the public by means of a pretended life, because all the power of deception is given to the performer. The performer is also a real presence, showing the construction (sometimes) and the operation (always) of the puppet. This serves to create a 'second-level' world – this time a world of fiction, which is also a world of reality as the product of a performer's actions. This 'second-level' world of fiction may be very 'poetic' and metaphorical, but its metonymical character is not thereby disturbed.

The passage from the metaphorical to the metonymical system of the concept of puppet theatre has been a revolution in many respects. The emphasis on the pretended autonomous acting of the puppet became anachronistic in a theatre that is meant to depend totally on the performer's talent and capacity. The puppet's properties in this theatre are not considered as given a priori, they do not exist as eidetic values to be discovered. On the contrary, they depend completely on the imagination of the designer and the invention of the performer. It is not

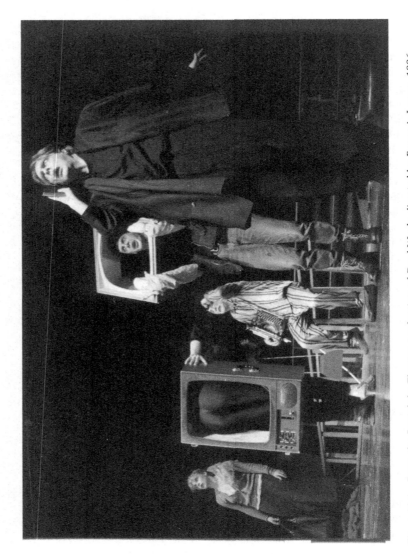

Figure 11.1 From the Banialuka Theatre production of *Dead Words*, directed by Francois Lezaro, 1996

surprising, then, that in such a theatre the puppet has been subjected to various experiments and is now often substituted by a simple object, a development that has enormously enriched the figurative potential of its theatrical language.

After many centuries of existence the puppet, endowed with the appearances of life or presented as an effect of a manipulator's action, is no longer perceived as a metaphor or as metonymy. Its borrowed life or its given form has become an obvious fact and hardly anybody treats it as a poetic trope. The use of a simple object as a stage character, meanwhile, has changed public perception, because it seems to be something out of the ordinary. A simple object, such as an umbrella, pillow, flask and so on, manufactured for everyday use, brings to the stage its own iconic value, representing a certain class of objects. The movement that is 'added to the object' may confirm its iconicity or oppose it. In the first case, we deal with the personification of the object, and the motion expresses a sort of possible, virtual movement of such an object. Thus we enter into the world of fiction and fantasy.

In the second case, that of opposition, we may decide on anthropomorphism. The object serves as a symbolic substitute of the human or other living being. Anthropomorphism demands from the performer the endowment of the object with properties that can be recognized as signs of a human being. The object's iconicity here cannot be of much help. In fact the performer has to work against it in order to make the public agree that the object does not represent itself but an imagined stage character. This work is done by the expedient application of motional and gestural signs. Naturally, the object is never completely forgotten. Its deceptive iconicity is a very important part of the play. It helps us to enter again into the kingdom of oxymoron. This time, however, its paradoxical structure appeals to the public with a new metaphor.

The aim of my study here was to discuss the basic functions of the components of the acting puppet. I have tried to present different aspects of the relationship between the puppet and its manipulator. We have seen that this relationship is dynamic and as such seems to be a generative force, supplying puppetry with its basic figures of speech. This essential relationship may be reproduced in any theatrical action and developed in different variations. The most popular of these concerns the relationship between the manipulator and the string puppet, and is interpreted as a model of a world in which the human being is dominated by some superior power. But there are, of course, many other such models.

This opens the door to the enormous fascination of poetic language within puppetry, based on the richness of its means of expression. The modern puppet theatre combines string, glove and other puppets, masks and people, movies and transparencies, props and simple objects, all of which create a fertile field for promoting poetic expression. Their mutual cooperation should be the next stage in our research into the metaphorical language of puppetry.

First published in *Present Trends in Research of World Puppetry*, Warsaw, 1992. Edited by Mischa Twitchin 2013.

Notes

1   Sinko G., *Opis przedstawienia teatralnego. Problem semiotyczny* (Description of the theatre performance. Semantic question), Wrocław 1982, 183.
2   Ibid., 187.
3   Bensky R.-D., *Recherches sur les structures et la symbolique de la marionnette*, Paris 1971, 18.
4   Paska R., 'Notes on puppet primitives', in *The Language of the Puppet*, Vancouver, WA 1990, 39.
5   Zich O., 'Drobne umeni – vytvarne snahy' (Small art – great endeavours), *Loutkove divadlo*, Praha 1923, 4.
6   Buschmeyer L., *Die Kunst des Puppenspiels* (The art of puppet play), Erfurt 1931.
7   Eichler F., *Das Wesen des Handpuppen- und Marionettenspiels* (The essence of hand puppet and marionette performance), Emsdetten 1937.
8   Elam K., *The Semiotics of Theatre and Drama*, London and New York 1980, 28.
9   Słowacki J., *Dzieła I*, Works Wrocław 1949, 12.
10   Elam, op. cit., 28.

Index

Made in the USA
Coppell, TX
05 April 2021